Lecture Notes in Computer Science　11882

T0214653

More information about this series at http://www.springer.com/series/7407

Mary Hall · Hari Sundar (Eds.)

Languages and Compilers for Parallel Computing

31st International Workshop, LCPC 2018
Salt Lake City, UT, USA, October 9–11, 2018
Revised Selected Papers

 Springer

Editors
Mary Hall (iD)
University of Utah
Salt Lake City, UT, USA

Hari Sundar (iD)
University of Utah
Salt Lake City, UT, USA

ISSN 0302-9743   ISSN 1611-3349   (electronic)
Lecture Notes in Computer Science
ISBN 978-3-030-34626-3   ISBN 978-3-030-34627-0   (eBook)
https://doi.org/10.1007/978-3-030-34627-0

LNCS Sublibrary: SL1 – Theoretical Computer Science and General Issues

This Springer imprint is published by the registered company Springer Nature Switzerland AG
The registered company address is: Gewerbestrasse 11, 6330 Cham, Switzerland

Preface

This volume contains the papers presented at LCPC 2018: the 31th International Workshop on Languages and Compilers for Parallel Computing, held during October 9–11, 2018, in Salt Lake City, Utah. Since its founding in 1988, the LCPC workshop has been a leading venue for research on parallelizing compilers and related topics in concurrency, parallel languages, parallel programming models, runtime systems, and tools. The workshop spans the spectrum from foundational principles to practical experience, and from early ideas to polished results. LCPC encourages submissions that go outside the scope of scientific computing and enable parallel programming in new areas, such as mobile computing and data centers. The value of LCPC stems largely from its focused topics and personal interaction. This year's location, in Salt Lake City, Utah, was both scenic and convenient. Fall is beautiful in Utah, and Salt Lake City nestled between the Wasatch and Oquirrh ranges provided a scenic location. Specific topics of LCPC 2018 included: compiling for parallelism and parallel compilers; static, dynamic, and adaptive optimization of parallel programs; parallel programming models and languages; formal analysis and verification of parallel programs; parallel runtime systems and libraries; performance analysis and debugging tools for concurrency and parallelism; parallel algorithms and concurrent data structures; parallel applications; synchronization and concurrency control; software engineering for parallel programs; fault tolerance for parallel systems; and parallel programming and compiling for heterogeneous systems. LCPC received 26 submissions, and each submission was reviewed by at least 3, and on average 3.5, Program Committee members. The committee decided to accept 14 papers, of which 8 are regular papers, 5 are short papers and 1 an invited paper. The workshop program includes 9 invited talks:

1. "The Tensor Algebra Compiler" by Saman Amarasinghe, MIT
2. "Programming Model and Compiler Extensions for Unifying Asynchronous Tasks, Futures, and Events" by Vivek Sarkar, Georgia Tech
3. "The Sparse Polyhedral Framework: Composing Compiler-Generated Inspector-Executor code" by Michelle Strout, Arizona State University
4. "Cache Analysis and Optimization Based on Reuse-time Distribution" by Chen Ding, University of Rochester
5. "New Opportunities for Compilers in Computer Security" by Alex Viedenbaum, University of California, Irvine
6. "Putting Parallelizing Compilers into the Toolbox of Computational Scientists" by Rudi Eigenmann, University of Delaware
7. "Quantifying and Reducing Execution Variance in STMs via Model Driven Commit Optimization" by Santosh Pande, Georgia Tech
8. "UPC++" by Scott Baden, UC San Diego
9. "Tuning without Auto-Tuning" by Martin Kong, Stonybrook University

We would like to thank the School of Computing staff for the help in organizing the workshop and the financial support from Microsoft and Intel. The generation of the proceedings was assisted by the EasyChair conference system.

December 2018

Mary Hall
Hari Sundar

Organization

Program Committee Chairs

Mary Hall   University of Utah, USA
Hari Sundar   University of Utah, USA

Program Committee

Chen Ding   University of Rochester, USA
Maria Garzaran   Intel, USA
Ganesh Gopalakrishnan   University of Utah, USA
Chunhua Liao   Lawrence Livermore National Laboratory, USA
Eric Mercer   Brigham Young University, USA
Saurav Muralidharan   Nvidia, USA
Cathie Olschanowsky   Boise State University, USA
Santosh Pande   Georgia Tech, USA
Lawrence Rauchwerger   Texas A&M University, USA
Vivek Sarkar   Georgia Tech, USA
Jun Shirako   Georgia Tech, USA
Hiroyuki Takizawa   Tohoku University, Japan
Peng Wu   Huawei, USA

Contents

A Unified Approach to Variable Renaming for Enhanced Vectorization

Prasanth Chatarasi[1]([⊠]), Jun Shirako[1], Albert Cohen[2], and Vivek Sarkar[1]

[1] Georgia Institute of Technology, Atlanta, GA, USA
{cprasanth,shirako,vsarkar}@gatech.edu
[2] INRIA & DI ENS, Paris, France
albert.cohen@inria.fr

Abstract. Despite the fact that compiler technologies for automatic vectorization have been under development for over four decades, there are still considerable gaps in the capabilities of modern compilers to perform automatic vectorization for SIMD units. One such gap can be found in the handling of loops with dependence cycles that involve memory-based anti (write-after-read) and output (write-after-write) dependences. Past approaches, such as variable renaming and variable expansion, break such dependence cycles by either eliminating or repositioning the problematic memory-based dependences. However, the past work suffers from three key limitations: (1) Lack of a unified framework that synergistically integrates multiple storage transformations, (2) Lack of support for bounding the additional space required to break memory-based dependences, and (3) Lack of support for integrating these storage transformations with other code transformations (e.g., statement reordering) to enable vectorization.

In this paper, we address the three limitations above by integrating both Source Variable Renaming (SoVR) and Sink Variable Renaming (SiVR) transformations into a unified formulation, and by formalizing the "cycle-breaking" problem as a minimum weighted set cover optimization problem. To the best of our knowledge, our work is the first to formalize an optimal solution for cycle breaking that simultaneously considers both SoVR and SiVR transformations, thereby enhancing vectorization and reducing storage expansion relative to performing the transformations independently. We implemented our approach in PPCG, a state-of-the-art optimization framework for loop transformations, and evaluated it on eleven kernels from the TSVC benchmark suite. Our experimental results show a geometric mean performance improvement of $4.61\times$ on an Intel Xeon Phi (KNL) machine relative to the optimized performance obtained by Intel's ICC v17.0 product compiler. Further, our results demonstrate a geometric mean performance improvement of $1.08\times$ and $1.14\times$ on the Intel Xeon Phi (KNL) and Nvidia Tesla V100 (Volta) platforms relative to past work that only performs the SiVR transformation [5], and of $1.57\times$ and $1.22\times$ on both platforms relative to past work on using both SiVR and SoVR transformations [8].

© Springer Nature Switzerland AG 2019
M. Hall and H. Sundar (Eds.): LCPC 2018, LNCS 11882, pp. 1–20, 2019.
https://doi.org/10.1007/978-3-030-34627-0_1

Keywords: Vectorization · Renaming · Storage transformations ·
Polyhedral compilers · Intel KNL · Nvidia Volta · TSVC Suite · SIMD

1   Introduction

There is a strong resurgence of interest in vector processing due to the significant
energy efficiency benefits of using SIMD parallelism within individual CPU cores
as well as in streaming multiprocessors in GPUs. These benefits increase with
widening SIMD vectors, reaching vector register lengths of 512 bits in the Intel
Xeon Phi Knights Landing (KNL) processor, Intel Xeon Skylake processor and
2048 bits in the scalable vector extension of the Armv8 architecture [18]. Further,
there is a widespread expectation that compilers will continue to play a central
role in handling the complexities of dependence analysis, code transformation
and code generation necessary for vectorization for CPUs. Even in cases where
the programmer identifies a loop as being vectorizable, the compiler still plays
a major role in transforming the code to use SIMD instructions. This is in
contrast with multicore and distributed-memory parallelism (and even with GPU
parallelism in many cases), where it is generally accepted that programmers
manually perform the code transformations necessary to expose parallelism, with
some assistance from the runtime system but little or no help from compilers. It
is therefore important to continue advancing the state of the art of vectorizing
compiler technologies, so as to address the growing needs for enabling modern
applications to use the full capability of SIMD units.

This paper focuses on advancing the state of the art with respect to handling
memory-based anti (write-after-read) or *output* (write-after-write) dependences
in vectorizing compilers. These dependences can theoretically be eliminated by
allocating new storage to accommodate the value of the first write operation
thereby ensuring that the following write operation need not wait for the first
write to complete. However, current state-of-the-art vectorizing compilers only
perform such storage transformations in limited cases, and often fail to vectorize
loops containing cycles of dependences that include memory-based dependences.
This is despite a vast body of past research on storage transformations, such as
variable renaming [7,13–15] and variable expansion [10], which have shown how
removing storage-related dependences can make it possible to "break" dependence cycles.

We believe that the limited use of such techniques in modern compilers is
due to three key limitations that currently inhibit their practical usage:

1. Lack of a unified framework that synergistically integrates multiple storage
   transformations,
2. Lack of support for bounding the additional space required to break memory-
   based dependences, and
3. Lack of support for integrating these storage transformations with other code
   transformations (e.g., statement reordering) to enable vectorization.

The goal of this paper is to enhance the current state-of-the-art in vectorizing compilers to enable more loops to be vectorized via systematic storage transformations (variable renamings) that remove selected memory-based dependences to break their containing cycles, while optionally using a bounded amount of additional space. We view our tool, called *PolySIMD*, as an extension to vectorization technologies that can be invoked when a state-of-the-art vectorizer fails to vectorize a loop. Thus, we do not focus on replicating all state-of-the-art vectorization capabilities in *PolySIMD*. For example, we focus on enabling vectorization of innermost loops in *PolySIMD*, though many state-of-the-art compilers support outer loop vectorization as well (and we believe that our contributions can also be applied to outer loop vectorization). By default, our tool takes sequential code as input, and focuses on identifying the best use of variable renamings to maximize opportunities for vectorization. An input loop can optionally be annotated with a pragma that specifies a bound (*spacelimit*) on the maximum amount of extra storage that can be allocated to break dependences. As discussed later, the two main variable renaming transformations that we employ in our approach are *Source Variable Renaming* (SoVR) and *Sink Variable Renaming* (SiVR).

The main technical contributions of this paper are as follows:

- We formalize the problem of identifying an optimized set of SoVR and SiVR variable renaming transformations to break cycles of dependences as a minimum weighted set cover optimization problem, and demonstrate that it is practical to use ILP formulations to find optimal solutions to this problem. If the user provides an optional *spacelimit* parameter, our formalization ensures that the additional storage introduced by our transformations remains within the user-provided bounds.
- We created a new tool, *PolySIMD*, to implement our approach by selecting and performing an optimal set of SoVR and SiVR transformations, along with supporting statement reordering transformations. Given an input sequential loop, *PolySIMD* either generates transformed sequential CPU code that can be input into a vectorizing compiler like ICC or generates GPU code (CUDA kernels) that can be processed by a GPU compiler like NVCC. *PolySIMD* is implemented as a extension to the PPCG framework [1,20], so as to leverage PPCG's dependence analysis and code generation capabilities.
- We evaluated our approach on eleven kernels from the TSVC benchmark suite [16], and obtained a geometric-mean performance improvement of 4.61× on an Intel Xeon Phi (KNL) machine relative to the optimized performance obtained by Intel's ICC v17.0 product compiler.
- We also compared our approach with the two most closely related algorithms from past work, one by Calland et al. [5] that only performed SiVR transformations, and the other by Chu et al. [8]. that proposed a (not necessarily optimal) heuristic to combine SiVR and SoVR transformations.

Relative to Calland et al's approach, our approach delivered an overall geometric-mean performance improvement of 1.08× and 1.14× on the Intel KNL and Nvidia Volta platforms respectively, though our approach selected exactly the same (SiVR-only) transformations for six of the eleven benchmarks. Relative to Chu et al's approach, our approach delivered an overall geometric-mean performance improvement of 1.57× and 1.22× on the Intel KNL and Nvidia Volta platforms respectively.

Table 1. An example to illustrate SoVR and SiVR transformations.

Original program having cycles	Applying SoVR(s2, a[i+1]) on the original program	Applying SiVR(s1, a[i]) on the original program
``for i = 1 to N {
a[i] = b[i]+c[i];//s1
a[i+1] = a[i-1]+2*a[i+1];//s2
}```	```for i = 1 to N {
a[i] = b[i]+c[i];//s1
float k = a[i+1];//s21
a[i+1] = a[i-1]+2*k;//s2
}```	```float a_temp[N];
for i = 1 to N {
a_temp[i] = b[i]+c[i];//s11
a[i] = a_temp[i];//s1
a[i+1] = (i > 1) ? \ //s2
(a_temp[i-1] : a[i-1])+2*a[i+1]
}```
Dependence graph of the original program	Dependence graph after applying SoVR(s2, a[i+1]) on the original program	Dependence graph after applying SiVR(s1, a[i]) on the original program

2   Discussion on Variable Renaming Transformations

In this section, we discuss on two variable renaming transformations that are considered in this paper, and they are *Source variable renaming* (SoVR)[1] introduced by Kuck et al. in [15] and *Sink variable renaming* (SiVR) introduced by Chu et al. in [7]. Furthermore, these two renaming transformations were formalized by Calland et al. in [5], and referred SoVR and SiVR as T1 and T2 transformations respectively.

2.1   Source Variable Renaming (SoVR)

Source variable renaming transformation is introduced to handle anti-dependences in cycles of memory-based dependences, and the transformation is applied on a read access of a statement to reposition an outgoing anti-dependence edge from the read access [15]. Applying SoVR on a read access (say **r**) of a statement introduces a new assignment statement that copies the value of **r** into a temporary variable (say **k**), and then the original statement's read access is replaced with **k**. Since the transformation is renaming source (read access) of an anti-dependence, we call this transformation as a source variable renaming transformation.

Example. Applying SoVR on the read access a[i+1] of the statement s2 in the original program (shown in Table 1) introduces a new assignment statement s21

---

[1] SoVR was also referred as node splitting by Kuck et al. in [15].

copying the value of a[i+1] into a temporary variable k, and then the statement s2 refers to k in-place of a[i+1]. As a result, the source of the anti-dependence from the read access a[i+1] is repositioned to s21. This reposition helps in breaking one of the cycles through s2, i.e., the cycle involving a flow-dependence from a[i] of s1 to a[i-1] of s2, and an anti-dependence from a[i+1] of s2 to a[i] of s1.

Usefulness. Since SoVR transformation is applied on a read access of a statement, the transformation can modify only incoming flow- and outgoing anti-dependences related to that read access. Hence, applying a SoVR transformation on a statement is useful in breaking cycles if the statement has an incoming anti- or output-dependences and an outgoing anti-dependence [5]. Also, SoVR transformation can be useful if the statement's incoming flow-dependence and outgoing anti-dependence are on different accesses.

Space requirements & Additional memory traffic. The temporary variable introduced as part of a SoVR transformation is private to a loop carrying an anti-dependence that we are interested in repositioning. Hence, SoVR requires an additional space equivalent to the length of vector registers (i.e., VLEN) of target hardware. Furthermore, the transformation additionally introduces only one scalar load and one scalar store per every iteration of the target loop.

2.2 Sink Variable Renaming (SiVR)

Sink variable renaming transformation is introduced to handle both anti- and output-dependences in cycles of memory-based dependences [7]. The transformation is applied on a write access of a statement to reposition an outgoing flow-dependence from the write access and also an outgoing anti-dependence from the statement. Applying SiVR on a write access (say w) of a statement s introduces a new assignment statement that evaluates the right hand side of the statement into a temporary array (say temp), and then any references to the value of w are replaced by accessing the temp. Since SiVR transformation is applied on a write access of a statement, the transformation can modify only incoming anti- or output-dependences related to that write access. As a result, applying SiVR transformation is useful in breaking cycles if the statement has either an incoming anti- or output-dependences and either an outgoing flow- or anti-dependences [5]. Since the transformation is renaming the sink (the write access) of an incoming anti- or output-dependence, this transformation is called as sink variable renaming transformation [7].

Example. Applying SiVR on the write access a[i] of the statement s1 in the original program (shown in Table 1) introduces a new assignment statement s11 that evaluates the rhs of s1 into a temporary array a_temp, and then the transformation replaces the references to a[i] (such as a[i-1]) with the a_temp. As a result, the source of the flow-dependence from the write access a[i] is repositioned to s11. This repositioning helps in breaking all of the cycles present in the original program including the one that is not broken by the previous SoVR transformation, i.e., the cycle involving a flow-dependence from a[i] of s1 to a[i-1] of s2, and an output-dependence from a[i+1] of s2 to a[i] of s1.

Space requirements. The temporary array introduced as part of a SiVR transformation is not private to a loop unlike SoVR transformation, because references to the newly allocated storage can be across iterations. Hence, SiVR requires an additional space equivalent to the number of iterations of a loop. However, the additional storage can be reduced by strip mining the loop, and vectorizing only the strip [21]; whose space requirement is now proportional to the strip size, and the strip can be as minimal as vector length.

Additional memory traffic. SiVR transformation introduces pointer-based loads and stores, unlike the SoVR transformation which introduces only scalar loads and stores. The new assignment statement as part of a SiVR transformation introduces one additional pointer-based store and one pointer-based load per one iteration of the loop. Along with a new assignment statement, each reference to the newly allocated storage introduces one additional pointer-based load, leading to overall (1+#references) of pointer-based loads per one iteration of the loop. In this work, we focus on applying renaming transformations for vectorizing only inner-most loops, and this focus helps in conservatively counting the references to the newly allocated storage by traversing the loop body and ignoring conditionals.

2.3   Synergy Between SoVR and SiVR

In general, SoVR transformation is neater in code generation and performs more efficiently than SiVR since the SoVR transformation introduces scalar loads and stores. But, SoVR transformation has limited applicability (i.e., handling only anti-dependences) in breaking cycles compared to SiVR, which has broader applicability through breaking output-dependences. Table 2 shows a comparison between SoVR and SiVR transformations related to space requirements and additional stores and loads.

Table 2. A comparison between SoVR and SiVR transformations related to the space requirements and additional stores, loads introduced by these transformations in one iteration of the target loop. * – Additional scalar loads/stores for SiVR transformation may go negative in case of renaming scalars.

Storage	#Additional space	SoVR	SiVR
		Vector length	Loop length
Additional loads & stores	#scalar loads	1	0*
	#scalar stores	1	0*
	#pointer-based loads	0	1+#references
	#pointer-based stores	0	1

3   Motivating Example

To motivate the need of a unified framework that synergistically integrates multiple variable renaming transformations, we consider a running example (shown in Fig. 1) from [5] whose dependence graph consists of three cycles (i.e., s1-s3-s2-s4-s1, s1-s3-s4-s1, and s1-s2-s4-s1) which prohibit vectorization. Past work by Calland et al. [5] uses only SiVR transformations to eliminate all of the above three cycles by applying SiVR transformations on the statements s2 and s3. But, these transformations require an additional space close to 2 times the number of iterations of the loop-i, i.e., a total of $(2 \times T)$, and also introduce additional 2 pointer-based stores and 4 pointer-based loads per one iteration of the loop.

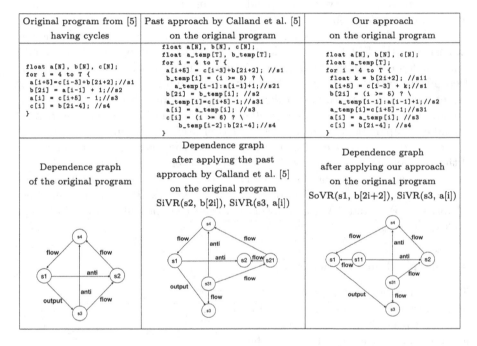

Original program from [5] having cycles	Past approach by Calland et al. [5] on the original program	Our approach on the original program

Fig. 1. A running example from [5] whose dependence graph consists of three cycles c1/c2/c3: s1-s3-s2-s4-s1/s1-s3-s4-s1/s1-s2-s4-s1 which prohibit vectorization. The table also lists dependence graphs and transformed codes after applying past approach [5] and our integrated approach on the original program.

However, instead of applying SiVR transformation on the statement s2 to break the cycle (c3), SoVR transformation can be applied on the s1 to break the same cycle (c3). This results in lesser additional space $(T + VLEN)$, and also introduces lesser additional 1 pointer-based store and 2 pointer-based loads per one iteration of the loop. Our approach identifies such optimal transformations from a set of valid SoVR and SiVR transformations by formalizing the "cycle-breaking" problem as a minimum weighted set cover optimization problem with a goal of reducing overhead arising from additional loads and stores introduced by these transformations. The speedup's after applying our approach over the original program is 5.06× and 4.02× compared to the original program and the transformed program after applying the Calland et al. approach [5] respectively on the Intel Knights Landing processor (More details about the architectures and compiler options can be found in Table 4).

4   Our Unified Approach to Variable Renaming

In this section, we introduce our approach that synergistically integrates SoVR and SiVR transformations into a unified formulation to break cycles of dependences involving memory-based dependences, and the approach is implemented in a tool called *PolySIMD*.

The overall approach is summarized in Fig. 2, which is implemented as an extension to the PPCG framework [20] (a state-of-the-art optimization framework for loop transformations), and consists of the following components: (1) Dependence cycles finder (Extracting flow-, anti-, and output-dependences on a target loop, then constructing a dependence graph, and then finding cycles in the graph using the *Johnson's algorithm* [12]), (2) Bipartite graph constructor (Building a bipartite mapping from a union over useful SoVR and SiVR transformations to the breakable cycles, in such a way that there is an edge between them if the transformation can break the cycle), (3) Solver (Reducing the problem of breaking cycles as a weighted set covering optimization problem and finding an optimal solution using the ILP solver of ISL framework [19]), (4) Transformer (Applying SoVR and SiVR transformation from the optimal solution to break cycles).

4.1   Dependence Cycles Finder

This component takes the polyhedral intermediate representation (also referred to as SCoP) extracted from a target loop as an input. Then, the loop-carried and loop-independent flow-, anti-, and output-dependences (including both data and control dependences) of the target loop are computed using the PPCG dependence analyzer. Afterwards, these dependences are represented as a directed graph, where a node denotes a statement, and an edge denotes a dependence between two statements. Also, each edge of a directed graph is annotated with a dependence type: flow-, anti-, or output-. Now, *PolySIMD* computes all strongly connected components (SCC's) of the directed

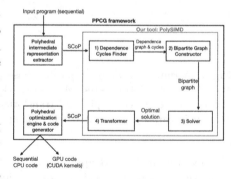

Fig. 2. Workflow of *PolySIMD* implemented as an extension to the PPCG [20].

graph using the *Tarjan's algorithm* [11]. Then, all elementary cycles[2] for every SCC of the dependence graph are identified using the *Johnson's algorithm* [12], an efficient algorithm to enumerate all elementary cycles of a directed graph. The worst case time complexity of the algorithm is $O((n + e)(c + 1))$ where n is the number of vertices, e is the number of edges and c is the number of distinct elementary cycles in a directed graph. For example, applying *Johnson*'s algorithm on a dependence graph of the running example (shown in Fig. 1 and has only one SCC) results in three elementary cycles c1/c2/c3: s1-s3-s2-s4-s1/s1-s3-s4-s1/s1-s2-s4-s1 on the `loop-i`.

Note that SoVR and SiVR transformation cannot break a cycle if the cycle is either a pure flow- or pure output-dependence cycle [5]. Since our approach considers only SoVR and SiVR into the formulation, if *PolySIMD* encounters any dependence cycle involving pure flow- or pure output-dependences in a SCC, then the tool ignores the SCC and continues with the rest of SCC's. If each SCC have either a pure flow- or pure output-dependence cycle, then *PolySIMD* will skip rest of steps in our approach, otherwise the tool continues with next steps. Since the three cycles c1, c2, and c3 of the running example are neither pure-flow nor pure-output dependence cycles, our approach proceeds to the next step.

4.2   Bipartite Graph Constructor

This component constructs a bipartite graph between a union of useful SoVR and SiVR transformations (see Sect. 2 for usefulness criteria) and breakable cycles of the dependence graph such that there is an edge between them if applying the transformation can break the cycle. As from the usefulness criteria, Table 3 shows a tabular version of the bipartite graph constructed for the running example.

Table 3. Bipartite graph constructed on the dependence graph of the original program in Fig. 1.

Transformations (T)	Cycles (C)
t1 = SoVR(s1, b[2i+2])	c3
t2 = SiVR(s2, b[2i])	c3
t3 = SiVR(s3, a[i])	c1, c2
t4 = SoVR(s3, c[i+5])	c2
t5 = SiVR(s4, c[i])	c2

4.3   Solver

After constructing the bipartite graph, the problem of finding an optimal set of transformations for cycle breaking is reduced to a minimum weighted set cover optimization problem (C, T, W) where C refers to a collection of cycles, T refers to a set of useful SoVR and SiVR transformations, and W refers to a set of weights for each transformation. The goal of the optimization problem is to identify the minimum weighted sub-collection of T whose union covers all cycles in C, and the optimization problem is known to be NP-hard. Hence, we

---

[2] An elementary cycle of a directed graph is a path in which no vertex appears twice except the first and last vertices. Since elementary cycles form a basis for enumerating all cycles in a directed graph, breaking all of them results in an acyclic graph.

formulate the minimum weighted set covering problem as the following integer
linear programming (ILP) in our tool-chain.

Variables:

– A variable t_i for each transformation of T

$$t_i \in \{0, 1\}, \forall t_i \in T$$

   where $t_i = 1$ indicates that the transformation t_i should be applied on the
   original program, otherwise it should be ignored.
– A weight parameter w_i for each transformation t_i to indicate an additional
   execution overhead (ignoring cache effects), and is measured using the additional loads and stores introduced by the transformation per one iteration of
   the target loop (See Table 2 for more details).
– A *latencyratio* parameter to indicate the ratio of access times of main memory
   to registers, and this parameter is used in converting weight parameters of
   SiVR transformations (introduced pointer-based loads/stores) into same units
   as of weight parameters of SoVR transformations (introduces scalar-based
   loads/stores).

Acyclicity constraint: The acyclic constraint on the dependence graph is modeled into a condition that each cycle of C should be covered by at-least one
transformation of T.

$$\forall c_j \text{ in } C, \left(\sum_{\substack{\forall t_i \text{ in } T \\ \text{such that } t_i \text{ can break } c_j}} t_i \right) \geq 1$$

Objective function: Our approach targets at minimizing additional overhead
introduced by the optimal set of transformations.

$$\text{Minimize} \left(\sum_{\forall t_i \text{ in } T} w_i \times t_i \right)$$

The ILP formulation for the example is as follows (Assuming *latencyratio* as
50).

$$T = \{t1, t2, t3, t4, t5\}, \quad C = \{c1, c2, c3\}, t_i \in \{0, 1\}, \forall t_i \in T,$$
$$w1 = w4 = 2, \quad w2 = w3 = w5 = 50 \times 3 = 150,$$
$$t3 \geq 1, t3 + t4 + t5 \geq 1, t1 + t2 \geq 1,$$
$$\text{Minimize} \left(2 \times (t1 + t4) + 150 \times (t2 + t3 + t5) \right)$$

   The optimal solution obtained for the above formulation is *(t1 = 1, t2 =
0, t3 = 1, t4 = 0, and t5 = 0)*, i.e., applying SoVR on **s2** and SiVR on **s3**
can break all cycles present in the running example with minimal additional

overhead introduced. Note that the above solution is different to the solution
(t2 = 1, t3 = 1) from the Calland et al's approach in [5] since our approach
considers both SoVR and SiVR transformations into the formulation, unlike the
Calland et al's approach which includes only SiVR transformations.

Heuristics. There can be simple heuristics such as applying SoVR transformation
in the beginning to break as many cycles it can and followed by applying SiVR
transformation to break rest of cycles, which can lead to the similar performance
improvements compared to our approach. The solution from such heuristics may
include redundant SoVR transformations, which can be observed on the running
example. Applying transformation t4 (SoVR) on the running example (ahead of
SiVR transformations) to break the cycle c2 is redundant because the transformation t3 (SiVR) will eventually break the cycle c2 and also can break cycle c1
that cannot be broken by any SoVR transformation.

There can exists other heuristics or greedy algorithms to the minimum
weighted set cover optimization problem. But, we believe that an ILP formulation formalizes the optimization problem without being tied to specific heuristics, which in turn reduces performance anomalies that can occur in optimization
heuristics; Also, the compile-times for the results in this experimental evaluation are less than half a second (see Table 5 for more details). We also believe
that our framework can be easily extended to include other heuristics or greedy
algorithms to the optimization problem.

4.4   Transformer

This component applies the optimal set of transformations obtained from the
solver onto the intermediate polyhedral representation of the target loop. It is
also mentioned in [5] that the order of applying SoVR and SiVR transformations
doesn't have any effect on the final program. Hence, *PolySIMD* first applies SoVR
transformations from the optimal solution, and then followed by SiVR transformations from rest of the optimal solution. The generation of new assignment
statements, modifying schedules of statements, and updating the references as
part of the code transformations are implemented using the dependence analyzer
and schedule trees of the PPCG framework.

After applying all transformations from the optimal solution, *PolySIMD* feeds
the transformed intermediate polyhedral representation to the PPCG optimization engine to perform statement reordering based on the topological sorting
of the transformed dependence graph. Note that all of the benchmarks in the
experimental evaluation required statement reordering transformation to be performed without which the Intel's ICC v17.0 product compiler couldn't vectorize.
This demonstrates the necessity of coupling storage optimizations with the loop
optimization framework. Finally, *PolySIMD* leverages code generation capabilities of the PPCG framework to generate transformed sequential CPU code that
can be input into a vectorizing compiler like ICC or generates GPU code (CUDA
kernels) that can be processed by a GPU compiler like NVCC.

4.5 Bounding Additional Space

We believe that one of the major key limitations in the unavailability of variable renaming techniques (especially on arrays) in modern compilers is due to the lack of support for bounding the additional space required to break memory-based dependences. Hence, we provide a clause (i.e., *spacelimit*) to the directive "#pragma vectorize" that can help programmers to limit the additional space to enable enhanced vectorization of inner-most loops, and the *spacelimit* is expressed in multiples of vector registers length. The clause *spacelimit* essentially helps our approach to compute strip size that can be vectorized, and the formula to compute the strip size (in multiples of vector length) is as follows.

$$\text{strip size} = \left\lfloor \frac{\text{spacelimit} \times VLEN - |T_{SoVR}| \times VLEN}{|T_{SiVR}| \times VLEN} \right\rfloor = \left\lfloor \frac{\text{spacelimit} - |T_{SoVR}|}{|T_{SiVR}|} \right\rfloor$$

where $|T_{SoVR}|$ and $|T_{SiVR}|$ refer to number of SoVR and SiVR transformations in the optimal solution respectively. If the strip size value is non-positive for a given *spacelimit*, then our approach ignores applying renaming transformations. Otherwise, our approach does strip mining of the target loop before applying any of the renaming transformations from the optimal solution.

5 Performance Evaluation

In this section, we present an evaluation of our *PolySIMD* tool relative to Intel's ICC v17.0 product compiler and to the two algorithms presented in past work [5,8] for performing SiVR and SoVR transformations to break cycles of a dependence graph. We begin with an overview of the experimental setup and the benchmark suite used in our evaluation, and then present experimental results for the three different comparisons.

5.1 Experimental Platforms

Our evaluation uses the following two SIMD architectures. (1) A many-core Intel Xeon Phi Knights Landing (KNL) processor with two 512-bit vector processing units (VPU) per core. Thus, each 512-bit VPU can perform SIMD operations on 16 single-precision floating point values, i.e., the VPU has an effective vector length of 16 (for 32-bit operands). Since we are evaluating vectorization for single-threaded benchmarks, we only use one core of the KNL processor in our evaluation, though our approach can be applied to multithreaded applications as well. (2) An Nvidia Volta accelerator (Tesla V100) with 80 symmetric multiprocessors (SMs), each of which can multiplex one or more thread blocks. A thread block can contain a maximum of 1024 threads, which are decomposed into 32-thread warps for execution on the SM. Thus, each SM can be viewed as being analogous to a VPU with an effective vector length of 32 (for 32-bit operands). For consistency with our KNL results, we only generate one block of

1024 threads per benchmark, thereby only using one SM in the GPU. However, our approach can be applied to multi-SM executions as well. Table 4 lists the system specifications and the compiler options used in our evaluations. The comparison with ICC could only be performed on KNL, since ICC does not generate code for Nvidia GPUs. The comparison with the two algorithms from past work [5, 8] were performed on both platforms.

Table 4. Summary of SIMD architectures and compiler flags used in our experiments. SP refers to Single Precision floating point operands, VPU refers to a KNL Vector Processing Unit, and SM refers to a GPU Streaming Multiprocessor.

	Intel Xeon Phi	Nvidia Volta
Microarch	Knights Landing	Tesla V100
SIMD lanes	16 SP per VPU (2 VPU's per core)	32 SP per SM
Compiler	Intel ICC v17.0	Nvidia NVCC v9.1
Compiler flags	-O3 -xmic-avx512	-O3 -arch=sm_70 -ccbin=icc

5.2 Benchmarks

We use the Test Suite for Vectorizing Compilers (TSVC) benchmark suite in our evaluation, originally developed in FORTRAN to assess the vectorization capabilities of compilers [4]. Later, the benchmark suite was translated into C with additional benchmarks to address limitations in the original suite [16], so we used this C version for our evaluations. A detailed study of these benchmarks, along with the vectorization capabilities of multiple compilers can be found in [9, 16]. Since our goal is to evaluate the effectiveness of renaming variables on breaking dependence cycles that inhibit vectorization, we restrict our attention to TSVC benchmarks that contain multi-statement dependence cycles containing at least one anti/output dependence and that cannot be broken by scalar privatization. Further, since *PolySIMD* is based on a polyhedral optimization framework, we further restricted our attention to the subset of these benchmarks that do not contain non-affine expressions that prevent polyhedral analysis[3]. This selection resulted in 11 benchmarks from the TSVC suite that will be the focus of our evaluation, and are summarized in Table 5.

5.3 Comparison with ICC

As discussed in Fig. 2, *PolySIMD* takes a sequential program as input, and generates sequential code as output with selected variable renamings and statement reorderings that enable enhanced vectorization. Figure 3 shows the speedups obtained by using *PolySIMD* as a preprocessor to Intel's ICC v17.0 product

---

[3] This constraint arises from the implementation of our algorithm in *PolySIMD*; our algorithm can be applied in a non-polyhedral compiler setting as well.

Table 5. Summary of the 11 benchmarks from the TSVC suite used in our evaluation, including the number of statements, number of dependences, and number of elementary cycles per benchmark (excluding self-loop cycles). The benchmarks were executed using $N = 2^{25}$ and $T = 200$ as input parameters. Number of SiVR and SoVR transformations performed by *PolySIMD* for the 11 benchmarks, and also the overall compilation times required. Coincidentally, none of these benchmarks triggered a case in which both SiVR and SoVR transformations had to be performed.

Benchmark	#Stmts	#Deps	#Elementary cycles	Our ILP solution		Compilation time (sec)	
				#SoVR's	#SiVR's	PolySIMD	Total
s116	5	5	1	1	0	0.08	0.10
s1244	2	2	1	1	0	0.01	0.02
s241	2	3	1	1	0	0.01	0.03
s243	3	6	2	1	0	0.02	0.04
s244	3	4	1	1	0	0.02	0.03
s2251	3	4	1	0	1	0.02	0.03
s252	3	5	2	0	2	0.02	0.04
s254	2	2	1	0	1	0.01	0.02
s255	3	6	3	0	2	0.02	0.04
s257	2	3	1	0	1	0.02	0.04
s261	4	9	3	0	2	0.02	0.04

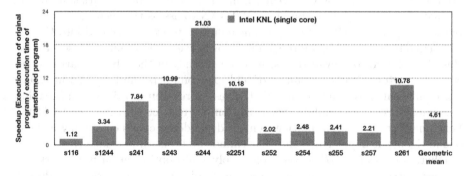

Fig. 3. Speedups using *PolySIMD* on the eleven benchmarks from the TSVC suite, compiled using the Intel's ICC v17.0 product compiler and running on a single core of Intel Knights Landing processor.

compiler on the KNL platform. The speedup represents the ratio of the execution time of the original program compiled with ICC to the execution time of the transformed program compiled with ICC, using the compiler options in Table 4 in both cases. As can be seen in Fig. 3, the use of *PolySIMD* as a preprocessor results in significant performance improvements for the 11 kernels. The transformations performed by *PolySIMD* are summarized in Table 5; the fact that no benchmark required both SiVR and SoVR transformations is a pure coincidence. We now discuss the two groups of benchmarks for which *PolySIMD* applied the SoVR and SiVR transformations respectively.

Source Variable Renaming (SoVR): The benchmarks s116, s1244, s241, s243, s244 in the first five entries of Table 5 contain multi-statement recurrences involving outgoing anti-dependences. Hence, *PolySIMD* applied the SoVR transformation on these benchmarks to reposition these outgoing anti-dependence edges to break the cycles, as dictated by the column titled *SoVR* under *ILP solution* of Table 5. There are a few interesting observations that can be made from the results in Table 5 for these five benchmarks: (1) The SoVR transformation enabled vectorization for all five benchmarks (as confirmed by the compiler log output), and resulted in speedups varying from 1.12× to 21.02× on Intel KNL relative to the original program using the Intel's ICC v17.0 product compiler. (2) The s1244 benchmark involves dead-write statements (i.e., there are no reads of a write before another statement writing to the same location) whose removal eliminate dependence cycles. Currently, *PolySIMD* doesn't check for dead-write statements unlike the Intel compiler (with O3 optimization flag enabled) which remove the dead writes to enable the vectorization. As a result, there is a lower speedup with our approach compared to the Intel compiler. (3) The reason for less speedup in case of the s116 benchmark is the generation of non-unit (unaligned) strided loads and stores leading to inefficient vectorization (as confirmed by the compiler log output describing the estimated potential speedup as 1.36×). (4) All these five benchmarks required statement reordering to be performed after the SoVR transformations, without which the Intel's compiler wasn't able to vectorize. This indicates the necessity of loop transformations framework to output the final code that can be vectorizable by the existing compilers.

Sink Variable Renaming (SiVR): The column titled *SiVR* under *ILP solution* indicates that the SiVR transformation should be performed on the remaining benchmarks (s2251, s252, s254, s255, s257, s261) in Table 5. These benchmarks have dependence cycles involving anti- and output-dependences, and hence our approach chose only the SiVR transformations to break these dependence cycles. As with the earlier five benchmarks, there are a few interesting observations that can be made from the results in Table 5 for these later three benchmarks: (1) The SiVR transformation enabled vectorization for all the remaining six benchmarks, and resulted in speedups varying from 2.02× to 10.77× on the Intel KNL platform relative to the original program. The compiler log output shows that vectorization was indeed performed in all cases. (2) The benchmarks s252, s254, s255, s257[4] have loop-carried flow-dependence and loop-independent anti-dependences on scalars, and resolving these dependences on scalars using our approach introduced higher overhead from temporary arrays pointer-based loads and stores. As a result, the performance improvements in these benchmarks are relatively low. (3) As seen with earlier five benchmarks benefited by the SoVR transformation along with the statement reordering, these six benchmarks also required statement reordering to be performed after the SiVR transformations, without which the Intel's compiler wasn't able to vectorize.

---

[4] Also, most of accesses in these benchmarks are dominated with scalars.

5.4   Comparison with Calland et al's Approach

The heuristics proposed by Calland et al. [5] aim to find the minimum number of SiVR transformations to break all dependence cycles involving memory-based dependences. As a result, the heuristics choose only SiVR transformations for vectorizing all the eleven benchmarks. However, our approach chooses to perform SoVR transformations on five of the eleven benchmarks (s116, s1244, s241, s243, s244), since SoVR incurs less overhead than SiVR. Hence, we observe speedups (shown in Table 6) with our approach relative to Calland et al, varying from 1.07× to 1.24× on the Intel KNL platform and 1.12× to 1.57× on the NVIDIA Volta. For the remaining six benchmarks, our approach chose exactly the same set of SiVR transformations as did their approach, and hence there is no performance improvement in these cases. The overall geometric-mean speedups on all of the eleven benchmarks are 1.08× and 1.14× relative to their approach on the KNL and Volta platforms.

Table 6. Speedups on the Intel KNL processor and NVIDIA Volta accelerator using *PolySIMD* on seven benchmarks from the eleven benchmarks relative to past approaches, i.e., Calland et al. [5] and Chu et al. [8]. We excluded the remaining four benchmarks from the table since our results were similar to both of the past works.

Benchmark	Intel KNL		NVIDIA Volta	
	Calland et al. approach	Chu et al. approach	Calland et al. approach	Chu et al. approach
s116	1.20×	1.03×	1.29×	1.27×
s1244	1.10×	4.03×	1.57×	1.51×
s241	1.07×	1.49×	1.31×	1.70×
s243	1.27×	1.59×	1.47×	1.61×
s244	1.24×	1.22×	1.12×	1.32×
s257	1.00×	9.74×	1.00×	1.08×
s261	1.00×	1.20×	1.00×	1.19×

5.5   Comparison with Chu et al's Approach

Chu et al. proposed an algorithm for resolving general multistatement recurrences which considers both SoVR and SiVR transformation [8]. The solution obtained by their algorithm depends on a traversal of the dependence graph, and may not be optimal in general. Further, their algorithm may include redundant SiVR transformations, which were observed when applying their algorithm to benchmarks s241, s243, s257 and 261, leading to lower performance compared to our approach. We observed performance improvements on these benchmarks with our approach (relative to Chu et al), varying from 1.20× to 9.74× on KNL and 1.08× to 1.70× on Volta. For the remaining three benchmarks s116, s1244 and s244 in Table 6, our approach chose the same solution as their approach, but we still obtained better performance because *PolySIMD* generates private scalars for SoVR transformations, unlike their algorithm which generates temporary arrays for the SoVR transformations. The generation of private scalars enabled our approach to achieve performance improvements speedups ranging from 1.03× to 4.03× on KNL and 1.27× to 1.51× on Volta. The overall geometric-mean speedups on all of the eleven benchmarks were 1.57× and 1.22× on the KNL and Volta platforms.

6 Related Work

Since there exists an extensive body of research literature in handling memory-based dependences, we focus on past contributions that are closely related to variable expansion [10], variable renaming including SoVR [5,15], SiVR [5–8] and Array SSA [14,17].

Comparison with past approaches involving SoVR and/or SiVR transformations. Calland et al. [5] formally defined both SoVR and SiVR transformations, and also explained the impact of these transformations on a dependence graph. Also, Calland et al. proved that the problem of finding the minimum number of statements to be transformed—to break artificial dependence paths involving anti- or output-dependences—is NP-complete, and proposed some heuristics. However, the implementation and impact of these techniques on the performance of representative benchmarks were not mentioned. But, *PolySIMD* utilizes both SoVR and SiVR in a complementary manner to coordinate each other, and is built on a polyhedral framework (PPCG), and leveraged it for statement reordering to enable vectorization. Also, we did not find a framework publicly available from the past approaches. Chu et al. work in [7,8] discussed dependence-breaking strategies in the context of recurrence relations, and developed an algorithm for the resolution of general multi-statement recurrences using the proposed strategies. But, the proposed algorithm for the resolution of cycles is not optimal and may generate solutions having redundant SoVR transformations.

Other works on storage transformations. Array SSA has been developed to convert a given program into a static single assignment form to enable automatic parallelization of loops involving memory-based dependences [14], and also to extend classical scalar optimizations to arrays [17]. However, applying renaming on writes of every statement of a loop body is significantly expensive in terms of additional space requirements, and may not be required for enabling vectorization. Other approaches such as variable expansion [10] can be used to break specific memory-based dependences. The variable expansion may be beneficial for applying onto scalars but expanding multi-dimensional arrays inside the inner-most loop for vectorization is expensive in terms of additional space. But, variable expansion can be useful in eliminating pure-output dependence cycles unlike with SoVR and SiVR, which is a part of our future work.

Bounding additional space. There has been lack of support for bounding the extra space required to break memory-based dependences in the past approaches [5,8]. But, our approach provides a *spacelimit* clause that can help programmers to specify the maximum amount of extra storage that can be allocated. An alternative approach to enable parallelization or vectorization has always been to convert the program to (dynamic) single assignment form, through array expansion, followed by affine scheduling [3] for vectorization, and then applying storage mapping optimization [2] (a generalized form of array contraction). Yet no such scheme can provide the guarantees that the affine transformations obtained on the fully expanded arrays will enable storage mapping optimization to restore a low-footprint implementation. Enforcing an a priori limit on memory usage would be even harder to achieve. Furthermore, no integrated system enabling vectorization through such a complex path of expansion and contraction has been available until now.

7 Conclusions and Future Work

Despite the fact that compiler technologies for automatic vectorization have been under development for over four decades, there are still considerable gaps in the capabilities of modern compilers to perform automatic vectorization for SIMD units. This paper focuses on advancing the state of the art with respect to handling *memory-based anti* (write-after-read) or *output* (write-after-write) dependences in vectorizing compilers. In this work, we integrate both Source Variable Renaming (SoVR) and Sink Variable Renaming (SiVR) transformations into a unified formulation, and formalize the "cycle-breaking" problem as a minimum weighted set cover optimization problem. Our approach also can ensure that the additional storage introduced by our transformations remains within the user-provided bounds.

We implemented our approach in PPCG, a state-of-the-art optimization framework for loop transformations, and evaluated it on eleven kernels from the TSVC benchmark suite. Our experimental results show a geometric mean performance improvement of $4.61\times$ on an Intel Xeon Phi (KNL) machine relative to the optimized performance obtained by Intel's ICC v17.0 product compiler. Further, our results demonstrate a geometric mean performance improvement of $1.08\times$ and $1.14\times$ on the Intel Xeon Phi (KNL) and Nvidia Tesla V100 (Volta) platforms relative to past work that only performs the SiVR transformation [5], and of $1.57\times$ and $1.22\times$ on both platforms relative to past work on using both SiVR and SoVR transformations [8]. We believe that our techniques will be increasingly important in the current era of pervasive SIMD parallelism, since non-vectorized code will incur an increasing penalty in execution time on future hardware platforms.

As part of the future work, we plan to work on extending the unified formulation by including variable expansion [10] and forward propagation techniques [15] to break pure-output and to handle pure-flow dependence cycles respectively. Also, we plan to extend our approach and implementation to handle non-affine regions of codes, and also to support vectorization of outer loops as well. Furthermore, we plan to investigate into enabling loop transformations (such as tiling in case of cycles on tiles) using variable renaming transformations.

References

1. Baghdadi, R., et al.: PENCIL: a platform-neutral compute intermediate language for accelerator programming. In: Proceedings of the 2015 International Conference on Parallel Architecture and Compilation (PACT), PACT 2015, pp. 138–149. IEEE Computer Society, Washington, DC (2015). https://doi.org/10.1109/PACT.2015.17

2. Bhaskaracharya, S.G., Bondhugula, U., Cohen, A.: SMO: an integrated approach to intra-array and inter-array storage optimization. In: Proceedings of the 43rd Annual ACM SIGPLAN-SIGACT Symposium on Principles of Programming Languages, POPL 2016, pp. 526–538. ACM, New York (2016). https://doi.org/10.1145/2837614.2837636

3. Bondhugula, U., Acharya, A., Cohen, A.: The Pluto+ algorithm: a practical approach for parallelization and locality optimization of affine loop nests. ACM Trans. Program. Lang. Syst. **38**(3), 12:1–12:32 (2016). https://doi.org/10.1145/2896389

4. Callahan, D., Dongarra, J., Levine, D.: Vectorizing compilers: a test suite and results. In: Proceedings of the 1988 ACM/IEEE Conference on Supercomputing, Supercomputing 1988, pp. 98–105. IEEE Computer Society Press, Los Alamitos (1988). http://dl.acm.org/citation.cfm?id=62972.62987

5. Calland, P., Darte, A., Robert, Y., Vivien, F.: On the removal of anti- and output-dependences. Int. J. Parallel Program. **26**(2), 285–312 (1998). https://doi.org/10.1023/A:1018790129478

6. Chang, W.L., Chu, C.P., Ho, M.S.H.: Exploitation of parallelism to nested loops with dependence cycles. J. Syst. Arch. **50**(12), 729–742 (2004). https://doi.org/10.1016/j.sysarc.2004.06.001. http://www.sciencedirect.com/science/article/pii/S1383762104000670

7. Chu, C.P.: A theoretical approach involving recurrence resolution, dependence cycle statement ordering and subroutine transformation for the exploitation of parallelism in sequential code. Ph.D. thesis, Louisiana State University, Baton Rouge, LA, USA (1992). uMI Order No. GAX92-07498

8. Chu, C.P., Carver, D.L.: An analysis of recurrence relations in Fortran Do-loops for vector processing. In: Proceedings. The Fifth International Parallel Processing Symposium, pp. 619–625, April 1991. https://doi.org/10.1109/IPPS.1991.153845

9. Evans, G.C., Abraham, S., Kuhn, B., Padua, D.A.: Vector seeker: a tool for finding vector potential. In: Proceedings of the 2014 Workshop on Programming Models for SIMD/Vector Processing, WPMVP 2014, pp. 41–48. ACM, New York (2014). https://doi.org/10.1145/2568058.2568069

10. Feautrier, P.: Array expansion. In: Proceedings of the 2nd International Conference on Supercomputing, ICS 1988, pp. 429–441. ACM, New York (1988). https://doi.org/10.1145/55364.55406

11. Hopcroft, J., Tarjan, R.: Algorithm 447: efficient algorithms for graph manipulation. Commun. ACM **16**(6), 372–378 (1973). https://doi.org/10.1145/362248.362272

12. Johnson, D.B.: Finding all the elementary circuits of a directed graph. SIAM J. Comput. **4**(1), 77–84 (1975). https://doi.org/10.1137/0204007

13. Kennedy, K., Allen, J.R.: Optimizing Compilers for Modern Architectures: A Dependence-Based Approach. Morgan Kaufmann Publishers Inc., San Francisco (2002)

14. Knobe, K., Sarkar, V.: Array SSA form and its use in parallelization. In: Proceedings of the 25th ACM SIGPLAN-SIGACT Symposium on Principles of Programming Languages, POPL 1998, pp. 107–120. ACM, New York (1998). https://doi.org/10.1145/268946.268956

15. Kuck, D.J., Kuhn, R.H., Padua, D.A., Leasure, B., Wolfe, M.: Dependence graphs and compiler optimizations. In: Proceedings of the 8th ACM SIGPLAN-SIGACT Symposium on Principles of Programming Languages, POPL 1981, pp. 207–218. ACM, New York (1981). https://doi.org/10.1145/567532.567555

16. Maleki, S., Gao, Y., Garzarán, M.J., Wong, T., Padua, D.A.: An evaluation of vectorizing compilers. In: Proceedings of the 2011 International Conference on Parallel Architectures and Compilation Techniques, PACT 2011, pp. 372–382. IEEE Computer Society, Washington, DC (2011). https://doi.org/10.1109/PACT.2011.68

17. Rus, S., He, G., Alias, C., Rauchwerger, L.: Region array SSA. In: Proceedings of the 15th International Conference on Parallel Architectures and Compilation Techniques, PACT 2006, pp. 43–52. ACM, New York (2006). https://doi.org/10.1145/1152154.1152165

18. Stephens, N., et al.: The ARM scalable vector extension. IEEE Micro **37**(2), 26–39 (2017). https://doi.org/10.1109/MM.2017.35

19. Verdoolaege, S.: *isl*: an integer set library for the polyhedral model. In: Fukuda, K., Hoeven, J., Joswig, M., Takayama, N. (eds.) ICMS 2010. LNCS, vol. 6327, pp. 299–302. Springer, Heidelberg (2010). https://doi.org/10.1007/978-3-642-15582-6_49

20. Verdoolaege, S., Carlos Juega, J., Cohen, A., Ignacio Gómez, J., Tenllado, C., Catthoor, F.: Polyhedral parallel code generation for CUDA. ACM Trans. Archit. Code Optim. **9**(4), 54:1–54:23 (2013). https://doi.org/10.1145/2400682.2400713

21. Weiss, M.: Strip mining on SIMD architectures. In: Proceedings of the 5th International Conference on Supercomputing, ICS 1991, pp. 234–243. ACM, New York (1991). https://doi.org/10.1145/109025.109083

Design and Performance Analysis of Real-Time Dynamic Streaming Applications

Xuan Khanh Do[1]([⊠]), Stéphane Louise[1], and Albert Cohen[2]

[1] CEA, LIST, 91191 Gif-sur-Yvette Cedex, France
{xuankhanh.do,stephane.louise}@cea.fr
[2] INIRA and ENS, 45 rue d'Ulm, 75005 Paris, France
albert.cohen@inria.fr

Abstract. Static dataflow graphs enable powerful design, implementation and analysis methods for embedded systems. Nevertheless, complex signal and media processing applications—such as cognitive radio or modern video codecs—display dynamic behavior that do not fit the classical cyclo-static restrictions. An approach to tackle this limitation combines integer parameters—to express dynamic rates—with control actors—to allow topology and mode changes as well as time-dependent scheduling and constraints, as introduced in the Transaction Parameterized Dataflow (TPDF) model of computation. In this paper we present a technique to automatically analyse the static properties of a TPDF application, including consistency, liveness, boundedness and worst-case throughput. Our implementation of these analyses is validated against a set of real-life dynamic applications, demonstrating significant buffer size and throughput improvements compared to the state of the art models, including Cyclo-Static Dataflow (CSDF) and Scenario-Aware Dataflow (SADF).

Keywords: Models of computation · Dataflow · Performance of systems

1 Introduction

The limits on power usage and dissipation is encouraging a trend towards on-chip parallelism in both HPC and embedded systems. Since the early 2000s, this trend has fostered the appearance of so-called many-core systems which are already available from several vendors, e.g., the MPPA-256 from Kalray (256 cores) [6] or Epiphany from Adapteva (64 cores). This broader availability of low-power many-core platforms opens new opportunities for system designers, but introduces also several challenges in expressing parallelism and facilitating the efficient mapping, performance tuning and analysis of applications.

Dataflow models of computation (MoC) are widely used to analyze and optimize streaming applications mapped onto embedded many-core platforms.

© Springer Nature Switzerland AG 2019
M. Hall and H. Sundar (Eds.): LCPC 2018, LNCS 11882, pp. 21–36, 2019.
https://doi.org/10.1007/978-3-030-34627-0_2

Applications are modeled as directed graphs where nodes represent actors (iterated execution of tasks) and edges represent communication channels. Among these, some dataflow models like SDF [14] and CSDF [5] families provide many decision procedures and optimization algorithms, they are useful for their predictability, formal abstraction, and amenability to powerful optimization techniques. However, it is not always possible or convenient to represent all of the functionality of a complex media and signal processing application in terms of a static dataflow representation; typical challenges include variable data rates, multi-standard or multi-mode signal processing, and data-dependent forms of adaptive behavior. For this reason, numerous dynamic dataflow modeling techniques—whose behavior is characterized by dynamic variations in resource requirements—have been proposed. In many of these, in exchange for the higher expressive power, translating into increased modeling flexibility, one must give up statically decidable guarantees on buffer underflow (deadlock), overflow (boundedness) or performance analysis (e.g., throughput).

Transaction Parameterized Dataflow (TPDF) [8] is a recently proposed model allowing dynamic changes of the graph topology, variable production/consumption rates and time constraints enforcement. The dynamic behaviour of TPDF can be viewed upon as a collection of different behaviours, called *cases*, occurring in certain unknown patterns. Each case of a TPDF graph is characterized by a value of its parameter and a graph topology. For this reason, each case is by itself fairly static and predictable in performance and resource usage and can be dealt with by traditional methods. In this paper we introduce a technique to automatically analyse a TPDF application for its static properties (i.e., consistency, liveness and boundedness) and its worst-case performance (e.g., throughput). TPDF would naturally fit larger frameworks such as Ptolemy [18], Open RVC-CAL [22], or dataflow visual programming languages such as LabView [12] or Matlab/Simulink. In this paper, We prefered to focus on the model's properties and specific algorithms, we will consider its interaction with wider semantical frameworks in future studies. In particular, while LabView and Simulink are widely and successfully deployed in industry, significantly reducing development time, they lacking the static guarantees and formal verification capabilities provided in TPDF. In summary, the contributions of this paper consist in:

- a formal model of TPDF based on the $(\max, +)$ algebra;
- methods to analyse the static properties and worst-case throughput of TPDF graphs;
- an implementation of the analysis algorithms, demonstrating significant buffer size and throughput improvements compared to CSDF and SADF.

The remainder of this paper is organised as follows. Section 2 recalls some technical preliminaries of CSDF, TPDF and introduces their $(\max, +)$ modeling. Then Sect. 3 presents the static analyses of this dynamic model for liveness, boundedness, worst-case throughput and a scheduling heuristic for TPDF. The latter is illustrated and evaluated in Sect. 4, considering different realistic case studies. Finally, we discuss the related work in Sect. 5 and summarize our contributions in Sect. 6.

2   Model of Computation

We first present CSDF [5], one of the reference dataflow MoC for applications in the signal processing domain. Then, TPDF [8] is introduced as a parameterized extension of CSDF with transaction processes. The dynamic behaviors of this model can be captured by using (max, +) algebra, as presented in Sect. 2.3.

2.1   Basic Model: CSDF

Cyclo-Static Dataflow (CSDF) [5] is chosen as the basic model for TPDF because it is deterministic and allows for checking conditions such as deadlocks and bounded memory execution at compile/design time, which is usually not possible for Dynamic Dataflow (DDF). In CSDF, a program is defined as a directed graph $G = \langle A, E \rangle$, where A is a set of actors and $E \subseteq A \times A$ is a set of communication channels. Actors represent functions that transform incoming data streams into outgoing data streams. An atomic data object carried by a channel is called a *token*. Each channel has an initial status, characterized by its *initial tokens*.

Every actor $a_j \in A$ has a cyclic *execution sequence* $[f_j(0), f_j(1), \cdots, f_j(\tau_j - 1)]$ of length τ_j. The interpretation of this sequence is: The n-th time that actor a_j is fired, it executes the code of function $f_j(n \mod \tau_j)$ and produces (consumes) $x_j^u(n \mod \tau_j)$ (or $y_j^u(n \mod \tau_j)$) tokens on its output (input) channel e_u. The firing rule of a cyclo-static actor a_j is evaluated as true for its n-th firing if and only if all input channels contain at least $y_j^u(n \mod \tau_j)$ tokens. The total number of tokens produced (consumed) by actor a_j on channel e_u during the first n invocations, denoted by $X_j^u(n) = \sum_{l=0}^{n-1} x_j^u(l)$ (or $Y_j^u(n) = \sum_{l=0}^{n-1} y_j^u(l)$).

Definition 1. *Given a connected CSDF graph G, a **valid static schedule** for G is a schedule that can be repeated infinitely while the buffer size remains bounded. A vector $\overrightarrow{q} = [q_1, q_2, ..., q_n]^T$ is a **repetition vector** of G if each q_j represents the number of invocations of an actor a_j in a valid static schedule for G. A CSDF graph is called **consistent** if and only if it has a non-trivial repetition vector [5].*

Theorem 1. *In a CSDF graph G, a repetition vector $\overrightarrow{q} = [q_1, q_2, ..., q_n]^T$ is given by [5]:*

$$\overrightarrow{q} = P \cdot \overrightarrow{r} \text{ , with } P = P_{jk} = \begin{cases} \tau_j & \text{, if } j = k \\ 0 & \text{, otherwise} \end{cases} \tag{1}$$

where $\overrightarrow{r} = [r_1, r_2, ..., r_n]^T$ is a solution of

$$\Gamma \cdot \overrightarrow{r} = 0 \tag{2}$$

and where the topology matrix $\Gamma \in \mathbb{Z}^{|E| \times |A|}$ is defined by

$$\Gamma_{uj} = \begin{cases} X_j^u(\tau_j) & ,\textit{if task } a_j \textit{ produces on edge } e_u \\ -Y_j^u(\tau_j) & ,\textit{if task } a_j \textit{ consumes from edge } e_u \\ 0 & ,\textit{otherwise} \end{cases} \qquad (3)$$

2.2   Transaction Parameterized Dataflow

TPDF [8] is introduced as an extension of CSDF, allowing rates to be *parametric* and a new type of *control* actor, channel and port. For a compact formal notations, kernels, which play the same role as computation units (actors) as in CSDF, have at most *one* control port. Kernels without control ports are considered to always operate in a *dataflow* way, i.e., a kernel starts its firings only when there is enough data tokens on all of its data input ports.

Definition 2. *A TPDF graph $\mathcal{G}$ is defined by a tuple $(K, G, E, P, R_k, R_g, \alpha, \phi^*)$ where:*

– *K is a non-empty finite set of kernels and G is a finite set of control actors such that $K \cap G = \varnothing$. For each kernel $k \in K$, M_k denotes the set of modes indicated by the control node connected to its unique control port c. The following modes are available within a TPDF graph:*
  - *Mode 1: Select one of the data inputs (outputs)*
  - *Mode 2: Select more than one data input (output)*
  - *Mode 3: Select available data input with the highest priority*
  - *Mode 4: Wait until all data inputs are available*
  In this context, the effect of control tokens can be also described as selecting between available data input and output ports besides choosing modes.
– *$E \in O \times (I \cup C)$ is a set of directed channels, where I, C, O is the union of all input, control and output port sets respectively. $E_c = E \setminus (O \times I)$ is the set of all control channels. A control channel can start only from a control actor and is connected to a control port. All other channel are data channels, which can start only from a kernel.*
– *P is a set of integer parameters.*
– *$R_k : M_k \times (I_k \cup C_k \cup O_k) \times \mathbb{N} \longrightarrow \mathbb{N}$ assigns the rate to the ports of the n-th firing of k for each mode. The rate $R_k(m, c, n) = \{0, 1\}$ for all modes $m \in M_k$ and for all firings of k. We restrict the case of zero values if both of the production and consummation rate of a channel is 0.*
– *$R_g : (I_g \cup C_g \cup O_g) \times \mathbb{N} \longrightarrow \mathbb{N}$ assigns the rate to each port of the n-th firing of a control actor g.*
– *$\alpha : (I \cup C \cup O) \longrightarrow \mathbb{N}$ returns for each port its priority. By default, the priority is the same for all ports.*
– *$\phi^* : E \longrightarrow \mathbb{N}$ is the initial channel status.*

A kernel $k \in K$ is assumed to wait until its control port becomes available to be fired by reading one token from this port. This token defines in which mode

$m \in M_k$ k will operate. One of the most important property of TPDF, which is different from (C)SDF, is that a kernel or a control actor does not have to wait until sufficient tokens are available at every data input port. This new property allows the capacity of dynamic graph reconfiguration depending on context and time.

In TPDF, the n-th firing of a control actor $g \in G$ starts by waiting until $R_g(i,n)$ and $R_g(c,n)$ tokens are available at every input $i \in I_g$ and $c \in C_g$, where $R_g(c,n) = \{0,1\}$. After performing its actions, the n-th firing of g ends by removing the $R_g(i,n)$ and $R_g(c,n)$ tokens from its input data and control ports and writing $R_g(o,n)$ tokens to each output control port $o \in O_g$.

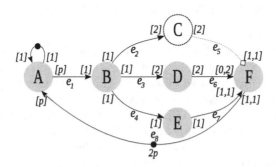

Fig. 1. Example of a TPDF graph with integer parameter p, control actor C and control channel e_5.

Example 1. Figure 1 depicts a TPDF graph with constant or parametric production/consumption rates (e.g., p for the rate of A). The repetition vector is $[2, 2p, p, p, 2p, 2p]$, respectively in the order A, B, C, D, E, F. C is a control actor and e_5 is a control channel. A sample execution of the graph is the following: A produces p tokens on e_1. Then B fires and produces one token on edge e_2, e_3, e_4. After, only E can fire because there are enough tokens on its input edge and produce one token on edge e_7. B (and A if necessary) will fire a second time and produce another token on edge e_2, e_3, e_4. Then C, D and E will fire and produce 2, 2 and 1 token, respectively, on edge e_5, e_6, e_7. Finally, F fires two times, each time it consumes one token from its control port. This token determines in which mode F will be fired. In this case, F can choose two tokens from e_6 or one from e_7 and remove the remaining tokens. This continues until each actor has fired a number of times equal to its repetition count.

In TPDF, two data distribution kernels *Select-duplicate, Transaction Box* [16] and a new type of control clock can be defined in a dataflow way.

- **Select-duplicate:** kernels with *one* entry and n outputs. At a given time, this actor has the ability to select a subset of its outputs to send the duplicated data tokens on.

- **Transaction:** symmetric processes with n inputs and *one* output. Its role is to atomically select a predefined number of tokens from one or several of its input to its output. By using special modes predefined by TPDF and combining with a control actor, the Transaction process implements important actions not available in usual dataflow MoC: Speculation, Redundancy with vote, Highest priority at a given deadline [16].
- **Clock:** can be considered as a watchdog timer with control tokens sent each time there is a timing out. The kernel which receives this time token will be awakened and fired immediately. In this way, TPDF can be applied to model streaming applications with time constraints, as can be seen in Sect. 4.1.

2.3   (max, +) Algebraic Semantics of TPDF

We use (max, +) algebra [1,11] to capture the semantics of modes introduced by TPDF graphs. In fact, this MoC can be considered as a dynamic switching between cases (each case is one graph iteration and can consist of different modes), each of which is captured by a CSDF graph with two fundamental characteristics of its self-timed execution: *synchronisation* (the *max* operator), when the graph (in a specific mode of TPDF) waits for sufficient input tokens to start its execution, and *delay* (the $+$ operator), when an actor starts firing it takes a fixed amount of time before it completes and produces its output tokens.

We briefly introduce some basic concepts of (max, +) (see [1] for background on (max, +) algebra, linear system theory of the (max, +) semiring). (max, +) algebra defines the operations of the maximum of numbers and addition over the set $\mathbb{R}_{max} = \mathbb{R} \cup \{-\infty\}$, where $\mathbb{R}$ is the set of real numbers. Let $a \oplus b = \max(a, b)$ and $a \otimes b = a + b$ for $a, b \in \mathbb{R}_{max}$. For scalars x and y, $x \cdot y$ (with short hand xy) denotes ordinary multiplication, not the (max, +) $\otimes$ operator. For $a \in R_{max}$, $-\infty \oplus a = a \oplus -\infty = a$ and $a \otimes -\infty = -\infty \otimes a = -\infty$. By using (max, +) algebra, we extend the linear algebra to matrices and vectors through the pair of operations $(\oplus, \otimes)$. The set of n dimensional (max, +) vectors is denoted $\mathbb{R}_{max}^n$ while $\mathbb{R}_{max}^{n \times n}$ denotes the set of $n \times n$ (max, +) matrices. The sum of matrices $A, B \in \mathbb{R}_{max}^{n \times n}$, denoted by $A \oplus B$ is defined by $[A \oplus B]_{ij} = a_{ij} \oplus b_{ij}$ while the matrix product $A \otimes B$ is defined by $[A \otimes B]_{ij} = \bigoplus_{k=1}^{n} a_{ik} \otimes b_{kj}$. For $a \in \mathbb{R}_{max}^n$, $||a||$ denotes the vector norm, defined as $||a|| = \bigoplus_{i=1}^{n} a_i = \max_i a_i$ (i.e., the maximum element). For a vector a with $||a|| > -\infty$, we use a^{norm} to denote $[a_i - ||a||]$. With $A \in \mathbb{R}_{max}^{n \times n}$ and $c \in \mathbb{R}$, we use denotations $A \oplus c$ or $c \oplus A$ for $[a_{ij} + c]$. The $\otimes$ symbol in the exponent indicates a matrix power in (max, +) algebra (i.e., $c^{\otimes n} = c \cdot n$).

Within an iteration, several modes can be evolved. Each mode corresponds to an element of the execution sequence of the kernel which receives the control token (e.g., for the TPDF graph in Fig. 1, with $p = 1$, F can be fired in two different modes within an iteration). Each combination of these modes and parameter's values forms a *case* of the TPDF graph, which can be represented by a CSDF graph. We record the production times of initial tokens after the

i−th case CSDF iteration using the *time-stamp* vector λ_i consisting of as many entries as there are initial tokens in the graph (e.g., $(2p + 1)$ initial tokens in Fig. 1). The relationship between the i−th and the $(i + 1)$-st case iteration is given by (4):

$$\lambda_{i+1} = M_{i+1} \otimes \lambda_i \tag{4}$$

M_i is the characteristic (max, +) matrix of case i. This matrix can be obtained by symbolic simulation of one iteration of the CSDF graph in case i. To illustrate, we use the first case of Example 1 in Fig. 1, where $p = 1$, the execution time vector $[2, 2, 1, 5, 2, 1.5]$, respectively in the order A, B, C, D, E, F and two tokens from the control actor set the kernel F in mode 4 (i.e., wait until all data inputs available). This graph has three initial tokens so $\lambda_i = [t_1, t_2, t_3]^T$. Entry t_k represents the time stamp of initial token k after the i−th case iteration. Initially, time-stamp t_1 corresponds to the symbolic time-stamp vector $[0, -\infty, -\infty]^T$, t_2 corresponds to the symbolic time-stamp vector $[-\infty, 0, -\infty]^T$ and finally t_3 to $[-\infty, -\infty, 0]^T$. We start by firing actor A consuming two tokens, one from the self edge and one from the edge from actor F, labelled t_1 and t_2 respectively. The tokens produced by A carry the symbolic time-stamp:

$$max([0, -\infty, -\infty]^T, [-\infty, 0, -\infty]^T) + 2 = [2, 2, -\infty]^T$$

which corresponds to the expression $max(t_1 + 2, t_2 + 2)$. The subsequent first firing of actor B with a duration of 2 consumes this token and produced output tokens labelled as:

$$max([2, 2, -\infty]^T) + 2 = [4, 4, -\infty]^T$$

If we continue the symbolic execution till the completion of the iteration, we obtain the symbolic time-stamp for the second firing of A $[4, 4, 2]^T$ which reproduces the token in the self edge for the next iteration. The tokens produced by the first and second firings of F in the back edge and reused by the next iteration has the time-stamp $[8.5, 8.5, 6.5]^T$ (by consuming t_2) and $[12.5, 12.5, 10.5]^T$ (by consuming t_3). If we collect the symbolic time-stamp vector of these new tokens into a new vector $\lambda_i' = [t_1', t_2', t_3']^T$, we obtain the following (max, +) equation:

$$\begin{bmatrix} t_1' \\ t_2' \\ t_3' \end{bmatrix} = \begin{bmatrix} 4 & 4 & 2 \\ 8.5 & 8.5 & 6.5 \\ 12.5 & 12.5 & 10.5 \end{bmatrix} \begin{bmatrix} t_1 \\ t_2 \\ t_3 \end{bmatrix} \tag{5}$$

If we assume that all initial tokens are available from time 0, the first time-stamp is $\lambda_0 = [0, 0, 0]^T$. After one iteration in the case where both the first and second tokens from C set F in mode 4, the time-stamp of initial tokens becomes $\lambda_1 = [4, 8.5, 12.5]^T$.

If this case followed by another case where the TPDF graph works in the mode 4 (i.e., wait until all data available) for the first token of C and mode 1 (i.e., select input E) for the second token of C, we obtain the following matrix:

$$\begin{bmatrix} t_1' \\ t_2' \\ t_3' \end{bmatrix} = \begin{bmatrix} 4 & 4 & 2 \\ 8.5 & 8.5 & 6.5 \\ 9.5 & 9.5 & 7.5 \end{bmatrix} \begin{bmatrix} t_1 \\ t_2 \\ t_3 \end{bmatrix} \tag{6}$$

With the initial tokens $\lambda_1 = [4, 8.5, 12.5]^T$, after this case, the time-stamp becomes $\lambda_2 = [14.5, 19, 20]^T$.

After analyzing all cases individually, the theory of (max, +) automata is used to capture the dynamic semantics of modes introduced by TPDF graphs. The completion time of a sequence of cases $cs_1 cs_2 cs_3 \ldots cs_n$ is given by:

$$\lambda_{i+1} = M_{i+1} \otimes M_i \otimes \ldots M_1 \otimes \lambda_0 \; \forall i \in [0, n-1] \tag{7}$$

A careful reader might have noticed that for the example in Fig. 1, the initial token vectors between the cases where $p = 1$ and $p = 2$ are not in the same dimensions and therefore the matrix multiplication of (7) will not be well-defined. However, case matrices can be extended with entries 0 and $-\infty$ to accommodate the initial tokens of the entire case sequence. For example, if p has a maximum value of 2 in the case sequence, the case iteration has five initial tokens so $\lambda_i = [t_1, t_2, t_3, t_4, t_5]^T$ we can extend the matrix of case cs_1 (Eq. (5)) to accommodate this case sequence and yield the following matrix:

$$M_1^{ext} = \begin{bmatrix} 4 & 4 & 2 & -\infty & -\infty \\ 8.5 & 8.5 & 6.5 & -\infty & -\infty \\ 12.5 & 12.5 & 10.5 & -\infty & -\infty \\ -\infty & -\infty & -\infty & 0 & -\infty \\ -\infty & -\infty & -\infty & -\infty & 0 \end{bmatrix} \tag{8}$$

The synchronization data between two different cases is made through the common initial tokens between two consecutive iterations. For the synchronization between different values of parameters, we use the initial token labelling to model inter-case synchronization. Initial tokens are explicitly defined by their identifier (e.g., t_1). Two initial tokens of two different cases are common only if they share the same identifier. With this approach, if we assume an initial case with five initial tokens ($p = 2$) followed by a case which has only three initial tokens ($p = 1$), only time-stamp value of initial tokens with the same identifier will be selected by using the extended case matrix. In the opposite case, the missing values for the *(i+1)*-th are replaced by $\|\lambda_i\|$ (i.e., the production time of the last token produced by the last iteration).

3   Throughput Analysis

Along with the three static analyses needed to consistency, boundedness, liveness [8], this section presents a method to evaluate the worst-case throughput of TPDF graphs.

The performance analysis of TPDF is challenging because TPDF is a dynamic dataflow model and the graph behavior is control-dependent. In this case, we introduce an analysis technique based on the work in [11]. We characterized the TPDF graphs by the possible orders in which certain cases may occur. It is possible by stochastically specifying each mode sequence (or graph case) by a Markov Chain. For worst-case analysis, we can abstract from these transition probabilities and obtain a Finite State Machine (FSM). Every state is labelled with a graph case and different states can be labelled with the same graph case.

Definition 3. *Given a set U of cases. A finite state machine F on U is a tuple $(S, s_0, \sigma, \varphi)$ consisting of a finite set S of states, an initial state $s_0 \in S$, a set of transitions between two states $\sigma \subseteq S \times S$ and a case labelling $\varphi : S \to U$.*

Each case of the graph is characterized by a (max, $+$) matrix, as can be seen in Sect. 2.3. Since TPDF is designed to be well adapted with streaming applications, we consider here infinite executions of the FSM to characterize the mode sequences that may occur. With this FSM and an initial time-stamp λ_0, we can associate a time-stamp sequence $\lambda_0 \lambda_1 \lambda_2 \ldots \lambda_n$ with $\lambda_{i+1} = M_{i+1} \otimes \lambda_i$ $\forall i \in [0, n-1]$. According to the theory of CSDF [5], each case is guaranteed to have an upper bound on the self-timed execution of the dataflow's execution, so we can derive straightforwardly that this case sequence has also an upper bound value.

To compute throughput, we have to check all possible case sequences. From the FSM of a TPDF graph, we define a state-space of case sequence executions as follows.

Definition 4. *Given a TPDF graph $\mathcal{G}$ characterized by the set of (max, $+$) matrices $\{M_i | i \in U\}$ and a FSM $F = (S, s_0, \sigma, \varphi)$, a state-space of $\mathcal{G}$ on F is a tuple (Q, q_0, θ), consisting of:*

- *A set $Q = S \times \mathbb{R}_{\max}^N$ of configurations (s, λ) with a state $s \in S$ of F and a time-stamp vector λ.*
- *q_0 is the initial configuration of the state-space.*
- *θ is the set of transitions between two configurations $\theta \subseteq Q \times \mathbb{R} \times Q$ consisting of the following transitions: $\{((s, \lambda), ||\lambda'||, (s', \lambda'^{norm}))|(s, \lambda) \in Q, (q, q') \in \sigma, \lambda' = M_{\Sigma(i)}\lambda\}$, where $M_{\Sigma(i)}$ is a multiplication of all case matrices between λ and λ', as defined in Eq. (7).*

A state in the state-space is a pair consisting of a state in the FSM and a normalized vector representing the relative distance in time of the time-stamp of the common initial tokens. An edge in this state-space $((s, \lambda), ||\lambda'||, (s', \lambda'^{norm}))$ represents the execution of a single iteration in the case of the destination of the edge. If we start with the initial tokens having time-stamp vector λ and we execute a single iteration in case s' then the new time-stamp vector of initial tokens are produced at $\lambda' = ||\lambda'|| + \lambda'^{norm}$ (or earlier). The state-space of a TPDF graph can be constructed in depth-first-search (DFS) or breadth-first-search (BFS) (or any other) manner incrementally. For a self-timed bounded graph with rational execution times, the state-space is finite. However, it can be large in some cases because of the number of modes used in each case and because of the complexity of the FSM. Further techniques (e.g., (max, $+$) automaton [10,11]) can be applied to reduce the size of the state-space and analyse the worst-case throughput in a faster way.

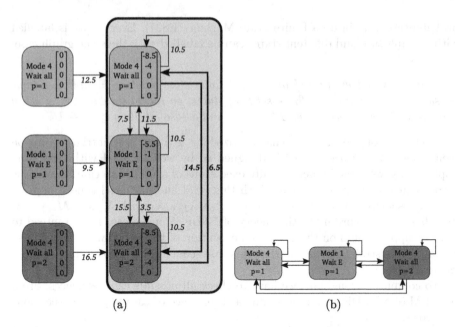

Fig. 2. (a) State-space of the example in Fig. 1 and (b) its Finite State Machine. The blue box and bold arrows highlight the cycle with the maximum cycle mean which determines the throughput. (Color figure online)

From Definition 4, according to [19], the throughput of a TPDF graph is equal to the inverse of the Maximum Cycle Mean (MCM) attained in any reachable simple cycles of the state-space. For example, Fig. 2 represents the reachable state-space of the example in Fig. 1 and its Finite State Machine. The blue box and bold arrows highlights the cycle with maximum cycle mean or lowest throughput (i.e., 10.5 for the MCM and 1/10.5 for the throughput).

4   Evaluation

Our method is implemented to check the static guarantees, compute the execution state-space and analyse the worst-case throughput of TPDF graphs in the publicly available SDF^3 software library for SDF, CSDF and SADF analysis [20]. We use a basic breadth-first-search to construct straightforwardly the state-space according to the definition of Sect. 3. During the exploration procedure, we enumerate the state-space and check timing constraints. Exploration continues until a state that our tool visited before is reached, we back-track and stop exploration in that direction.

4.1   Benchmarks

We have done experiments with a set of cognitive radio applications (e.g., OFDM [3], Adaptive Coding Transceiver and Receiver model [15]), on the well-known video codec VC-1 model [2], on the time-constrained application Edge Detection [17] as presented in Sect. 4.1 and on a large collection of randomly generated graphs, on a standard Intel Core i3@2.53 GHz based PC. Table 1 shows these applications with its number of kernels (N) in the eighth column and its number of states in the ninth column. These benchmarks are selected from different sources to check the expressiveness of TPDF and its performance results. The first source is several case studies of other dynamic dataflow models (e.g., VC-1 Decoder and OFDM). These applications are also official benchmarks of industrial tools such as LabView or Simulink. Another source is to build TPDF graph from real-life application programmed in C (e.g., Edge Detection). From this approach, dynamic code analysis tool, as the method introduced in [13], can be developed in the near future to transform automatically legacy code to TPDF graph.

Table 1. Throughput (iterations per cycle) obtained and the improvement of TPDF compared to the SADF and (C)SDF model (**Eff$_{SADF}$** and **Eff$_{(C)SDF}$**, respectively). N represents the number of kernels of each application. The last column represents the analysis time by using our tool set.

Application	TPDF	SADF	Eff$_{SADF}$	(C)SDF	Eff$_{(C)SDF}$	N	#States	Time (ms)
OFDM	2×10^{-2}	1.6×10^{-2}	25%	1.58×10^{-2}	26.58%	8	15	4
Adaptive coding	10×10^{-2}	8.5×10^{-2}	17.65%	4.6×10^{-2}	117.39%	14	6	16
VC-1 Decoder	4×10^{-1}	2.5×10^{-1}	60%	2.2×10^{-1}	81.81%	12	12	8
Edge detection	7.86×10^{-1}	-	-	-	-	8	18	12
Random graphs	1.5×10^{-1}	1.29×10^{-1}	15.51%	1.09×10^{-1}	36.6%	10~150	5~30	-

Case-Study on Edge Detection. Edge detection is one of the most significant tasks in image processing systems with various proposed algorithms: Quick Mask, Sobel, Prewitt, Kirsch, Canny [17]. When dealing with timing constraint, an average quality result at the right time is far better than an excellent result, later. The Canny filter may an excellent algorithm for edge detections, but the execution time depends on the input image. In contrast, Quick Mask or Sobel have image-independent execution time (i.e., depending only on the size of the input image, not on its contents). So a control actor of type clock can be used to implement this time constraint, as can be seen in [8].

Case-Study on Cognitive Radio. The TPDF approach is applied to model an OFDM demodulator from the domain of cognitive radio, which is one of the fundamental subsystems of LTE and WiMAX wireless communication systems. Figure 3 illustrates a runtime-reconfigurable OFDM demodulator that is modeled as a TPDF graph. Here, actor *SRC* represents a data source that generates random values to simulate a sampler. In a wideband OFDM system, information is encoded on a large number of carrier frequencies, forming an OFDM symbol stream. In baseband processing, a symbol stream can be viewed in terms of consecutive vectors of length N. The symbol is usually padded with a cyclic prefix (CP) of length L to reduce inter-symbol inference (ISI) [3]. In Fig. 3, the CP is removed by actor *RCP*. Then, actor *FFT* performs a fast Fourier transform (FFT) to convert the symbol stream to the frequency domain. This kernel is connected to a M-ary *QAM* demodulation, with a configurable *QPSK* configuration ($M = 2$ or $M = 4$). Finally, the output bits are collected by the data sink *SNK*.

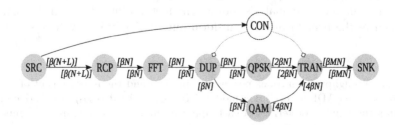

Fig. 3. TPDF model of an OFDM demodulator with a configurable *QPSK* ($M = 2$) or *QAM* ($M = 4$) configuration. Omitted rates equal to 1.

In summary, there are four principal parameters: β, M, N and L, where L depends on the cyclic prefix, N is the OFDM symbol length ($N = 512$ or $N = 1024$) and β, which varies between 1 and 100, is the number of OFDM symbols to be processed in a single activation of the actor. For example, if $M = 4$ and $\beta = 10$, this means that the system is operating in a mode that uses QAM as the demapping scheme, and executes actors in blocks of 10 firings each. Figure 4 presents the minimum buffer size required by the application, depending on the vectorization degree β and the symbol length N ($L = 1$ and M is chosen by the control node). We find out that the buffer size increases proportionally to the vectorization degree and we have an improvement of 29% in comparison with the implementation by using CSDF. This result can be explained by the fact that the dynamic topology obtained using TPDF is more flexible than the static topology of CSDF, allowing to remove unused edges and decrease the minimum buffer size required by one iteration of the TPDF graph. In a similar way, several StreamIt benchmarks (e.g., FM Radio [21]) must perform redundant calculations that are not needed with models allowing dynamic topology changes such as TPDF.

4.2   Experimental Results

These applications are implemented by using TPDF, SADF and a conservative CSDF/SDF model, without modes. Table 1 shows the throughput obtained using these models as well as the improvement of the results using TPDF compared to the SADF and CSDF/SDF model. For the OFDM application, a conservative

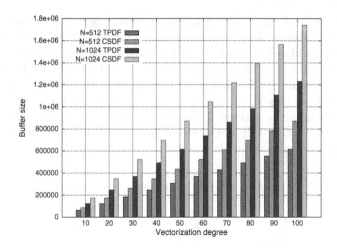

Fig. 4. Minimum buffer size increased proportionally to β, given by $Buff = 3 + \beta \times (12 \times N + L)$ for TPDF and $Buff = \beta \times (17 \times N + L)$ for CSDF.

CSDF model, without modes, can guarantee a throughput of 1.58×10^{-2} iterations per cycle. This result by using SADF is 1.6×10^{-2}. Experiments with the TPDF graph show that the OFDM graph can achieve a guaranteed throughput of 2×10^{-2} iterations per processors cycle, 25% and 26.58% higher than SADF and CSDF implementations, respectively. This result can be explained as follows: TPDF maximizes the degree of parallelism and driving around some sequential limitations by using speculation, a technique often used in hardware design to reduce the critical data-path, all kernels and cases which receive enough data tokens will be fired immediately and in parallel. Moreover, the kernel which receives the control token will also be fired instantly and choose the input or output data channel depending on the control token. All unnecessary kernels will be stopped, then computation will be accelerated and parallelized.

VC-1 Decoder is another application modelled by BPDF, a recent dynamic dataflow model [2]. The existing analysis method of this model takes only into account the maximum throughput. Our technique focuses on the worst-case throughput (i.e., a guaranteed lower bound on the application throughput), which is a more interested performance metric. Experiments with the TPDF model shows that we have an improvement of 60% compared to the SADF model and 81% to the conservative CSDF model. For the Edge Detection case study, as discussed in Sect. 4.1, our tool succeeds to analyse the throughput of the graph with a state-space of 18 states and the analysis took only 12 ms. This type of time constraint is complicated, even impossible by using SADF or (C)SDF model.

These results are also extended by testing the capacity of pipelining canonical periods of TPDF graphs. This experiment consists in testing the ability of TPDF to adapt the compile tool chain used for MPPA-256, which constructs for each CSDF application a canonical period per iteration and optimise the parallelism by pipelining these canonical periods. Figure 5 shows the ratios of the throughput by using a degree of pipelining of 2, 3 and 4 compared to the case when only one canonical period is used. We can see that a higher level of pipelining (under 4) gives always a higher throughput. In this way, we can conclude that TPDF is well adapted to the existing parallelism method used for ΣC and its real-world many-core platform, the Kalray's MPPA. We have also analysed a collection of more than 200 random TPDF graphs between 10 and 150 actors with an entry in the repetition vector between 1 and 10 and between 5 and 30 modes to use, giving an average of 15.51% and 36.6% higher throughput guarantee than from a SADF and a conservative CSDF model of the same graph, respectively.

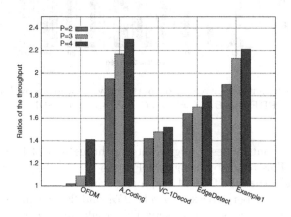

Fig. 5. Ratios of the throughput under different degrees of pipelining.

5   Related Work

Dataflow models are widely used in modeling and analyzing applications in the domain of digital signal processing. Moreover, they are also used for designing and analyzing concurrent multimedia applications realized using multiprocessor systems-on-chip. The main aim is to realize predictable performance and among the performance indicators, throughput is a prominent one. Throughput of static models, such as SDF and CSDF, and its static guarantees has been extensively studied in the literature [7,19,20]. However, the desire to extend the range of applicability to more dynamic dataflow models has lead to use of extensions, for instance PSDF [4] and SPDF [9]. In contrast to CSDF, these models allow a dynamic variation of the production and consumption rates of actors to change at runtime according to the manipulated data. However, none of these models provide any of the static analyses enabled by TPDF: rate consistency, boundedness, liveness and performance analysis, nor do they support parametric rates without dynamic topology changes.

6   Conclusion

In this paper, we have introduced a formal model of Transaction Parameterized Dataflow graphs based on the theory of (max, +) automata. From this theory, we derived static analyses to guarantee the boundedness, liveness and evaluate the worst-case throughput when executing a TPDF application. An implementation of the TPDF model has been presented and experimentally evaluated on realistic applications, showing that this approach can give much tighter performance guarantees than state of the art analyses. We believe the proposed model is an important step towards the design of a programming model suitable for high performance applications with safety-critical requirements.

References

1. Baccelli, F., Cohen, G., Olsder, G., Quadrat, J.: Synchronization and Linearity. Wiley, New York (1992)
2. Bebelis, V., Fradet, P., Girault, A., Lavigueur, B.: BPDF: a statically analyzable dataflow model with integer and Boolean parameters. In: EMSOFT, pp. 3:1–3:10 (2013)
3. van de Beek, J.J., Sandell, M., Isaksson, M., Ola Borjesson, P.: Low-complex frame synchronization in OFDM systems. In: ICUPC (1995)
4. Bhattacharya, B., Bhattacharyya, S.: Parameterized dataflow modeling for DSP systems. IEEE Trans. Signal Process. **49**(10), 2408–2421 (2001)
5. Bilsen, G., Engels, M., Lauwereins, R., Peperstraete, J.: Cyclo-static data flow. In: ICASSP, vol. 5, pp. 3255–3258, May 1995
6. de Dinechin, B.D., et al.: A distributed run-time environment for the Kalray MPPA-256 integrated manycore processor. Procedia Comput. Sci. **18**, 1654–1663 (2013)
7. Do, X., Louise, S., Cohen, A.: Managing the latency of data-dependent tasks in embedded streaming applications. In: MCSoc (2015)
8. Do, X., Louise, S., Cohen, A.: Transaction parameterized dataflow: a model for context-dependent streaming applications. In: 2016 Design, Automation Test in Europe Conference Exhibition (DATE), pp. 960–965, March 2016
9. Fradet, P., Girault, A., Poplavko, P.: SPDF: a schedulable parametric data-flow MoC. In: DATE, pp. 769–774, March 2012
10. Gaubert, S.: Performance evaluation of (max,+) automata. IEEE Trans. Autom. Control **40**(12), 2014–2025 (1995)
11. Geilen, M., Stuijk, S.: Worst-case performance analysis of synchronous dataflow scenarios. In: CODES+ISSS, pp. 125–134, October 2010
12. Johnson, G.: LabVIEW Graphical Programming: Practical Applications in Instrumentation and Control. McGraw-Hill School Education Group, New York (1997)
13. Lazarescu, M.T., Lavagno, L.: Interactive trace-based analysis toolset for manual parallelization of C programs. ACM Trans. Embed. Comput. Syst. **14**(1), 13:1–13:20 (2015)
14. Lee, E.A., Messerschmitt, D.G.: Synchronous data flow. Proc. IEEE **75**(9), 1235–1245 (1987)
15. Lotze, J., Fahmy, S., Noguera, J., Doyle, L.: A model-based approach to cognitive radio design. IEEE J-SAC **29**(2), 455–468 (2011)

16. Louise, S., Dubrulle, P., Goubier, T.: A model of computation for real-time applications on embedded manycores. In: MCSoC, September 2014
17. Phillips, D.: Image Processing in C, Part 5: Basic Edge Detection, pp. 47–56 (1994)
18. Ptolemaeus, C. (ed.): System Design, Modeling, and Simulation Using Ptolemy II. Ptolemy.org (2014). http://ptolemy.org/books/Systems
19. Sriram, S., Bhattacharyya, S.S.: Embedded Multiprocessors: Scheduling and Synchronization, 2nd edn. Marcel Dekker, Inc., New York (2009)
20. Stuijk, S., Geilen, M., Basten, T.: SDF^3: SDF for free. In: Proceedings of ACSD, pp. 276–278 (2006)
21. Thies, W., Amarasinghe, S.: An empirical characterization of stream programs and its implications for language and compiler design. In: Proceedings of PACT (2010)
22. Wipliez, M., Roquier, G., Nezan, J.F.: Software code generation for the RVC-CAL language. J. Signal Process. Syst. **63**(2), 203–213 (2009)

A Similarity Measure for GPU Kernel Subgraph Matching

Robert Lim$^{(\boxtimes)}$, Boyana Norris, and Allen Malony

University of Oregon, Eugene, OR, USA
{roblim1,norris,malony}@cs.uoregon.edu

Abstract. Accelerator architectures specialize in executing SIMD (single instruction, multiple data) in lockstep. Because the majority of CUDA applications are parallelized loops, control flow information can provide an in-depth characterization of a kernel. CUDAflow is a tool that statically separates CUDA binaries into basic block regions and dynamically measures instruction and basic block frequencies. CUDAflow captures this information in a control flow graph (CFG) and performs subgraph matching across various kernel's CFGs to gain insights into an application's resource requirements, based on the shape and traversal of the graph, instruction operations executed and registers allocated, among other information. The utility of CUDAflow is demonstrated with SHOC and Rodinia application case studies on a variety of GPU architectures, revealing novel control flow characteristics that facilitate end users, autotuners, and compilers in generating high performing code.

1 Introduction

Structured programming consists of base constructs that represent how programs are written [4,27]. When optimizing programs, compilers typically operate on the intermediate representation (IR) of a control flow graph (CFG), which is derived from program source code analysis and represents basic blocks of instructions (nodes) and control flow paths (edges) in the graph. Thus, the overall program structure is captured in the CFG and the IR abstracts machine-specific intrinsics that the compiler ultimately translates to machine code. The IR/CFG allows the compiler to reason more efficiently about optimization opportunities and apply transformations. In particular, compilers can benefit from prior knowledge of optimizations that may be effective for specific CFG structures.

In the case of accelerated architectures that are programmed for SIMD parallelism, control divergence encountered by threads of execution presents a major challenge for applications because it can severely reduce SIMD computational efficiency. It stands to reason that by identifying the structural patterns of a CFG from an accelerator (SIMD) program, insight on the branch divergence problem [22] might be gained to help in their optimization. Current profiling approaches to understanding thread divergence behavior (e.g., [10,21,24]) do not map performance information to critical execution paths in the CFG.

© Springer Nature Switzerland AG 2019
M. Hall and H. Sundar (Eds.): LCPC 2018, LNCS 11882, pp. 37–53, 2019.
https://doi.org/10.1007/978-3-030-34627-0_3

While accelerator devices (e.g., GPUs) offer hardware performance counters for measuring computational performance, it is more difficult to apply them to capture divergence behavior [17].

Our research focuses on improving the detail and accuracy of control flow graph information in accelerator (GPU) programs. We study the extent to which CFG data can provide sufficient context for understanding a GPU kernel's execution performance. Furthermore, we want to investigate how effective knowledge of CFG shapes (patterns) could be in enabling optimizing compilers and autotuners to infer execution characteristics without having to resort to running execution experiments. To this end, we present CUDAflow, a scalable toolkit for heterogeneous computing applications. Specifically, CUDAflow provides a new methodology for characterizing CUDA kernels using control flow graphs and instruction operations executed. It performs novel kernel subgraph matching to gain insights into an application's resource requirements. To the knowledge of the authors, this work is a first attempt at employing subgraph matching for revealing control flow behavior and generating efficient code.

Contributions described in this paper include the following.

- Systematic process to construct control flow graphs for GPU kernels.
- Techniques to perform subgraph matching on various kernel CFGs and GPUs.
- Approaches to reveal control flow behavior based on CFG properties.

The rest of the paper is organized as follows. Section 2 discusses prior work, and Sect. 3 provides background information. Section 4 describes the methodology behind our CUDAflow tool and our implementation approach. Sections 5 and 6 summarizes the findings of our application characterization studies. Section 7 outlines future work.

2   Prior Work

Control flow divergence in heterogeneous computing applications is a well known and difficult problem, due to the lockstep nature of the GPU execution paradigm. Current efforts to address branch divergence in GPUs draw from several fields, including profiling techniques in CPUs, and software and hardware architectural support in GPUs. For instance, Sarkar demonstrated that the overall execution time of a program can be estimated by deriving the variances of basic block regions [23]. Control flow graphs for flow and context sensitive profiling were discussed in [2,3], where instrumentation probes were inserted at selected edges in the CFG, which reduced the overall profiling overhead with minimal loss of information. Hammock graphs were constructed [30] that mapped unstructured control flow on a GPU [11,28]. By creating thread frontiers to identify early thread reconvergence opportunities, dynamic instruction counts were reduced by as much as 633.2%.

Lynx [12] creates an internal representation of a program based on PTX and then emulates it, which determines the memory, control flow and parallelism of the application. This work closely resembles ours but differs in that we perform workload characterization on actual hardware during execution. Other performance measurement tools, such as HPCToolkit [1] and DynInst [20], provide a way for users to construct control flow graphs from CUDA binaries, but do not analyze the results further. The MIAMI toolkit [19] is an instrumentation framework for studying an application's dynamic instruction mix and control flow but does not support GPUs.

Subgraph matching has been explored in a variety of contexts. For instance, the DeltaCon framework matched arbitrary subgraphs based on similarity scores [15], which exploited the properties of the graph (e.g., clique, cycle, star, barbell) to support the graph matching. Similarly, frequent subgraph mining was performed on molecular fragments for drug discovery [5], whereas document clustering was formalized in a graph database context [14]. The IsoRank authors consider the problem of matching protein-protein interaction networks between distinct species [25]. The goal is to leverage knowledge about the proteins from an extensively studied species, such as a mouse, which when combined with a matching between mouse proteins and human proteins can be used to hypothesize about possible functions of proteins in humans. However, none of these approaches apply frequent subgraph matching for understanding performance behavior of GPU applications.

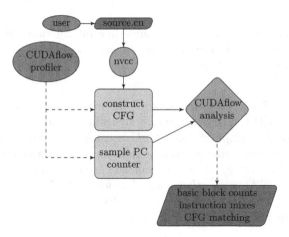

Fig. 1. Overview of our proposed `CUDAflow` methodology.

3 Background

Our `CUDAflow` approach shown in Fig. 1 works in association with the current `nvcc` toolchain. Control flow graphs are constructed from static code analysis and program execution statistics are gathered dynamically through program counter sampling. This measurement collects counts of executed instructions and corresponding source code locations, among other information. In this way, the `CUDAflow` methodology provides a more accurate characterization of the application kernel, versus hardware performance counters alone, which lack the

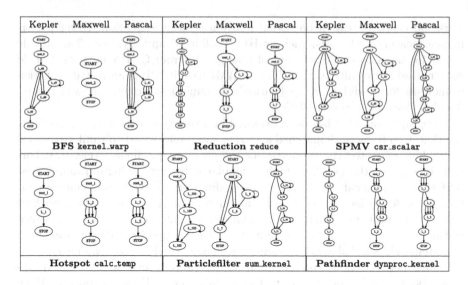

Kepler	Maxwell	Pascal	Kepler	Maxwell	Pascal	Kepler	Maxwell	Pascal
BFS kernel_warp			**Reduction reduce**			**SPMV csr_scalar**		
Hotspot calc_temp			**Particlefilter sum_kernel**			**Pathfinder dynproc_kernel**		

Fig. 2. Control flow graphs generated for each CUDA kernel, comparing architecture families (Kepler, Maxwell, Pascal).

ability to correlate performance with source line information and are prone to miscounting events [16]. In particular, it gives a way to understand the control flow behavior during execution.

Kernel Control Flow Graphs. One of the more complex parameters used to characterize SIMD thread divergence is by using a control flow graph (CFG) representation of the computation. A CFG is constructed for each GPU kernel computation in program order and can be represented as a directed acyclic graph $G = (N, E, s)$, where (N, E) is a finite directed graph, and a path exists from the $START$ node $s \in N$ to every other node. A unique $STOP$ node is also assumed in the CFG. A node in the graph represents a basic block (a straight line of code without jumps or jump targets), whereas directed edges represent jumps in the control flow.

Each basic block region is incremented with the number of times the node is visited. Upon sampling the program counter, the PC address is referenced internally to determine to which basic block region the instruction corresponds to.

```
.L_41:
    /*04a0*/   DSETP.LE.AND P0,PT,|R6|,+INF,PT;
    /*04a8*/   @P0 BRA '(.L_43);
    /*04b0*/   LOP32I.OR R5, R7, 0x80000;
    /*04b8*/   MOV R4, R6;

    /*04c8*/   BRA '(.L_42);
```

The SASS assembly code illustrates how a control flow graph is constructed. Each basic block is labeled in the left margin (e.g. ".L_41"), with predication and branch instructions representing edges that lead to corresponding block regions (e.g. ".L_43," ".L_42"). The PC offsets are listed in hexadecimal between the comments syntax (**). In other words, ".L_41" represents a node n_i, with ".L_43," and ".L_42" as its children.

Example control flow graphs for selected SHOC (top) [9] and Rodinia (bottom) [6] GPU benchmarks are displayed in Fig. 2. Different GPU architecture types will result in the nvcc compiler producing different code and possibly control flow, as seen in the CFGs from Fig. 2 for Kepler, Maxwell and Pascal architectures. Section 5 discusses the differences in GPU architectures. The CFG differences for each architecture are due in part to the architecture layout of the GPU and its compute capability (NVIDIA virtual architecture). The Maxwell generally uses fewer nodes for its CFGs, as evident in kernel_warp. Our approach can expose these important architecture-specific effects on the CFGs. Also, note that similarities in structure exist with several CFGs, including csr_scalar and sum_kernel. Part of the goal of this research is to predict the required resources for the application by inferring performance through CFG subgraph matching, with the subgraphs serving as building blocks for more nested and complex GPU kernels. For this purpose, we introduce several metrics that build on this CFG representation.

Transition Probability. Transition probabilities represent frequencies of an edge to a vertex, or branches to code regions, which describes the application in a way that gets misconstrued in a flat profile. A stochastic matrix could also facilitate in eliminating dead code, where states with 0 transition probabilities represent node regions that will never be visited. Kernels employing structures like loops and control flow increase the complexity analysis, and knowledge of transition probabilities of kernels could help during code generation.

A canonical adjacency matrix M represents a graph G such that every diagonal entry of M is filled with the label of the corresponding node and every off-diagonal entry is filled with the label of the corresponding edge, or zero if no edge exists [29]. The adjacency matrix describes the transition from N_i to N_j. If the probability of moving from i to j in one time step is $Pr(j|i) = m_{i,j}$, the adjacency matrix is given by $m_{i,j}$ as the ith row and the jth column element. Since the total transition probability from a state i to all other states must be 1, this matrix is a right stochastic matrix, so that $\sum_j P_{i,j} = 1$.

Figure 3 illustrates transition probability matrices for a kernel from the Pathfinder application (Table 2, bottom-rt.), comparing Kepler (left) and Maxwell (right) versions. Note that the Pascal version was the same as Maxwell, as evident in Fig. 2, lower-right, and was left out intentionally. The entries of the transition probability matrix were calculated by normalizing over the total number of observations for each observed node transition i to j. Although the matrices differ in size, observe that a majority of the transitions take place in the upper-left triangle, with a few transitions in the bottom-right, for all matrices. The task is to match graphs of arbitrary sizes based on its transition probability matrix and instruction operations executed, among other information.

$$\begin{array}{c}
\begin{array}{cccccc} R_1 & L_1 & L_4 & L_3 & L_2 & L_5 \end{array} \\
\begin{bmatrix}
.21 & - & - & - & - & - \\
0 & .04 & - & - & - & - \\
0 & .04 & .38 & - & - & - \\
0 & 0 & 0 & .08 & - & - \\
0 & 0 & 0 & 0 & .21 & - \\
0 & 0 & 0 & 0 & .02 & 0
\end{bmatrix}
\end{array}
\quad
\begin{array}{c}
\begin{array}{cccc} R_1 & L_3 & L_2 & L_1 \end{array} \\
\begin{bmatrix}
.30 & - & - & - \\
0 & .51 & - & - \\
0 & 0 & 0 & - \\
0 & 0 & 0 & .21
\end{bmatrix}
\end{array}$$

Fig. 3. Transition probability matrices for Pathfinder (`dynproc_kernel`) application, comparing Kepler (left) and Maxwell (right) versions.

Hybrid Static and Dynamic Analysis. We statically collect instruction mixes and source code locations from generated code and map the instruction mixes to the source locator activity as the program is being run [17]. The static analysis of CUDA binaries produces an objdump file, which provides assembly information, including instructions, program counter offsets, and source line information. The CFG structure is stored in iGraph format [8]. We attribute the static analysis from the objdump file to the profiles collected from the source code activity to provide runtime characterization of the GPU as it is being executed on the architecture. This mapping of static and dynamic profiles provides a rich understanding of the behavior of the kernel application with respect to the underlying architecture.

4   Methodology

Based on the kernel CFG and transition probability analysis, the core of the `CUDAflow` methodology focuses on the problem of subgraph matching. In order to perform subgraph matching, we first scale the matrices to the same size by taking for graphs G_1 and G_2 the maximal proper submatrix, constructed by $\mathcal{B}(G_i) = \max(|V_1|, |V_2|)$ for a given $G_i = \min(|V_1|, |V_2|)$ using spline interpolation. The similarities in the shapes of the control flow graphs, the variants generated for each GPU (Table 2) and the activity regions in the transition probability matrices (Fig. 3) provided motivation for this approach. In our case, the dense hotspots in the transition matrix should align with their counterparts if the matrices are similar enough.

4.1   Bilinear Interpolation

To scale the transition matrix before performing the pairwise comparison, we employ a spline interpolation procedure. Spline interpolation is general form of linear interpolation for functions of n-order polynomial, such as bilinear and cubic. For instance, a spline on a two-order polynomial performs bilinear interpolation on a rectilinear 2D grid (e.g. x and y) [13]. The idea is to perform linear interpolation in both the vertical and horizontal directions. Interpolation works by using known data to estimate values at unknown points. Refer to [13] for the derivation of bilinear interpolation.

Table 1. Distance measures considered in this paper.

Abbrev	Name	Result
Euc	Euclidean	$\sqrt{\sum_{i=1}^{n} \lvert x_i - y_i \rvert^2}$
Iso	IsoRank	$(\mathbf{I} - \alpha \mathbf{Q} \times \mathbf{P})\mathbf{x}$
Man	Manhattan	$\sum_{i=1}^{n} \lvert x_i - y_i \rvert$
Min	Minkowski	$\sqrt[p]{\sum_{i=1}^{n} \lvert x_i - y_i \rvert^p}$
Jac	Jaccard	$\frac{\sum_{i=1}^{n}(x_i - y_i)^2}{\sum_{i=1}^{n} x_i^2 + \sum_{i=1}^{n} y_i^2 - \sum_{i=1}^{n} x_i y_i}$
Cos	Cosine	$1 - \frac{\sum_{i=1}^{n} x_i y_i}{\sqrt{\sum_{i=1}^{n} x_i^2}\sqrt{\sum_{i=1}^{n} y_i^2}}$

4.2 Pairwise Comparison

Once the matrix is interpolated, the affinity scores (S_1 and S_2 for graphs G_1' and G_2', respectively) are matched via a distance measure, which includes the Euclidean distance, the IsoRank solution [25], Manhattan distance, Minkowski metric, Jaccard similarity, and Cosine similarity. The distance measures considered in this work are listed in Table 1. By definition, $sim(G_i, G_j) = 0$ when $i = j$, with the similarity measure placing progressively higher scores for objects that are further apart.

5 Experimental Setup

To demonstrate our CUDAflow methodology, we measured the performance of applications on several GPU architectures.

5.1 Execution Environment

The graphic processor units used in our experiments are listed in Table 2. The selected GPUs reflect the various architecture family generations, and performance results presented in this paper represent GPUs belonging to the same family. For instance, we observed that the performance results from a K80 architecture and a K40 (both Kepler) were similar, and, as a result, did not include comparisons of GPU architectures within families. Also, note the changes in architectural features across generations (global memory, MP, CUDA cores per MP), as well as ones that remain fixed (constant memory, warp size, registers per block). For instance, while the number of multiprocessors increased in successive generations, the number of CUDA cores per MP (or streaming multiprocessors, SM) actually decreased. Consequently, the number of CUDA cores ($MP \times CUDA_{cores\_per\_mp}$) increased in successive GPU generations.

Table 2. Graphical processors used in this experiment.

	K80	M40	P100
CUDA capability	3.5	5.2	6.0
Global memory (MB)	11520	12288	16276
Multiprocessors (MP)	13	24	56
CUDA cores per MP	192	128	64
CUDA cores	2496	3072	3584
GPU clock rate (MHz)	824	1140	405
Memory clock rate (MHz)	2505	5000	715
L2 cache size (MB)	1.572	3.146	4.194
Constant memory (bytes)	65536	65536	65536
Shared mem blk (bytes)	49152	49152	49152
Registers per block	65536	65536	65536
Warp size	32	32	32
Max threads per MP	2048	2048	2048
Max threads per block	1024	1024	1024
CPU (Intel)	Haswell	Ivy Bridge	Haswell
Architecture family	Kepler	Maxwell	Pascal

5.2   Applications

Rodinia and SHOC application suite are a class of GPU applications that cover a wide range of computational patterns typically seen in parallel computing. Table 3 describes the applications used in this experiment along with source code statistics, including the number of kernel functions, the number of associated files and the total lines of code.

Rodinia. Rodinia is a benchmark suite for heterogeneous computing which includes applications and kernels that target multi-core CPU and GPU plat-forms [6]. Rodinia covers a wide range of parallel communication patterns, synchronization techniques, and power consumption, and has led to architectural insights such as memory-bandwidth limitations and the consequent importance of data layout.

SHOC Benchmark Suite. The Scalable HeterOgeneous Computing (SHOC) application suite is a collection of benchmark programs testing the performance and stability of systems using computing devices with non-traditional architectures for general purpose computing [9]. SHOC provides implementations for CUDA, OpenCL, and Intel MIC, and supports both sequential and MPI-parallel execution.

Table 3. Description of SHOC (top) and Rodinia (bottom) benchmarks studied.

	Name	Ker	File	Ln	Description
SHOC	FFT	9	4	970	Forward and reverse 1D fast Fourier transform
	MD	2	2	717	Compute the Lennard-Jones potential from molecular dynamics
	MD5Hash	1	1	720	Computate many small MD5 digests, heavily dependent on bitwise operations
	Reduction	2	5	785	Reduction operation on an array of single or double precision floating point values
	Scan	6	6	1035	Scan (parallel prefix sum) on an array of single or double precision floating point values
	SPMV	8	2	830	Sparse matrix-vector multiplication
	Stencil2D	2	12	1487	A 9-point stencil operation applied to a 2D dataset
Rodinia	Backprop	2	7	945	Trains weights of connecting nodes on a layered neural network
	BFS	2	3	971	Breadth-first search, a common graph traversal
	Gaussian	2	1	1564	Gaussian elimination for a system of linear equations
	Heartwall	1	4	6017	Tracks changing shape of walls of a mouse heart over a sequence of ultrasound images
	Hotspot	1	1	1199	Estimate processor temperature based on floor plan and simulated power measurements
	Nearest Neighbor	1	2	385	Finds k-nearest neighbors from unstructured data set using Euclidean distance
	Needleman-Wunsch	2	3	1878	Global optimization method for DNA sequence alignment
	Particle Filter	4	2	7211	Estimate location of target object given noisy measurements in a Bayesian framework
	Pathfinder	1	1	707	Scan (parallel prefix sum) on an array of single or double precision floating point values
	SRAD v1	6	12	3691	Diffusion method for ultrasonic and radar imaging applications based on PDEs
	SRAD v2	2	3	2021	...

6   Analysis

To illustrate our new methodology, we analyzed the SHOC and Rodinia applications at different granularities.

6.1   Application Level

Figure 4 projects goodness as a function of efficiency, which displays the similarities and differences of the benchmark applications. The size of bubble represents the number of operations executed, whereas the shade represents the GPU type. Efficiency describes how gainfully employed the GPU floating-point units remained, or FLOPs per second:

$$efficiency = \frac{op_{fp} + op_{int} + op_{simd} + op_{conv}}{time_{exec}} \cdot calls_n \qquad (1)$$

The *goodness* metric describes the intensity of the floating-point and memory operation arithmetic intensity:

$$goodness = \sum_{j \in J} op_j \cdot calls_n \qquad (2)$$

Note that efficiency is measured via runtime, whereas goodness is measured statically. Figure 4 (left) shows a positive correlation between the two measures, where the efficiency of an application increases along with its goodness. Static metrics, such as *goodness*, can be used to derive dynamic behavior of an application. This figure also demonstrates that merely counting the number of executed operations is not sufficient to characterize applications because operation counts do not fully reveal control flow, which is a source of bottlenecks in large-scale programs.

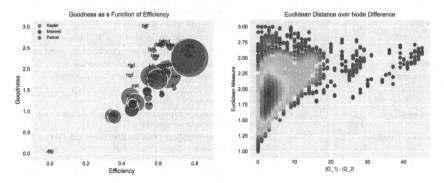

Fig. 4. Left: The *static* goodness metric (Eq. 2) is positively correlated with the *dynamic* efficiency metric (Eq. 1). The color represents the architecture and the size of bubbles represents the number of operations. Right: Differences in vertices between two graphs, as a function of Euclidean metric for all GPU kernel combinations. Color represents intensity.

6.2   CFG Subgraph Matching

Distribution of Matched Pairs. Figure 4 (right) projects the distribution of differences in vertices $|V|$ for all 162 CFG kernel pairs (Table 3, 2nd col. + 3 GPUs) as a function of the Euclidean measure (application, architecture, kernel), with shade representing the frequency of the score. Note that most matched CFGs had a similarity score of 1.5 to 2.2 and had size differences under 10 vertices. Figure 4 (right) also shows that as the differences in vertices increase, similarity matching becomes degraded due to the loss of quality when interpolating missing information, which is expected. Another observation is that strong similarity results when node differences of the matched kernel pairs were at a minimum, between 0 and 8 nodes.

Error Rates from Instruction Mixes. Here, we wanted to see how far off our instruction mix estimations were from our matched subgraphs. Figure 5 displays instruction mix estimation error rates, calculated using mean squared error, for MD, Backprop, and SPMV kernels as a function of matched kernels (x-axis) with IsoRank scores between 1.00 to 1.30. Naming convention for each kernel is as follows: ⟨*gpu_arch.suite.app.kernel*⟩. In general, CUDAflow is able

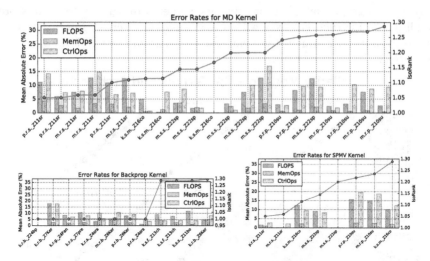

Fig. 5. Error rates when estimating instruction mixes statically from runtime observations for selected matched kernels (x-axis), with IsoRank scores near 1.30.

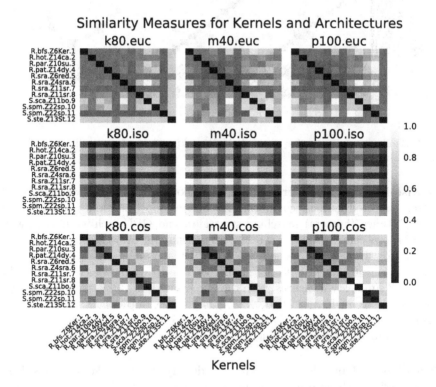

Fig. 6. Similarity measures for Euclidean, IsoRank and Cosine distances for 12 arbitrarily selected kernels.

to provide subgraph matching for arbitrary kernels through the IsoRank score in addition to instruction mixes within a 8% margin of error. Note that since relative dynamic performance is being estimated from static information, the error rates will always be high.

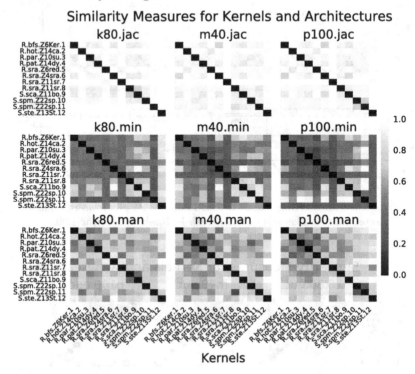

Fig. 7. Similarity measures for Jaccard, Minkowski and Manhattan distances for 12 arbitrarily selected kernels.

Pairwise Matching of Kernels. Figure 6 shows pairwise comparisons for 12 arbitrary selected kernels, comparing Euclidean (top), IsoRank (middle), and Cosine distance (bottom) matching strategies, and GPU architectures (rows). Figure 7 shows comparisons for the Jaccard measure, Minkowski, and Manhattan distances for the same 12 kernels. Note that the distance scores were scaled to 0 and 1, where 0 indicates strong similarity and 1 denotes weak similarity. In general, all similarity measures, with the exception of IsoRank, is able to match against itself, as evident in the dark diagonal entries in the plots. However, this demonstrates that using similarity measures in isolation alone is not sufficient for performing subgraph matching for CUDA kernels.

Clustering of Kernels. We wanted to identify classes of kernels, based on characteristics such as instruction mixes, graph structures and distance measures. The Ward variance minimization algorithm minimizes the total within-cluster variance by finding a pair of clusters that leads to a minimum increase in

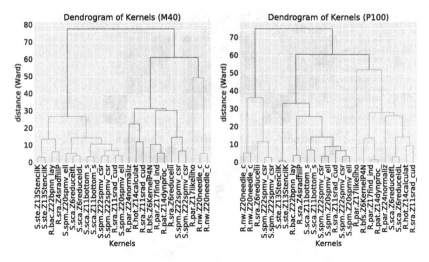

Fig. 8. Dendrogram of clusters for 26 kernels, comparing Maxwell (left) and Pascal (right) GPUs.

a weighted squared distances. The initial cluster distances in Ward's minimum variance method is defined as the squared Euclidean distance between points: $d_{ij} = d(\{X_i\}, \{X_j\}) = ||X_i - X_j||^2$. Figure 8 shows a dendrogram of clusters for 26 kernels calculated with Ward's method all matched with Rodinia Particle-filter sum_kernel, comparing the Maxwell (left) and Pascal (right) GPUs, which both have 4 edges and 2 vertices in their CFGs. sum_kernel performs a scan operation and is slightly memory intensive ($\sim$26% on GPUs). As shown, our tool is able to categorize kernels by grouping features, such as instruction mixes, graph structures, and distance measures that show strong similarity. This figure also demonstrates that different clusters can be formed on different GPUs for the same kernel, where the hardware architecture may result in different cluster of kernel classes.

Finally, we wanted to see if our technique could identify the same kernels running on a different GPU. Figure 9 shows distance measures when comparing three kernels across three GPUs, for a total of 9 comparisons, whereas Fig. 10 shows pairwise comparisons for the same three kernels across 3 GPUs, for a total of 27 comparisons (x-axis), considering pairwise comparisons in both directions (e.g. $\text{sim}(G_1, G_2)$ and $\text{sim}(G_2, G_1)$). Figure 9 displays patches of dark regions in distance measures corresponding to the same kernel when compared across different GPUs. As shown in Fig. 10, our tool not only is able to group the same kernel that was executed on different GPUs, as evident in the three general categories of clusters, but also kernels that exhibited similar characteristics when running on a particular architecture, such as instructions executed, graph structures, and distance measures.

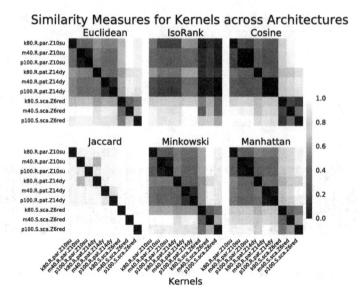

Fig. 9. Dendrogram of clusters for pairwise comparison for 3 kernels across 3 GPUs (9 total).

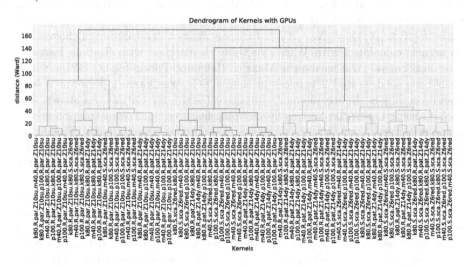

Fig. 10. Dendrogram of clusters for pairwise comparison for 3 kernels across 3 GPUs (27 total).

6.3   Discussion

These metrics can be used both for guiding manual optimizations and by compilers or autotuners. For example, human optimization effort can focus on the code fragments that are ranked high by kernel impact, but low by the goodness metric. An autotuner can also use metrics such as the goodness metric to explore the space of optimization parameters more efficiently, such as by excluding cases where we can predict a low value of the goodness metric without having to execute and time the actual generated code. A benefit to end users (not included in paper, due to space purposes) would be providing the ability to compare an implementation against a highly optimized kernel. By making use of subgraph matching strategy as well as instruction operations executed, `CUDAflow` is able to provide a mechanism to characterize unseen kernels.

7   Conclusion

We have presented `CUDAflow`, a control-flow-based methodology for analyzing the performance of CUDA applications. We combined static binary analysis with dynamic profiling to produce a set of metrics that not only characterizes the kernel by its computation requirements (memory or compute bound), but also provides detailed insights into application performance. Specifically, we provide an intuitive visualization and metrics display, and correlate performance hotspots with source line and file information, effectively guiding the end user to locations of interest and revealing potentially effective optimizations by identifying similarities of new implementations to known, autotuned computations through subgraph matching. We implemented this new methodology and demonstrated its capabilities on SHOC and Rodinia applications.

Future work includes incorporating memory reuse distance statistics of a kernel to characterize and help optimize the memory subsystem and compute/memory overlaps on the GPU. In addition, we want to generate robust models that will discover optimal block and thread sizes for CUDA kernels for specific input sizes without executing the application [18]. Last, we are in the process of developing an online web portal [7,26] that will archive a collection of control flow graphs for all known GPU applications. For instance, the web portal would be able to make on-the-fly comparisons across various hardware resources, as well as other GPU kernels, without burdening the end user with hardware requirements or software package installations, and will enable more feature rich capabilities when reporting performance metrics.

References

1. Adhianto, L., et al.: HPCToolkit: tools for performance analysis of optimized parallel programs. Concurr. Comput. Pract. Exp. **22**(6), 685–701 (2010)
2. Ammons, G., Ball, T., Larus, J.R.: Exploiting hardware performance counters with flow and context sensitive profiling. ACM Sigplan Not. **32**(5), 85–96 (1997)
3. Ball, T., Larus, J.R.: Optimally profiling and tracing programs. ACM Trans. Program. Lang. Syst. (TOPLAS) **16**(4), 1319–1360 (1994)
4. Böhm, C., Jacopini, G.: Flow diagrams, turing machines and languages with only two formation rules. Commun. ACM **9**(5), 366–371 (1966)
5. Borgelt, C., Berthold, M.R.: Mining molecular fragments: finding relevant substructures of molecules. In: Proceedings of the IEEE International Conference on Data Mining, pp. 51–58. IEEE (2002)

6. Che, S., et al.: Rodinia: a benchmark suite for heterogeneous computing. In: IEEE International Symposium on Workload Characterization, IISWC 2009, pp. 44–54. IEEE (2009)
7. Collective Knowledge (CK). http://cknowledge.org
8. Csardi, G., Nepusz, T.: The iGraph software package for complex network research
9. Danalis, A., et al.: The scalable heterogeneous computing (SHOC) benchmark suite. In: Proceedings of the 3rd Workshop on General-Purpose Computation on Graphics Processing Units, pp. 63–74. ACM (2010)
10. Allinea DDT. http://www.allinea.com/products/ddt
11. Diamos, G., Ashbaugh, B., Maiyuran, S., Kerr, A., Wu, H., Yalamanchili, S.: SIMD re-convergence at thread frontiers. In: Proceedings of the 44th Annual IEEE/ACM International Symposium on Microarchitecture, pp. 477–488. ACM (2011)
12. Farooqui, N., Kerr, A., Eisenhauer, G., Schwan, K., Yalamanchili, S.: Lynx: a dynamic instrumentation system for data-parallel applications on GPGPU architectures. In: International Symposium on Performance Analysis of Systems and Software (ISPASS), pp. 58–67. IEEE (2012)
13. Gonzales, R.C., Woods, R.E.: Digital Image Processing. Addison-Wesley, Reading (1993)
14. Huan, J., Wang, W., Prins, J.: Efficient mining of frequent subgraphs in the presence of isomorphism. In: Third IEEE International Conference on Data Mining, ICDM 2003, pp. 549–552. IEEE (2003)
15. Koutra, D., Vogelstein, J.T., Faloutsos, C.: DeltaCon: a principled massive-graph similarity function. SIAM
16. Lim, R., Carrillo-Cisneros, D., Alkowaileet, W., Scherson, I.: Computationally efficient multiplexing of events on hardware counters. In: Linux Symposium (2014)
17. Lim, R., Malony, A., Norris, B., Chaimov, N.: Identifying optimization opportunities within kernel execution in GPU codes. In: Hunold, S., et al. (eds.) Euro-Par 2015. LNCS, vol. 9523, pp. 185–196. Springer, Cham (2015). https://doi.org/10.1007/978-3-319-27308-2_16
18. Lim, R., Norris, B., Malony, A.: Autotuning GPU kernels via static and predictive analysis. In: 2017 46th International Conference on Parallel Processing (ICPP), pp. 523–532. IEEE (2017)
19. Marin, G., Dongarra, J., Terpstra, D.: MIAMI: A framework for application performance diagnosis. In: 2014 IEEE International Symposium on Performance Analysis of Systems and Software (ISPASS), pp. 158–168. IEEE (2014)
20. Miller, B.P., et al.: The paradyn parallel performance measurement tool. Computer 28(11), 37–46 (1995)
21. Nvidia Visual Profiler. https://developer.nvidia.com/nvidia-visual-profiler
22. Sabne, A., Sakdhnagool, P., Eigenmann, R.: Formalizing structured control flow graphs. In: Ding, C., Criswell, J., Wu, P. (eds.) LCPC 2016. LNCS, vol. 10136, pp. 153–168. Springer, Cham (2017). https://doi.org/10.1007/978-3-319-52709-3_13
23. Sarkar, V.: Determining average program execution times and their variance. In: ACM SIGPLAN Notices, vol. 24, pp. 298–312. ACM (1989)
24. Shende, S.S., Malony, A.D.: The TAU parallel performance system. Int. J. High Perform. Comput. Appl. 20(2), 287–311 (2006)
25. Singh, R., Xu, J., Berger, B.: Pairwise global alignment of protein interaction networks by matching neighborhood topology. In: Speed, T., Huang, H. (eds.) RECOMB 2007. LNCS, vol. 4453, pp. 16–31. Springer, Heidelberg (2007). https://doi.org/10.1007/978-3-540-71681-5_2

26. Sreepathi, S., et al.: Application characterization using Oxbow toolkit and PADS infrastructure. In: Proceedings of the 1st International Workshop on Hardware-Software Co-Design for High Performance Computing, pp. 55–63. IEEE Press (2014)

27. Williams, M.H., Ossher, H.: Conversion of unstructured flow diagrams to structured form. Comput. J. **21**(2), 161–167 (1978)

28. Wu, H., Diamos, G., Li, S., Yalamanchili, S.: Characterization and transformation of unstructured control flow in GPU applications. In: 1st International Workshop on Characterizing Applications for Heterogeneous Exascale Systems (2011)

29. Yan, X., Han, J.: gSpan: graph-based substructure pattern mining. In: Proceedings of 2002 IEEE International Conference on Data Mining, ICDM 2003, pp. 721–724. IEEE (2002)

30. Zhang, F., D'Hollander, E.H.: Using hammock graphs to structure programs. IEEE Trans. Softw. Eng. **30**(4), 231–245 (2004)

New Opportunities for Compilers in Computer Security

Junjie Shen[1], Zhi Chen[1], Nahid Farhady Ghalaty[2], Rosario Cammarota[3], Alexandru Nicolau[1], and Alexander V. Veidenbaum[1(✉)]

[1] Department of Computer Science, University of California, Irvine, USA
{junjies1,zhi2,nicolau,alexv}@ics.uci.edu
[2] Accenture Cyber Security Technology Labs, Arlington, VA, USA
nahid.farhady@accenture.com
[3] Qualcomm Technologies, Inc., San Diego, USA
rosarioc@qti.qualcomm.com

Abstract. Compiler techniques have been deployed to prevent various security attacks. Examples include mitigating memory access corruption, control flow integrity checks, race detection, software diversity, etc.

Hardware fault and side-channel attacks, however, are typically thought to require hardware protection. Attempts have been made to mitigate some timing and fault attacks via compiler techniques, but these typically adversely affected performance and often created opportunities for other types of attacks. More can and should be done in this area by the compiler community.

This paper presents such a compiler approach that simultaneously mitigates two types of attacks, namely a fault and a side-channel attacks. Continued development in this area using compiler techniques can further improve security.

1 Introduction

Compiler techniques have been successfully deployed to prevent various security attacks. Examples include mitigating memory access corruption, such as buffer overflow, in which the attacker attempts to subvert the control flow, e.g., via code reuse attack. Static analysis techniques are used to examine source code to eliminate bugs that can be exploited. Control-Flow Integrity checks the validity of the control-flow of an application. Software diversity is used to generate at compile time a unique binary layout for each compilation, limiting code reuse attacks. It is also applied at binary loading time to provide a different program memory layout for each execution, while the binary is fixed.

Hardware fault and side-channel attacks are harder to deal with and are typically thought to require hardware protection. A fault attack (FA) injects faults into the underlying microprocessor hardware to alter values in registers or memory and affect the execution of instructions. The attacker can then observe the faulty output and finally break the security of the system using systematic fault analysis models, such as Differential Fault Intensity Analysis (DFIA) [11].

© Springer Nature Switzerland AG 2019
M. Hall and H. Sundar (Eds.): LCPC 2018, LNCS 11882, pp. 54–60, 2019.
https://doi.org/10.1007/978-3-030-34627-0_4

A side-channel attack (SCA) may record sequences of measurements (traces), taken across cryptographic operations, such as operation counts, power consumption, execution time, etc. Statistical methods, such as Differential Power Analysis (DPA) [13] and Correlation Power Analysis (CPA) [4], on traces are then used to identify secret key dependent correlations and perform key extraction.

Mitigation strategies for FA and SCA are designed and deployed independently from each other. The former are built on redundancy [2] while the latter are based on masking and hiding [3]. Integration of both mitigation strategies is complex because of the interaction between them. The overhead usually exceeds the combined overhead of the individual mitigation strategies. A single strategy that mitigates both threats at the same time with overhead comparable to a typical mitigation strategy against FA or SCA [16] would be highly beneficial. Equally beneficial would be the integration of the combined mitigation in a compiler, because current implementations rely on manual effort by experts, which is complex and error-prone.

This work highlights one of many opportunities for compiler writers to address physical security, in collaboration with security experts. A compilation flow is developed to use vectorization to make code resistant to both fault and power/electromagnetic attacks. Vectorization is used for operation duplication and data redundancy in registers/memory, *not* for ILP. Furthermore, the duplication is performed in such a way that the Hamming weight of data in a vector register stays constant. The combined approach is referred to as *Twofer*.

To the best of our knowledge, this is the first work that exploits vector extensions to protect cryptographic algorithms against both fault and side-channel attacks within a unified framework.

2   Proposed Mitigation Technique

The compilation framework and the implementation details of the proposed mitigation technique are briefly described next. [8] proposed an approach to code vectorization for vector register value redundancy and operation duplication to mitigate fault attacks. Checking is performed at certain program points, such as stores, function calls, and branches, by comparing the equivalence of two result values in a vector register. In addition, vector gather/scatter instructions were utilized to duplicate address computations.

Memory contents was not duplicated in [8], however, in line with much prior work that relied on memory/cache ECC. This is no longer sufficient due to the recent proliferation of "Rowhammer" based memory attacks. This work, therefore duplicates all variables of the cryptographic primitives and checks the memory contents integrity using the duplicated values.

The proposed mitigation uses 1's complement to compensate the Hamming weight variance. The compiler can insert additional instructions to invert the result of a memory load before packing the original and inverted values in a vector register to form a Hamming weight-constant vector. However, this will affect the performance significantly since memory loads are very common in block ciphers. More importantly, key-dependent scalar loads are vulnerable to DPA. The size of key-dependent storage, such as *S-box* and cipher state arrays in AES, is therefor increased by 4x. In *Twofer*, the new array duplicates and interleaves the value of each element *val* in the original array with its 1's complement: $(val, \sim val, val, \sim val)$. The array indices need to be multiplied by four to reflect the correct location in the new array (i.e., stride-indexing). Arrays are also aligned to the cache line size so that every $(val, \sim val)$ pair fits in a cache line.

A vector memory load reads four consecutive values from the original memory address simultaneously using the masked vector load primitive. Two data items are used to counter fault attacks and the other two are used to prevent side-channel leakage. Stores are handled similar to loads, but are protected using masked stores. However, vector load and store instructions are more expensive than their scalar counterparts.

Most ALU instructions can be effectively protected against both FA and SCA using the proposed 1's complement approach, but the *xor* operation can cancel the masking effect and increase the Hamming weight. This is because both operand registers for *xor* always contain the original values and their inverted values. Hence, the two related lanes of a result vector register will be identical. An *xor* operation will produce a vector result with two values where one is the inverted value of the other if we invert one of the vector lanes in a vector operand before a *xor* operation. For example, if the two operands are $\langle a, \neg a \rangle$ and $\langle b, \neg b \rangle$, either $\neg a$ or $\neg b$ needs to be inverted. This pre-processing requires an additional *xor* operation, but the performance cost is very low.

3   Evaluation

The evaluation of *Twofer* was performed by comparing it with *Scalar* in defending against side-channel and fault attacks. It used the cryptographic library GNU Libgcrypt. Pin [14] was used as the base to build a binary instrumentation tool to collect traces, by recording Hamming weights corresponding to a discrete instant in time when data is written into registers during the execution of cryptographic software. This tool provides an accurate representation of the Hamming weight leakage model for cryptographic implementations in software. The evaluation of fault attack resistance was performed by injecting 1,000 single-bit faults at random positions in a cryptographic algorithm execution.

3.1   Resistance Against Side-Channel Attacks

Attacking with DPA. The cumulative differential for each key guess is calculated. DPA will generate 256 differential traces corresponding to each key byte guess. The key byte guess with the highest cumulative differential will be the speculation for the correct byte. The differential analysis is applied on all 16 key byte positions. For brevity, we only include a single key byte in the analysis.

The differential analysis results of a key byte are presented in Fig. 1. DPA is applied on a set of randomly generated keys. The unprotected *Scalar* is completely broken in the DPA attack with 20,000 traces. On the other hand, *Twofer*

remains invulnerable after the differential analysis to the limits of compliance–
FIPS 140 [10] and BSI AIS [12] series of recommendations for side-channel resistance of cryptographic software modules. The correct byte is indistinguishable
as its cumulative differential is perfectly blended into other guesses. More importantly, the correct byte in *Twofer* shows no trend of standing out as more traces
are added in the differential attack.

Attacking with CPA. A more powerful attack, correlation power analysis,
is applied on both *Scalar* and *Twofer*. For a given key guess, CPA calculates the
Pearson's correlation coefficient between the power hypothesis for the Hamming
weight of `SubBytes` output and the actual power usage (traces).

Figure 2 shows the CPA results on a key byte position. The correlation of the
correct byte in *Scalar* remains 1 throughout the experiment. In fact, *Scalar* is
completely broken with merely 5 traces. However, *Twofer* shows full mitigation
against CPA, benefiting from the constant Hamming weight of key-dependent
instructions.

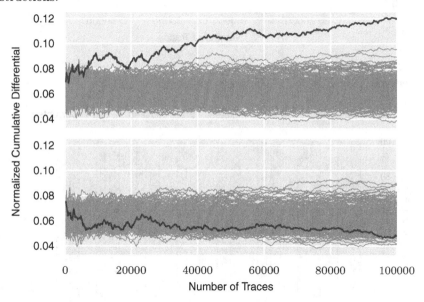

Fig. 1. DPA results of *Scalar* (top) and *Twofer* (bottom) on a key byte.

3.2 Resistance to Fault Attacks

1,000 single-bit faults were injected to each of the ciphers, similar to the approach
in [8]. Figure 3 presents the results, where **detected** are the faults detected by
our error checking code; **incomplete** are faults causing segmentation faults or
causing the cipher to enter an infinite loop; **masked** are the faults with no effect
on the cipher result (i.e. was masked); and **corrupted** shows the faults for which
the cipher finishes and generates an incorrect result. The unprotected ciphers
have a 24.34% corruption rate, on average, while *Twofer* reduces it significantly
– down to 0.53%.

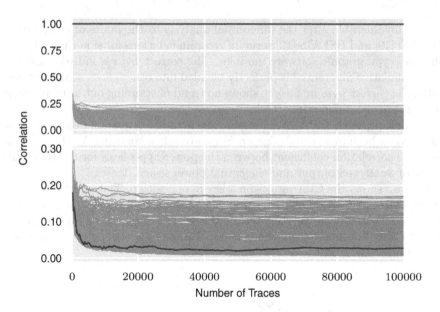

Fig. 2. CPA results of *Scalar* (top) and *Twofer* (bottom) on a key byte. The attacks were performed using 200 to 100,000 traces with a step size of 200.

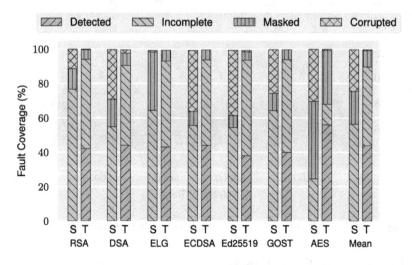

Fig. 3. Fault injection results. *S* for *Scalar* and *T* for *Twofer*.

3.3 Overhead Evaluation

The run time and energy overheads of *Twofer* were collected over 1000 consecutive cipher operations (private and public for public key ciphers, and encryption and decryption for AES). *Twofer* incurs a reasonable 2.38x slowdown in performance. The overhead is primarily due to (a) extra instructions required for error checking, and (b) the high latency of AVX-512 vector instructions.

The energy consumption was measured with Likwid 4.2.1 [17] using hardware performance counters. The results show that applying *Twofer* imposes a 2.32x energy overhead in comparison to *Scalar*.

Twofer memory overhead is also negligible because cipher states and *S-boxes* only occupy a small fraction of the overall memory footprint in execution. Public ciphers generally have a small cipher state and are dominated by arithmetic calculations.

4   Related Work

Prior work for the mitigation of both fault and side-channel attacks exists. For instance, Wiretap codes that provide resistance against SCA can be used for fault detection up to a certain level of injection [6]. Bringer et al. proposed a smart card friendly Orthogonal Direct Sum Masking technique to protect the AES algorithm against both SCA and FA [5]. This technique is not fully protected against fault attacks because of the author's assumption that generating a fault with a higher Hamming distance is more difficult. An example of such an attack can be DFA attacks that require random byte fault injection [18]. Similar ideas have been proposed in [7]. These proposed techniques also have not been automated, however, unlike the work presented here. The need for combined countermeasures is also increasing due to recent advances towards combined attacks. Examples of such attacks are discussed in [1,9,15].

5   Conclusion

Compiler techniques have not been fully examined in the context of physical attacks and especially in mitigating multiple types of attacks simultaneously. For instance, countermeasures against fault and side-channel attacks rely on different techniques. Integrating both countermeasures is a nontrivial task and often imposes overhead that exceeds the sum of individual countermeasures.

This work demonstrated that a unified compiler-based approach is possible to tackle both fault and side-channel attacks by leveraging redundancy through vectorization along with masking.

References

1. Amiel, F., Villegas, K., Feix, B., Marcel, L.: Passive and active combined attacks: combining fault attacks and side channel analysis. In: FDTC 2007, pp. 92–102. IEEE (2007)
2. Bar-El, H., Choukri, H., Naccache, D., Tunstall, M., Whelan, C.: The sorcerer's apprentice guide to fault attacks. Proc. IEEE **94**(2), 370–382 (2006)
3. Bayrak, A.G., Velickovic, N., Regazzoni, F., Novo, D., Brisk, P., Ienne, P.: An EDA-friendly protection scheme against side-channel attacks. In: DATE 2013, pp. 410–415. EDA Consortium (2013)

4. Brier, E., Clavier, C., Olivier, F.: Correlation power analysis with a leakage model. In: Joye, M., Quisquater, J.-J. (eds.) CHES 2004. LNCS, vol. 3156, pp. 16–29. Springer, Heidelberg (2004). https://doi.org/10.1007/978-3-540-28632-5_2

5. Bringer, J., Carlet, C., Chabanne, H., Guilley, S., Maghrebi, H.: Orthogonal direct sum masking. In: Naccache, D., Sauveron, D. (eds.) WISTP 2014. LNCS, vol. 8501, pp. 40–56. Springer, Heidelberg (2014). https://doi.org/10.1007/978-3-662-43826-8_4

6. Bringer, J., Chabanne, H., Le, T.H.: Protecting AES against side-channel analysis using wire-tap codes. J. Cryptogr. Eng. **2**, 1–13 (2012)

7. Carlet, C., Guilley, S.: Complementary dual codes for counter-measures to side-channel attacks. In: Pinto, R., Malonek, P.R., Vettori, P. (eds.) Coding Theory and Applications. CSMS, vol. 3, pp. 97–105. Springer, Cham (2015). https://doi.org/10.1007/978-3-319-17296-5_9

8. Chen, Z., Shen, J., Nicolau, A., Veidenbaum, A., Farhady, N.: CAMFAS: a compiler approach to mitigate fault attacks via enhanced SIMDization. In: FDTC 2017, pp. 57–64. IEEE (2017)

9. Clavier, C., Feix, B., Gagnerot, G., Roussellet, M.: Passive and active combined attacks on AES combining fault attacks and side channel analysis. In: FDTC 2010, pp. 10–19. IEEE (2010)

10. FIPS, PUB: 140-2. Security Requirements for Cryptographic Modules **25** (2001)

11. Ghalaty, N.F., Yuce, B., Taha, M., Schaumont, P.: Differential fault intensity analysis. In: FDTC 2014, pp. 49–58. IEEE (2014)

12. Killmann, W., Lange, T., Lochter, M., Thumser, W., Wicke, G.: Minimum requirements for evaluating side-channel attack resistance of elliptic curve implementations (2011). http://www.bsi.bund.de

13. Kocher, P., Jaffe, J., Jun, B.: Differential power analysis. In: Wiener, M. (ed.) CRYPTO 1999. LNCS, vol. 1666, pp. 388–397. Springer, Heidelberg (1999). https://doi.org/10.1007/3-540-48405-1_25

14. Luk, C.K., et al.: Pin: building customized program analysis tools with dynamic instrumentation. ACM SIGPLAN Not. **40**, 190–200 (2005)

15. Roche, T., Lomné, V., Khalfallah, K.: Combined fault and side-channel attack on protected implementations of AES. In: Prouff, E. (ed.) CARDIS 2011. LNCS, vol. 7079, pp. 65–83. Springer, Heidelberg (2011). https://doi.org/10.1007/978-3-642-27257-8_5

16. Schneider, T., Moradi, A., Güneysu, T.: ParTI – towards combined hardware countermeasures against side-channel and fault-injection attacks. In: Robshaw, M., Katz, J. (eds.) CRYPTO 2016. LNCS, vol. 9815, pp. 302–332. Springer, Heidelberg (2016). https://doi.org/10.1007/978-3-662-53008-5_11

17. Treibig, J., Hager, G., Wellein, G.: LIKWID: a lightweight performance-oriented tool suite for x86 multicore environments. In: ICPPW 2010, pp. 207–216. IEEE (2010)

18. Tunstall, M., Mukhopadhyay, D., Ali, S.: Differential fault analysis of the advanced encryption standard using a single fault. In: Ardagna, C.A., Zhou, J. (eds.) WISTP 2011. LNCS, vol. 6633, pp. 224–233. Springer, Heidelberg (2011). https://doi.org/10.1007/978-3-642-21040-2_15

Footmark: A New Formulation for Working Set Statistics

Liang Yuan[1]([✉]), Wesley Smith[2], Sicong Fan[3], Zixu Chen[3], Chen Ding[3], and Yunquan Zhang[1]

[1] SKL of Computer Architecture, ICT, CAS, Beijing, China
yuanliang@ict.ac.cn
[2] University of Edinburgh, Edinburgh, UK
[3] University of Rochester, Rochester, USA

Abstract. The working set (WS) model pioneered by Denning and others is the foundation for analyzing memory performance and optimizing memory management. An important measure is the average working set size (WSS). In 1968, Denning derived a recursive formula to compute the average WSS. The Denning recursion was originally derived for infinitely long program executions and later adapted to use on finite length traces. All previous adaptations, however, have had to modify the Denning recursion for boundary correction.

This paper presents footmark, which redefines average WSS for finite length traces. It has three benefits. By definition, footmark satisfies a new type of symmetry. Mathematically, the paper gives four equivalent formulas for computing footmark including one that is identical to the Denning recursion. The mathematical simplicity is beneficial in both formal and practical analysis of working sets. Based on the new formulas, the paper proves a previously unknown equivalence relation between two working set definitions. Finally, the paper evaluates three WSS definitions using six test programs from the SPEC 2017 benchmark suite.

Keywords: Locality · Footprint · Working set

1 Introduction

The memory system of a modern computer is organized as a hierarchy. Locality is the fundamental principle to support memory hardware design and guide software optimization. We focus on locality metrics, which are widely used in software and hardware based analyses to manage and optimize a system's use of its memory hierarchy. For locality analysis, the basic unit of information is a data access, and the basic relation is a data reuse. Locality analysis shows the underlying relation between cache performance and data reuses.

The research was conducted when the first author visited University of Rochester from September 2017 to September 2018 and when the second author worked at the university in summer 2018.

© Springer Nature Switzerland AG 2019
M. Hall and H. Sundar (Eds.): LCPC 2018, LNCS 11882, pp. 61–69, 2019.
https://doi.org/10.1007/978-3-030-34627-0_5

In locality analysis, an important concept is the working set (WS), and a useful measure is average working set size (WSS). In 1968, Denning derived the formula to compute the average WSS [5, Sec. 4.4]. The formula was later expressed as a recursion [7]. We call it the *Denning working set recursion* or the Denning recursion in short and will review it in Sect. 2.

The Denning recursion was originally derived for infinite long program executions. It was later adapted to use on finite length traces by adding special boundary corrections [8,13]. More recently, Ding et al. defined a form of average WSS called the footprint [9,14]. The footprint definition has the property that it considers all windows of the same length, regardless whether a window is at the boundary or not. In this paper, we refer to this property as *window-length symmetry*. The footprint calculation has to use first- and last-access times, which are unneeded by the Denning recursion [14].

In this paper, we present *footmark*, which redefines average WSS. The new definition combines elements of past work but offers several advantages.

The first is *window-count symmetry*, which means that every trace element, whether it is at the boundary or in the middle of the trace, is considered in the same number of windows when calculating footmark. The second is simplicity. The paper presents three formulas to compute footmark, which are more succinct than previous formulas (for finite length traces). Furthermore, footmark can be computed using the Denning recursion.

We show a proof that footmark numerically differs from the footprint by at most 1 for small window sizes, even though the two definitions treat boundary windows differently, and the footprint uses significantly more information about the trace than footmark does. Finally, we demonstrate the equivalence in experiments using a set of SPEC 2017 benchmark programs.

Although the paper does not show any use of footmark, we note here that its mathematical simplicity has benefits in both practical and theoretical analysis of working sets. Operationally, footmark requires only the reuse interval, which can be measured efficiently through sampling, either at run time [10,12,15] or by a compiler [3]. In formal analysis, a recent discovery is the effect of interleaving on the footprint [2]. The simpler footmark formulas may significantly reduce the complexity of the symbolic reasoning.

In the remainder of the paper, we present the background in Sect. 2 and footmark in Sect. 3 including its derivation and equivalence relations.

2   Background

A *trace* is a sequence of references to data or memory locations. Each reference may be an object identifier or the address of a memory cell, block, or page. We also call a reference a *trace element*, and its target a *data item*. The length of a trace is n. The number of distinct items is m.

A *window* $A(t, \tau)$ is the τ-length substring of trace A beginning at the tth element. The window's *working set* $W(t, \tau)$ is the set of distinct elements in it. The *working set size* is the size of its working set, $\omega(t, \tau) = |W(t, \tau)|$ [4]. Note that the original working set definition by Denning uses backward windows [6]. Here we depart from the convention slightly and use forward windows, i.e. the first parameter is the *first* element of the window. The choice is to make boundary windows more easily distinguishable, i.e. all head windows start from 0.

A *reuse* is defined as two consecutive references of the same data. The *reuse interval* is the elapse of logical or physical time between these two references. It is the same as the *interreference interval* used in the literature on virtual memory management [4] and the *reuse time* used in our earlier papers. The reuse interval is at most $n - 1$. The *reuse interval histogram* is represented by $ri(i)$ for $i \in [1, \ldots, n-1]$, each is the number of reuses with reuse interval i. For example, in the trace *aabb*, the reuse interval for a is 1, and $ri(1) = 2$.

In the working set theory, Denning [6] defines *the average working set size* $S_n(x)$ for a trace of finite length n: $S_n(x) \triangleq \frac{1}{n}(\sum_{t=0}^{x-1} w(0,t) + \sum_{t=0}^{n-x} w(t,x))$. The average working set size $S(x)$ for an infinite length trace is given by $S(x) \triangleq \lim_{n \to \infty} S_n(x)$. It is impossible to calculate $S(x)$ directly by enumerating all windows since the trace is infinite. By adopting a probabilistic approach, Denning [7] derives the recursive formula for $S(x)$ using a distribution of reuse interval frequencies $ri(i)/n$: $S(x + 1) = S(x) + \lim_{n \to \infty} \sum_{i=x+1}^{n-1} ri(i)/n$. For a trace of a finite length, Denning and Slutz derived the recursion as $s(x + 1) = s(x) + mwh(x)$ [8], which we will discuss in Sect. 3.2.

Xiang et al. defined the *footprint fp(x)*. For integer $x \in [0, n]$, $fp(x)$ is the average working set size among all windows of length x: $fp(x) \triangleq \frac{1}{n-x+1} \sum_{t=0}^{n-x} w(t,x)$. We denote the total WSS of length-x windows as $FP(x) \triangleq \sum_{t=0}^{n-x} w(t,x)$ and have $FP(x) = (n - x + 1)fp(x)$. Every trace element and every working set are considered for windows of the same length. We call it the *window-length symmetry*.

Xiang gave the formula to compute the footprint using the reuse interval $ri(i)$ for each reuse interval i and the first- and last-access time, $ft(e)$ and $< (e)$, for each data item e. The Xiang formula uses $ri(x + 1 \ldots n - 1)$ to compute the footprint for window size x. Yuan et al. [16] derived two methods for calculating the footprint using the same information. They rely on $ri(1 \ldots n - 1)$ and $ri(1 \ldots x - 1)$ for window size x respectively. Let $d(x) = x$ if $x > 0$ and $d(x) = 0$ otherwise. The three formulas for the footprint are as follows.

$$FP(x) = m(n - x + 1) - \sum_{i=x+1}^{n-1} (i - x) \times ri(i) - \sum_{e=1}^{m} d(ft(e) - x + 1)$$

$$- \sum_{e=1}^{m} d(n - x - < (e))$$

$$= xm + \sum_{i=1}^{n-1} \min(i, x) \times ri(i) - \sum_{e=1}^{m} d(x - 1 - ft(e))$$

$$- \sum_{e=1}^{m} d(< (e) - (n - x))$$

$$= xn - \sum_{i=1}^{x-1}(x-i) \times ri(i) - \sum_{e=1}^{m} d(x-1-ft(e))$$

$$- \sum_{e=1}^{m} d(< (e) - (n-x)) \tag{1}$$

We call the second the additive formula (since the ri term is additive) and the third the incremental formula (since it uses ri incrementally). In all these formulas, the boundary effect is computed by the $2m$ terms (based on the first- and last-access times), which add considerable complexity.

3   Footmark

3.1   Definition and Calculation

The footmark is $fm(x) = FM(x)/n$ for $0 < x \le n$, which is the total WSS $FM(x)$ divided by the trace length n. The total WSS is as follows and includes all windows of length x and all head and tail windows of lengths *less* than x.

$$FM(x) = \sum_{t=1}^{x-1} \omega(0,t) + \sum_{t=0}^{n-x} \omega(t,x) + \sum_{t=1}^{x-1} \omega(n-x+t,x-t)$$

The novel feature of this definition is taking the total WSS of $n + x - 1$ windows but dividing the total by n. Because head and tail windows are shorter than x, and their total length is $(x-1)x$, they are treated as $x-1$ windows.

For example, consider the trace $abcdef$, we have $n = 6, x = 4$. The first sum in $FM(x)$ includes all head windows of length smaller than 4: a, ab and abc; the second sum all windows of length 4, $abcd$, $bcde$ and $cdef$; and the last sum all tail windows of length smaller than 4, def, ef and f. $FM(x)$ adds the WSS of $5 + x$ windows, and the footmark is this sum divided by 6. In particular, $fm(x) = x$ for $1 \le x \le 6$.

Footmark does not have window-length symmetry, since head and tail windows have different lengths. Instead, it has *window-count symmetry*: for $fm(x)$, every trace element is considered in x windows, i.e. x working sets. By itself, the new symmetry does not seem more useful. In fact, it has to consider more windows, yet the extra (tail) windows have dubious importance in practice.

The benefit of the new definition, however, is mathematical simplicity. For the trace $abcdef$, footmark and footprint actually compute the same result, i.e. $fp(x) = x$ for $1 \le x \le 6$. However, the calculation differs. The denominator in footprint decrements from n to 1 as x increases from 1 to n. It is simpler in footmark — it is always n. Moreover, it is also simpler to represent and compute the enumerator $FM(x)$.

The middle term of $FM(x)$ is the total WSS of all length-x windows, which can be computed by the formulas shown in Eq. (1). The other two terms are for the head and tail windows, which we compute using the following lemma:

Lemma 1.

$$\sum_{t=1}^{x-1} \omega(0,t) = \sum_{e=1}^{m} d(x-1-\mathit{ft}(e))$$

$$\sum_{t=1}^{x-1} \omega(n-x+t, x-t) = \sum_{e=1}^{m} d(< (e) - (n-x))$$

where $\mathit{ft}, <$ are first- and last-access times, and $d(x) = x$ if $x > 0$ and $d(x) = 0$ otherwise.

Proof. The first equation computes the total WSS of $x-1$ head windows, i.e. $A(0,t)$ for $1 \leqslant t \leqslant x-1$, by calculating the contribution to the total WSS by each data item e in the trace. A data item e appears in a head window if it is first accessed before time $x-1$, i.e. $\mathit{ft}(e) \leq x-1$. The number of windows is appears in is simply $x-1-\mathit{ft}(e)$, i.e. the windows $A(0,\mathit{ft}(e)) \ldots A(0, x-1)$. Since all windows start from 0, any data reuse does not add to the total WSS. Therefore, the summing of $d(x-1-\mathit{ft}(e))$ is the total WSS, and the first equation holds. The second equation can be proved with similar reasoning. □

Combining Eq. (1) and Lemma 1, we have

$$FM(x) = mx + \sum_{i=1}^{n-1} \min(i,x) \times \mathit{ri}(i)$$

$$= nx - \sum_{i=1}^{x-1} (x-i) \times \mathit{ri}(i)$$

$$= mx - \sum_{i=x+1}^{n-1} (i-x) \times \mathit{ri}(i) + \sum_{e=1}^{m} (< (e) - \mathit{ft}(e)) \qquad (2)$$

We call them the additive, incremental and Xiang formula style respectively. The incremental formula computes the total WSS iteratively using the reuse interval histogram. The Xiang formula style uses the ft and $<$ terms, but they are not strictly necessary, as evident by its equality to the first two formulas.

By considering more windows, footmark achieves the window-count symmetry, and it is simpler than the footprint, which uses the window-length symmetry. Since footmark requires only the reuse interval and does not need first- and last-access times, it can be used in a recent compiler technique of static locality analysis [3]. In formal analysis, footmark has the same denominator n, which can simply derivations of mathematical properties, for example, computing the effect of trace interleaving [2].

3.2   Equivalence

We first show that footmark can be computed by the Denning recursion. In a finite length trace, we must consider the first accesses of data, i.e. the m accesses that are not reuses. We use a "trick" to consider them as reuses with the reuse interval n (actual reuse intervals are at most $n - 1$).[1]

From the additive formula $FM(x) = \sum_{i=1}^{n} \min(i, x) \times ri(i)$, we have the recursive formula for fm, which is the Denning recursion:

$$fm(x + 1) - fm(x) = \sum_{i=x+1}^{n} ri(i)/n.$$

For a finite length trace, Denning and Slutz derived the recursion as $s(x+1) = s(x) + mwh(x)$, where $mwh(x)$ includes the reuse intervals but also additional terms for boundary correction [8]. Footmark does not use additional corrections and shows what the unchanged Denning recursion means for a finite length trace.

Next we prove a theorem that the footmark and the footprint are practically numerically identical for small window sizes.

Theorem 1. $-1 \leqslant fm(x) - fp(x) \leqslant 1$, When $x \leqslant \sqrt{n}$.

Proof. We only prove the right inequality. Let $FM_{end}(x) = FM(x) - FP(x)$, we have:

$$fm(x) - fp(x) = \frac{FM(x)}{n} - fp(x)$$
$$= \frac{FM_{end}(x)}{n} + \frac{FP(x)}{n} - fp(x)$$
$$= \frac{FM_{end}(x)}{n} + \frac{n - x + 1}{n} fp(x) - fp(x)$$
$$= \frac{1}{n}(FM_{end}(x) + (1 - x)fp(x))$$

It is easy to see that the upper bound for $FM_{end}(x)$ is $x(x-1)$, and lower bound for $fp(x)$ is 1. It then follows that $fm(x) - fp(x) \leq \frac{1}{n}(x(x-1) + (1-x))$. For $x \leq \sqrt{n}$, we have $fm(x) - fp(x) \leq \frac{1}{x^2}(x^2 - 2x + 1) = (1 - \frac{2}{x} + \frac{1}{x^2}) \leq 1$. □

However, there is no such constant bound in general cases. Consider a trace of length n where the first and last $n/4$ accesses are all distinct, while the middle $n/2$ accesses are all the same. The difference $fm(n/2) - fp(n/2) \approx n/16$. In real-world applications, the windows in FM_{end} tend to contain more distinct data items, and we can expect $fm(x) > fp(x)$.

3.3   Experimental Evaluation

In Theorem 1, we have proved that the footmark is practically identical to the Xiang footprint for window sizes up to the square root of n. Next we show the actual results on 6 test programs in the SPEC CPU2017 suite. The programs are *bwaves*, *cactusBSSN*, *gcc*, *mcf*, *perlbench*, and *namd*. They are profiled by the

---

[1] This trick was first used by Denning and Slutz to count the end corrections for space-time working set [8].

Loca tool [1], which is based on a binary rewriter tool Pin [11]. Loca instruments a program and outputs the first- and last-access times and the reuse intervals as a logarithmic-scale histogram.

From these histograms, we compute average working-set size using three definitions. We use the first- and last-access time histogram and the reuse interval histogram to compute the footprint. In addition, we simplify the Xiang formula to use only the reuse interval. We call it *reuse-term footprint*. Specifically, it is $rtfp(x) = m - \sum_{i=x+1}^{n-1}(i-x)rt(i)/n$. Finally, we compute footmark, which is the same as the Denning recursion.

Figure 1 shows a comparison between the three definitions. Footmark and reuse-term footprint use only the reuse interval histogram. Both can be viewed as an approximation of the footprint. We see that footmark closely matches footprint. For infinitely long traces, the reuse-term footprint is the same as footprint, i.e. $\lim_{n\to\infty}(fp(x) - rtfp(x)) = 0$. For our tests, however, reuse-term footprint deviates significantly from footprint especially in *gcc* and *perlbench*, making it unsuitable to model finite length traces.

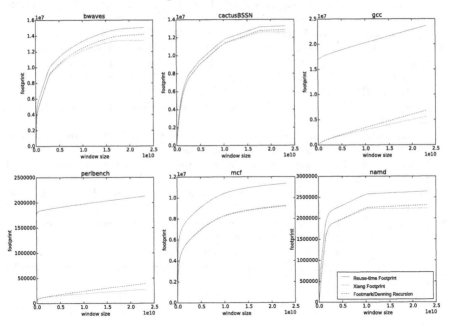

Fig. 1. Comparison of three definitions. The footmark closely matches the footprint, while the reuse-term footprint does not.

4 Conclusion

We have presented a new working set metric for finite length traces called footmark. It has the window-count symmetry and shows what the unmodified Denning recursion means for finite length traces. We have derived non-recursive including additive and incremental formulas to compute footmark, proved its equivalence relations with footprint, and demonstrated its accuracy experimentally.

Acknowledgement. The authors wish to thank Peter Denning for the feedback and suggestions on the presentation of the paper's contributions and William Wilson for help on the use of the loca tool. The funding was provided in part by National Key R&D Program of China (2016YFB0200803) and NFSC (61432018, 61402441, 61521092, 61502450, 61602443), by the National Science Foundation of the United States (Contract No. CCF-1717877 and CCF-1629376), by an IBM CAS Faculty Fellowship, and by Guangdong Province Key Laboratory of Popular High Performance Computers (2017B030314073).

References

1. Loca: Program locality analysis tools (2018). https://github.com/dcompiler/loca
2. Brock, J., Ding, C., Lavaee, R., Liu, F., Yuan, L.: Prediction and bounds on shared cache demand from memory access interleaving. In: Proceedings of the International Symposium on Memory Management, pp. 96–108 (2018). https://doi.org/10.1145/3210563.3210565. http://doi.acm.org/10.1145/3210563.3210565
3. Chen, D., Liu, F., Ding, C., Pai, S.: Locality analysis through static parallel sampling. In: Proceedings of the ACM SIGPLAN Conference on Programming Language Design and Implementation, pp. 557–570 (2018). https://doi.org/10.1145/3192366.3192402. http://doi.acm.org/10.1145/3192366.3192402
4. Coffman Jr., E.G., Denning, P.J.: Operating Systems Theory. Prentice-Hall, Englewood Cliffs (1973)
5. Denning, P.J.: Resource Allocation in Multiprocess Computer Systems. Ph.D. thesis, Massachusetts Institute of Technology (1968)
6. Denning, P.J.: The working set model for program behaviour. Commun. ACM **11**(5), 323–333 (1968)
7. Denning, P.J., Schwartz, S.C.: Properties of the working set model. Commun. ACM **15**(3), 191–198 (1972)
8. Denning, P.J., Slutz, D.R.: Generalized working sets for segment reference strings. Commun. ACM **21**(9), 750–759 (1978)
9. Ding, C., Chilimbi, T.: All-window profiling of concurrent executions. In: Proceedings of the ACM SIGPLAN Symposium on Principles and Practice of Parallel Programming (2008). Poster paper
10. Hu, X., et al.: Fast miss ratio curve modeling for storage cache. ACM Trans. Storage **14**(2), 12:1–12:34 (2018). https://doi.org/10.1145/3185751. http://doi.acm.org/10.1145/3185751
11. Luk, C.K., et al.: Pin: building customized program analysis tools with dynamic instrumentation. In: Proceedings of the ACM SIGPLAN Conference on Programming Language Design and Implementation, pp. 190–200 (2005)
12. Pan, C., Hu, X., Zhou, L., Luo, Y., Wang, X., Wang, Z.: PACE: penalty aware cache modeling with enhanced AET. In: 9th ACM SIGOPS Asia-Pacific Workshop on Systems (APSys 2018) (2018)
13. Slutz, D.R., Traiger, I.L.: A note on the calculation working set size. Commun. ACM **17**(10), 563–565 (1974). https://doi.org/10.1145/355620.361167. http://doi.acm.org/10.1145/355620.361167

14. Xiang, X., Bao, B., Ding, C., Gao, Y.: Linear-time modeling of program working set in shared cache. In: Proceedings of the International Conference on Parallel Architecture and Compilation Techniques, pp. 350–360 (2011)
15. Xiang, Y., Wang, X., Huang, Z., Wang, Z., Luo, Y., Wang, Z.: DCAPS: dynamic cache allocation with partial sharing. In: Proceedings of the EuroSys Conference, pp. 13:1–13:15 (2018). https://doi.org/10.1145/3190508.3190511. http://doi.acm.org/10.1145/3190508.3190511
16. Yuan, L., Ding, C., Denning, P.J., Zhang, Y.: A measurement theory of locality. CoRR abs/1802.01254 (2018). http://arxiv.org/abs/1802.01254

Towards an Achievable Performance for the Loop Nests

Aniket Shivam[1]([✉]), Neftali Watkinson[1], Alexandru Nicolau[1], David Padua[2], and Alexander V. Veidenbaum[1]

[1] Department of Computer Science, University of California, Irvine, Irvine, USA
{aniketsh,watkinso,nicolau,alexv}@ics.uci.edu
[2] Department of Computer Science, University of Illinois at Urbana-Champaign, Champaign, USA
padua@illinois.edu

Abstract. Numerous code optimization techniques, including loop nest optimizations, have been developed over the last four decades. Loop optimization techniques transform loop nests to improve the performance of the code on a target architecture, including exposing parallelism. Finding and evaluating an optimal, semantic-preserving sequence of transformations is a complex problem. The sequence is guided using heuristics and/or analytical models and there is no way of knowing how close it gets to optimal performance or if there is any headroom for improvement.

This paper makes two contributions. First, it uses a comparative analysis of loop optimizations/transformations across multiple compilers to determine how much headroom may exist for each compiler. And second, it presents an approach to characterize the loop nests based on their hardware performance counter values and a Machine Learning approach that predicts which compiler will generate the fastest code for a loop nest. The prediction is made for both auto-vectorized, serial compilation and for auto-parallelization. The results show that the headroom for state-of-the-art compilers ranges from 1.10x to 1.42x for the serial code and from 1.30x to 1.71x for the auto-parallelized code. These results are based on the Machine Learning predictions.

1 Introduction

Modern architectures have been evolving towards greater number of cores on the chip, as well as, improving the processing capabilities of individual cores. Each core in the current multi-core architectures includes the capability to process Single Instruction Multiple Data (SIMD) or Vector instructions. State-of-the-art compilers, or code optimizers, use advanced loop transformation techniques to modify the loop nests so as to take advantage of these SIMD instructions. The underlying code optimization techniques in the compilers to *auto-vectorize* the loop nests [1, 19, 26] require careful analysis of data dependences, memory access patterns, etc. Similarly, a serial version of the loop nest may be parallelized i.e. transformed such that loop iterations can be reordered and scheduled for parallel

© Springer Nature Switzerland AG 2019
M. Hall and H. Sundar (Eds.): LCPC 2018, LNCS 11882, pp. 70–77, 2019.
https://doi.org/10.1007/978-3-030-34627-0_6

execution across the multiple cores. These transformations are characterized as *auto-parallelization* techniques [3, 7, 13–16, 18] and the end product is a multi-threaded code.

Some key transformations for optimizing loop nests [12, 26] are Distribution, Fusion, Interchange, Skewing, Tiling and Unrolling. The best set of transformations for a given loop nest can be any possible sequence of these transformations with even repeating transformations. Even though the compilers may have the ability to perform important loop transformations, the built-in heuristics and analytical models that drive these optimizations to determine the order and the profitability of these transformations may lead to sub-optimal results. Evaluation studies [10, 17, 23] have shown that state-of-the-art compilers may miss out on opportunities to optimize the code for modern architectures. But a major challenge in developing heuristics and profitability models is predicting the behavior of a multi-core processor which has complex pipelines, multiple functional units, memory hierarchy, hardware data prefetching, etc. Parallelization of loop nests involve further challenges for the compilers, since communication costs based on the temporal and spatial data locality among iterations have an impact on the overall performance too. These heuristics and models differ between compilers which leads to different quality of the generated code for the loop nests and therefore, the performance may vary significantly. There are various compilers and domain specific loop optimizers that perform auto-vectorization and, in some cases, auto-parallelization such Intel ICC, GNU GCC, LLVM Clang, etc. By observing their relative performance one can identify relative headroom.

Embedding Machine Learning models in compilers is continuously being explored by the research community [2, 5, 6, 9, 22–25]. Most of the previous work used Machine Learning in the domain of auto-vectorization, phase-ordering and parallelism runtime settings. This work applies Machine Learning on a coarser level, in order to predict the most suited code optimizer - for serial as well as parallel code.

Previous studies have shown that hardware performance counters can successfully capture the characteristic behavior of the loop nests. In those studies, Machine Learning models either use a mix of static features (collected from source code at compile time) and dynamic features (collected from profiling) [23, 24], or exclusively use dynamic features [2, 6, 25]. This work belongs to the second class and exclusively uses hardware performance counters collected from profiling a serial (-O1) version of a loop nest and uses these dynamic features as the input for the Machine Learning classifiers. It also shows that it is feasible to use hardware performance counters from an architecture to make predictions for similar multi-core architectures.

The focus of this work is to consider state-of-the art code optimizers and then use Machine Learning algorithms to make predictions for better, yet clearly achievable performance for the loop nests using these code optimizers. This is what defines a possible headroom. We believe that recognizing the inherent behavior of loop nests using hardware performance counters and Machine Learning algorithms will present an automated mechanism for compiler writers to identify where to focus on making improvements in order to achieve better performance.

2   Experimental Methodology

This section describes the candidate code optimizers and the architectures that we considered for this work and methodology for conducting the experiments.

2.1   Code Optimizers

In this work we considered 4 candidate code optimizers, as shown in Table 1, including Polly [11,20], a Polyhedral Model based optimizer for LLVM. 2 out of those 4 optimizers can perform auto-parallelization of the loop nests. The hardware performance counters are collected using an executable generated by icc with flags -O1 -no-vec, in order to disable all loop transformations, and disable vector code and parallel code generation.

2.2   Benchmarks

The first benchmark suite that we use for our experiment is Test Suite for Vectorizing Compilers (TSVC) as used by Callahan et al. [4] and Maleki et al. [17] for their works. This benchmark was developed to assess the auto-vectorization capabilities of compilers. Therefore, we only use those loop nests in the serial code related experiments. The second benchmark suite that we collect loop nests from is Polybench [21]. This suite consists of 30 benchmarks that perform numerical computations used in various domains such as linear algebra computations, image processing, physics simulation, etc. We use Polybench for experiments involving both serial and auto-parallelized code. We use the two largest datasets from Polybench to create our ML dataset. In our experience, the variance of both the hardware performance counter values and the most suited code optimizer for the loop nests across the two datasets, was enough to treat them as two different loop nests. This variance can be attributed to two main reasons. First, a different set of optimizations being performed by the optimizers based on the built-in analytical models/heuristics that drive those optimizations, since properties like loop trip counts usually vary across datasets. Second, the performance across datasets on an architecture with a memory hierarchy, where

Table 1. Candidate Code Optimizer and their flags

Code optimizer	Version	Flags (Auto-Parallelization flags)	Auto-Parallelization
clang (LLVM)	6.0.0	-Ofast -march=native	No
gcc (GNU)	5.4.0	-Ofast -march=native	No
icc (Intel)	18.0.0	-Ofast -xHost (-parallel)	Yes
polly	6.0.0	-O3 -march=native -polly -polly-vectorizer=stripmine -polly-tiling (-polly-parallel)	Yes

the behavior of memory may change on one or more levels. This analysis was required to prevent the ML algorithms from *overfitting*.

2.3 Experimental Platforms

For the experiments, we used two recent Intel architectures. The first architecture is a four-core Intel Kaby Lake Core i7-7700K. This architecture supports Intel's SSE, AVX and AVX2 SIMD instruction set extensions. The second architecture we use is a two sixteen-core Intel Skylake Xeon Gold 6142. The Skylake architecture supports two more SIMD instruction set extensions, i.e., AVX-512CD and AVX-512F than the Kaby Lake architecture. For the auto-parallelization related experiments, only one thread is mapped per core.

We skip dynamic instruction count as a feature and normalize the rest of the hardware performance counters in terms of *per kilo instructions* (PKI). We exclude loop nests that have low value for crucial hardware performance counters such as instructions retired. From our experiments, we discovered two interesting correlations among hardware performance counters and the characteristic behavior of the loop nests. First, the hardware performance counters values from Kaby Lake architecture (after disabling loop transformations and vector code generation) were sufficient to get well trained ML model to make predictions for a similar architecture like the Skylake architecture. Second, for predicting the most suited candidate for serial code and for the auto-parallelized code for a loop nest, the same set of hardware performance counters, collected from profiling a serial version, can be used to train the ML model and achieve satisfactory results.

2.4 Machine Learning Model Evaluation

For training and evaluating our Machine Learning model, we use Orange [8]. We use Random Forest (RF) as the classifier for all the experiments. We randomly partition our dataset into Training dataset (75%) and Validation dataset (25%). The training dataset allows us to train and tune the ML models. We evaluate our trained models on Accuracy and Area Under Curve (AUC). Whereas, the validation dataset is a set of unseen loop nests that we use to make predictions. For serial code experiments, there are 209 instances (loop nests) in the training dataset and 69 instances in the validation dataset. For auto-parallelized code experiments, there are 147 instances in the training dataset and 49 instances in the validation dataset. The predicted optimizer's execution time as compared to that of the most suited optimizer's execution time will be same in case of correct predictions and higher in case of mispredictions.

We repeat our ML experiments thrice in order to validate our results, i.e., we randomly split the dataset, train new ML models and then make the predictions. We take into account the unique instances from the three validation datasets for measurements. Therefore, the number of instances differ between similar experiments.

3   Experimental Analysis

For evaluating the results, we calculate the speedup of ML predictions over candidate code optimizers, i.e., the speedup obtained if the code optimizer recommended by the ML model was used to optimize loop nests instead of a candidate.

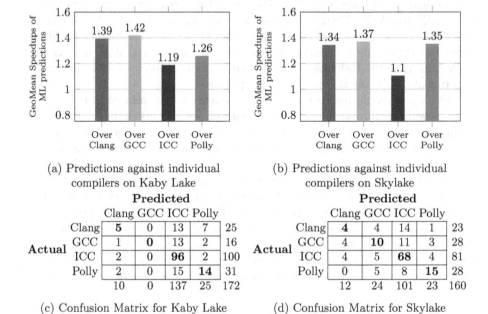

(a) Predictions against individual compilers on Kaby Lake

(b) Predictions against individual compilers on Skylake

		Predicted				
		Clang	GCC	ICC	Polly	
	Clang	**5**	0	13	7	25
Actual	GCC	1	**0**	13	2	16
	ICC	2	0	**96**	2	100
	Polly	2	0	15	**14**	31
		10	0	137	25	172

		Predicted				
		Clang	GCC	ICC	Polly	
	Clang	**4**	4	14	1	23
Actual	GCC	4	**10**	11	3	28
	ICC	4	5	**68**	4	81
	Polly	0	5	8	**15**	28
		12	24	101	23	160

(c) Confusion Matrix for Kaby Lake

(d) Confusion Matrix for Skylake

Fig. 1. Speedup of predictions for serial code

3.1   Predicting the Most Suited Code Optimizer for Serial Code

Figure 1a and b show the results for the performance gains from the predictions for the Kaby Lake and Skylake architectures, respectively. These predicted gains can be viewed as the achievable headroom for each compiler. On the validation dataset, RF classifier predicted with an overall accuracy of 67% for Kaby Lake and 61% for Skylake as shown in the confusion matrices in Fig. 1c and d respectively.

Across both architectures, Intel compiler performs well on majority of the loop nests. Therefore, the Majority Classifier predicted ICC with 58% overall accuracy for Kaby Lake and 50% overall accuracy for Skylake. The distribution of performance of the ML predictions compared to ICC, the maximum performance gain on a loop nest was 27x, whereas the maximum slowdown was 0.2x.

3.2 Predicting the Most Suited Code Optimizer for Auto-Parallelized Code

For the auto-parallelization experiments, there are only two candidates: ICC and Polly. The RF classifier predicted with an overall accuracy of 85% for Kaby Lake and 72% for Skylake as shown in Fig. 2c. Since the validation dataset was well balanced for the two targets, the Majority Classifier produced an overall accuracy of 64% for Kaby Lake and 50% for Skylake. Based on the distribution of performance of the ML predictions, when compared to ICC, the maximum gain on a loop nest was 91x whereas the maximum slowdown was 0.09x.

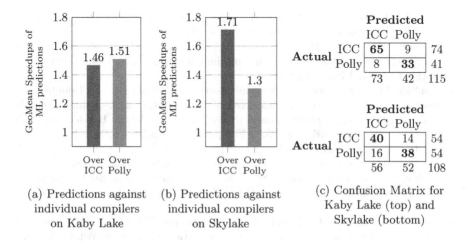

(a) Predictions against individual compilers on Kaby Lake

(b) Predictions against individual compilers on Skylake

(c) Confusion Matrix for Kaby Lake (top) and Skylake (bottom)

Fig. 2. Speedup of predictions for auto-parallelized code

4 Overall Analysis and Discussion

The performance gain from the ML predictions over the candidate code optimizers range from 1.10x to 1.42x for the serial code and from 1.30x to 1.71x for the auto-parallelized code across two multi-core architectures. Counters related to Cycles Per Instruction (CPI), D-TLB, memory instructions, cache performance (L1, L2 and L3) and stall cycles were crucial indicators of the inherent behavior of the loop nests.

On analyzing the validation datasets for serial code experiments, we found that on an average for 95% of the loop nests, there was at least 5% performance difference between the most suited code optimizer and the worse suited code optimizer. For auto-parallelized code experiments, on an average for 91.5% of the loop nests, there was at least 5% performance difference between the most suited code optimizer and the worse suited code optimizer.

On the other hand, for the serial code experiments, for 68% of the loop nests, there was at least 5% performance difference between the most suited code optimizer and the second most suited code optimizer. That suggests that for the remaining 32% of the loop nests, it would be harder to make a distinction between the most suited code optimizer and the second one. Since the ML models' overall accuracy are 67% for Kaby Lake and 61% for Skylake, we can infer that they are doing very well on the loop nests that have a clear distinction about the most suited code optimizer.

Acknowledgments. This work was supported by NSF award XPS 1533926.

References

1. Allen, R., Kennedy, K.: Automatic translation of fortran programs to vector form. ACM Trans. Program. Lang. Syst. **9**(4), 491–542 (1987)
2. Ashouri, A.H., et al.: MiCOMP: mitigating the compiler phase-ordering problem using optimization sub-sequences and machine learning. ACM Trans. Arch. Code Optim. (TACO) **14**(3), 29 (2017)
3. Bondhugula, U., Baskaran, M., Krishnamoorthy, S., Ramanujam, J., Rountev, A., Sadayappan, P.: Automatic transformations for communication-minimized parallelization and locality optimization in the polyhedral model. In: Hendren, L. (ed.) CC 2008. LNCS, vol. 4959, pp. 132–146. Springer, Heidelberg (2008). https://doi.org/10.1007/978-3-540-78791-4_9
4. Callahan, D., Dongarra, J., Levine, D.: Vectorizing compilers: a test suite and results. In: Proceedings of the 1988 ACM/IEEE Conference on Supercomputing, Supercomputing 1988, pp. 98–105. IEEE Computer Society Press, Los Alamitos (1988)
5. Cammarota, R., Beni, L.A., Nicolau, A., Veidenbaum, A.V.: Optimizing program performance via similarity, using a feature-agnostic approach. In: Wu, C., Cohen, A. (eds.) APPT 2013. LNCS, vol. 8299, pp. 199–213. Springer, Heidelberg (2013). https://doi.org/10.1007/978-3-642-45293-2_15
6. Cavazos, J., et al.: Rapidly selecting good compiler optimizations using performance counters. In: International Symposium on Code Generation and Optimization, CGO 2007, pp. 185–197. IEEE (2007)
7. Darte, A., Robert, Y., Vivien, F.: Scheduling and Automatic Parallelization. Springer, New York (2012). https://doi.org/10.1007/978-1-4612-1362-8
8. Demšar, J., et al.: Orange: data mining toolbox in python. J. Mach. Learn. Res. **14**(1), 2349–2353 (2013)
9. Fursin, G., et al.: Milepost GCC: machine learning enabled self-tuning compiler. Int. J. Parallel Program. **39**(3), 296–327 (2011)
10. Gong, Z., et al.: An empirical study of the effect of source-level loop transformations on compiler stability. Proc. ACM Program. Lang. **2**(OOPSLA), 126:1–126:29 (2018)
11. Grosser, T., Groesslinger, A., Lengauer, C.: Polly - performing polyhedral optimizations on a low-level intermediate representation. Parallel Process. Lett. **22**(04), 1250010 (2012)
12. Kennedy, K., Allen, J.R.: Optimizing Compilers for Modern Architectures: A Dependence-Based Approach. Morgan Kaufmann Publishers Inc., San Francisco (2002)

13. Li, W., Pingali, K.: A singular loop transformation framework based on non-singular matrices. In: Banerjee, U., Gelernter, D., Nicolau, A., Padua, D. (eds.) LCPC 1992. LNCS, vol. 757, pp. 391–405. Springer, Heidelberg (1993). https://doi.org/10.1007/3-540-57502-2_60

14. Lim, A.W., Cheong, G.I., Lam, M.S.: An affine partitioning algorithm to maximize parallelism and minimize communication. In: Proceedings of the 13th International Conference on Supercomputing, ICS 1999, pp. 228–237. ACM, New York (1999)

15. Lim, A.W., Lam, M.S.: Maximizing parallelism and minimizing synchronization with affine partitions. Parallel Comput. **24**(3–4), 445–475 (1998)

16. Lim, A.W., Liao, S.-W., Lam, M.S.: Blocking and array contraction across arbitrarily nested loops using affine partitioning. In: Proceedings of the Eighth ACM SIGPLAN Symposium on Principles and Practices of Parallel Programming, PPoPP 2001, pp. 103–112. ACM, New York (2001)

17. Maleki, S., et al.: An evaluation of vectorizing compilers. In: 2011 International Conference on Parallel Architectures and Compilation Techniques, pp. 372–382, October 2011

18. Padua, D.A., Kuck, D.J., Lawrie, D.H.: High-speed multiprocessors and compilation techniques. IEEE Trans. Comput. **C-29**(9), 763–776 (1980)

19. Padua, D.A., Wolfe, M.: Advanced compiler optimizations for supercomputers. Commun. ACM **29**(12), 1184–1201 (1986)

20. Polly: LLVM Framework for High-Level Loop and Data-Locality Optimizations. http://polly.llvm.org

21. PolyBench/C 4.1. http://web.cse.ohio-state.edu/~pouchet/software/polybench/

22. Stock, K., Pouchet, L.-N., Sadayappan, P.: Using machine learning to improve automatic vectorization. ACM Trans. Arch. Code Optim. (TACO) **8**(4), 50 (2012)

23. Tournavitis, G., et al.: Towards a holistic approach to auto-parallelization: integrating profile-driven parallelism detection and machine-learning based mapping. In: Proceedings of the 30th ACM SIGPLAN Conference on Programming Language Design and Implementation, PLDI 2009, pp. 177–187. ACM, New York (2009)

24. Wang, Z., O'Boyle, M.F.: Mapping parallelism to multi-cores: a machine learning based approach. In: Proceedings of the 14th ACM SIGPLAN Symposium on Principles and Practice of Parallel Programming, PPoPP 2009, pp. 75–84. ACM, New York (2009)

25. Watkinson, N., et al.: Using hardware counters to predict vectorization. In: Languages and Compilers for Parallel Computing, LCPC 2017. Springer, in Press

26. Wolfe, M.J.: High Performance Compilers for Parallel Computing. Addison-Wesley Longman Publishing Co. Inc., Boston (1995)

Extending Index-Array Properties
for Data Dependence Analysis

Mahdi Soltan Mohammadi[1]([✉]), Kazem Cheshmi[2], Maryam Mehri Dehnavi[2],
Anand Venkat[3], Tomofumi Yuki[4], and Michelle Mills Strout[1]

[1] University of Arizona, Tucson, USA
{kingmahdi,mstrout}@cs.arizona.edu
[2] University of Toronto, Toronto, Canada
{kazem,mmehride}@cs.toronto.edu
[3] Intel, Santa Clara, United States
anand.venkat@intel.com
[4] Univ Rennes, Inria, Rennes, France
tomofumi.yuki@inria.fr

Abstract. Automatic parallelization is an approach where a compiler
analyzes serial code and identifies computations that can be rewritten
to leverage parallelism. Many data dependence analysis techniques have
been developed to determine which loops in a code can be parallelized.
With code that includes indirect array accesses through what are commonly called index arrays, such data dependence analysis is restricted in
the conclusions that can be drawn at compile time. Various approaches
that use index array properties such as monotonicity have been shown
to more effectively find parallel loops. In this paper, we extend the kinds
of properties about index arrays that can be expressed, show how to
convert loop-carried data dependence relations and relevant index-array
properties to constraints that can be provided to the Z3 SMT solver, and
evaluate the impact of using such index-array properties on identifying
parallel loops in a set of numerical benchmarks.

Keywords: Data dependence analysis · Sparse matrices · Automatic
parallelization · SMT solvers

1 Introduction

Many numerical computations involve sparse tensors, which are vectors, matrices, and their higher-dimensional analogs, that have so few non-zeros that
compressed storage of some kind is used. These compressed formats result in
indirect array accesses such as x[col[i]] and non-affine loop bounds such as
rowptr[i+1]. The arrays used to index other arrays are referred to as index
arrays as well as subscripted subscripts in the compiler literature [12]. The index
arrays cause difficulties for compile-time data dependence analyses used to find
parallelizable loops. However, there is an opportunity to use properties about

© Springer Nature Switzerland AG 2019
M. Hall and H. Sundar (Eds.): LCPC 2018, LNCS 11882, pp. 78–93, 2019.
https://doi.org/10.1007/978-3-030-34627-0_7

```
1 for (i=0; i<nnz_y; i++) {
2    x[ idx[i] ] = x[ idx[i] ] + y[i];
3 }
```

Fig. 1. Addition of a sparse vector with a dense vector.

the values in such arrays such as monotonicity to determine at compile time that some of these loops are parallelizable.

As an example, Fig. 1 contains code that performs a vector add of a dense vector x and a sparse vector y. Since y has been compressed, it only stores non-zero values while the idx index array stores what dense index is associated with each value. The values stored in the idx index array are all unique since they should indicate dense locations of unique non-zeroes in y array. In other words, the idx index array has the injectivity property.

To determine whether the i-loop in Fig. 1 is fully parallelizable, one must show there are no loop-carried dependences on the loop. Since the idx index array is injective, this implies that no two values in the idx array are the same and therefore each iteration reads and writes to and from different locations of the x array with the x[idx[i]] access. And, since there is no overlap between the writes and reads to x[idx[i]] in different iterations of the loop, there is no loop carried dependence. If the injectivity property is not known, then the compiler has to assume that any two values in idx[] might be the same and therefore conservatively assume a loop-carried dependence.

In the past, other research has used index-array properties for finding loop parallelism. McKinley [12] first pointed out index array properties can be used to facilitate data dependence analysis, but automating the approach was left as future work. She detailed how injectivity and monotonicity of index arrays can show lack of flow, anti, and output dependences for some common access patterns. Wonnacott and Pugh [16] represented index arrays as uninterpreted function symbols in their constraint based dependence analysis. That resulted in them inherently utilizing functional consistency property about index arrays. Lin and Padua [11] formulated five index array properties including monotonicity, and four properties about values and bounds of index array being closed-formed under loop iterators. Fuzzy data dependence analysis [5] uses the range of index arrays to conservatively approximate dependences. The Hybrid Analysis research formulated the monotonicity and injectivity properties and used them to find full parallelism in the PERFECT CLUB and SPEC benchmarks [13,15,18,19].

We can express all of the previously studied index-array properties as universally quantified affine constraints on index array values, similar to approaches used in program verification community to formulate properties about general arrays [6,9,10]. We use constraint-based data dependence analysis to determine lack of loop-carried data dependences for finding fully parallel loops in number of popular sparse computations that are building blocks of bigger numerical applications. Just like [16], we represent index arrays as uninterpreted functions. For example, the injectivity property for an index array like idx[] in Fig. 1 can be specified by indicating that for all indices x_1 and x_2 into the index array where

x_1 is not equal to x_2, the values in the index array are also not equal:

$$(\forall x_1, x_2)(x_1 \neq x_2 \implies index(x_1) \neq index(x_2)).$$

In this paper, we experiment with more index-array properties that can be expressed with such universally quantified constraints including information about sparse matrix formats, matrix triangularity information, and periodic monotonicity and injectivity. Oancea and Rauchwerger [14] observed that periodic monotonicity could help prove loop parallelism, but did not provide a mechanism for applying the property automatically.

This paper makes the following contributions:

– Specification of more index-array properties, namely triangularity, and periodic monotonicity.
– A constraint-based data dependence analysis that uses an SMT solver to apply the index array properties for finding fully parallel loops.
– Experimental results showing that the index array properties introduced in this paper lead to more loops being parallelized and that those loops when parallelized exhibit improved performance.
– An in-depth comparison of related work based on what index array properties used and what impact on automatic parallelization such work reported.

2   Background: Data-Dependence Analysis

This section reviews how loop carried array dependence analysis can be specified as a constraint problem, and how index arrays found in sparse codes can be represented in these constraints as uninterpreted functions [17].

2.1   Loop-Carried Dependence Constraints for Sparse Codes

A fully parallel loop will not have any loop-carried dependences. A data dependence occurs between two iterations of a loop when both of the iterations access the same memory location and at least one of the accesses is a write. Such data dependence constraints can be expressed in the following generic form:

$$\{I \to I' | \overbrace{I \prec I'}^{lexicographical\ Ordering} \wedge \underbrace{F(I) = G(I')}_{Array\ Access\ Equality} \wedge \overbrace{Constraints(I) \wedge Constraints(I')}^{Loop\ Bounds\ and\ Conditional\ Constraints\ (if,...)}\}$$

where I and I' are iteration vector instances from the same loop nest, $I \prec I'$ denotes that iteration I happens lexicographically before iteration I', F and G are macro functions that define array index expressions to the same array with at least one of the accesses being a write, $Constraints$ is the macro function that defines conditional expressions, and the loop bounds for the I iteration vectors.

```
1 for (int j = 0 ; j < n ; j++){
2   x[j] /= Lx[colPtr[j]] ;
3   for(int p = colPtr[j]+1 ; p < colPtr[j+1] ; p++){
4     x[row[p]] -= Lx[p] * x[j];
5 }}
```

Fig. 2. Forward Solve computation assuming matrices are stored in CSC sparse matrix format, code from Cheshmi et al. [7]

In this paper, the term *dependence relation* is used interchangeably with dependence constraints by viewing them as a relation between I and I'. If the constraints in the data dependence relation are shown to be satisfiable, then a loop-carried dependence exists and the loop is not fully parallelizable. Therefore, our goal is to find as many UNsatisfiable data dependence relations as possible.

2.2   Data Dependence Analysis Example

As an example, Fig. 2 shows a forward solve computation implemented for any lower triangular sparse matrix stored in compressed sparse column (CSC) format. In this code the outer loop j traverses over compressed column indices in colPtr index array, and the p loop goes over nonzeros. Also, the row index array stores the row indices, while Lx and x store the values of nonzeros. Consider a read x[j], and a write x[row[p]] to array x, both in line 4 of Figure 2. The read after write dependence for the j-loop has the following constraints:

$$\{[j] \to [j'] : \exists p, p' : \overbrace{j < j'}^{lexicographical\ Ordering} \wedge \overbrace{row(p) = j'}^{Array\ Access\ Equality} \wedge$$
$$\underbrace{0 \le j, j' < n \wedge colPtr(j) < p < colPtr(j+1) \wedge colPtr(j') < p' < colPtr(j'+1)}_{Loop\ Bounds}\}$$

Also note that, if we define the flow dependence based on the same accesses for the loop carried dependence of inner loop p it would be as follows:

$$\{[j, p] \to [j', p'] : \overbrace{j = j' \wedge p < p'}^{lexicographical\ Ordering} \wedge \overbrace{row(p) = j'}^{Array\ Access\ Equality} \wedge$$
$$\underbrace{0 \le j, j' < n \wedge colPtr(j) < p < colPtr(j+1) \wedge colPtr(j') < p' < colPtr(j'+1)}_{Loop\ Bounds}\}$$

The difference between two dependences is in the lexicographical ordering.

3   Disproving Dependences with Index-Array Properties

With no information about uninterpreted functions, it is important to assume they can take on any value. Nonetheless, the index arrays that uninterpreted

```
1  for(i = 0; i < n; i++) {
2    val[colPtr[i]] = sqrt(val[colPtr[i]]);
3
4    for(m=colPtr[i]+1; m<colPtr[i+1]; m++){
5      val[m] = val[m] / val[colPtr[i]];
6    }
7    for(m=colPtr[i]+1; m<colPtr[i+1]; m++){
8      for(k = colPtr[row[m]];
9          k < colPtr[row[m]+1]; k++){
10       for(l = m; l < colPtr[i+1]; l++){
11         if(row[l] == row[k]
12            && row[l+1] <= row[k]){
13           val[k] -= val[m]* val[l];
14 }}}}}
```

$$\{[i, m] \rightarrow [i', m'] : \exists k, l, k', l' :$$
$$i = i' \wedge m < m' \wedge k = m'$$
$$0 \le i, i' < n \wedge row(l) = row(k)$$
$$colPtr(i) < m < colPtr(i + 1)$$
$$colPtr(row(m)) \le k$$
$$k < colPtr(row(m) + 1)$$
$$colPtr(i') < m' < colPtr(i' + 1)$$
$$colPtr(row(m')) \le k'$$
$$k' < colPtr(row(m') + 1)$$
$$m \le l < colPtr(i + 1)$$
$$m' \le l' < colPtr(i' + 1)$$
$$row(l') = row(k')$$
$$row(l' + 1) \le row(k')\}$$

Fig. 3. Incomplete Cholesky0 implementation from SparseLib++ library [2]

functions represent have various properties that can be used to add more constraints to data dependence relations and in some cases can enable showing more dependences are unsatisfiable. In this section, we first give an example illustrating a case where a combination of two index array properties enables showing a dependence is unsatisfiable, show how to implement this approach using an SMT solver, and present the index array properties we have found useful.

3.1   Example Using New Index Array Properties

For the Incomplete Cholesky code shown in Fig. 3 on the left, the data dependence relation due to the write val[k], and a read val[m] in Line 13 for m-loop in line 7 is shown on the right side of the figure. Using only original constraints above, it is not possible to prove this dependence unsatisfiable. Nonetheless, using additional constraints instantiated from the triangularity and monotonicity index array properties, explained in Sect. 3.3, can show us that the dependence is unsatisfiable. Figure 4 depicts the partial ordering between key constraints from the dependence in question, derivation of new constraints from index array properties assertions, and the contradiction that proves unsatisfiability.

3.2   Leveraging SMT Solvers

We can leverage SMT solvers to use index array properties to determine the satisfiability of data dependence relations. A common approach used in verification community to obtain more precise results [6,9,10] is to express array properties as universally quantified assertions, combine them with their originally extracted constraints about a program, and ask a SMT solver whether the constraints are satisfiable. We use the same approach by utilizing Z3 SMT solver [3]. The Z3 SMT solver uses the interface format SMTLIB2 [4]. Therefore, we specify all the

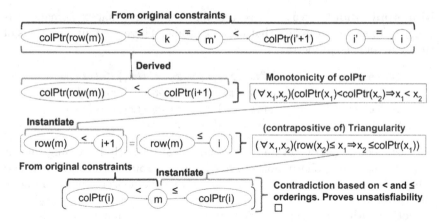

Fig. 4. Proving a dependence of Incomplete Cholesky unsatisfiable.

constraints from the original dependence and all the user asserted index array properties for Z3 SMT solver in SMTLIB format. For instance, the following shows some of the constraints from original dependence used in the unsatisfiability proof in Sect. 3.1 in SMTLIB format:

Original constraint	Z3 specification
$colPtr(i) = k'$	(assert (= (colPtr i) k'))
$colPtr(row(m')) <= k'$	(assert (<= (colPtr (row m')) k'))
$(\forall x_1, x_2)(x_1 < x_2 \iff$ $colPtr(x_1) < colPtr(x_2))$	(assert (forall ((e1 Int) (e2 Int)) (=> (< e1 e2) (< (colPtr e1) (colPtr e2))))) (assert (forall ((e1 Int) (e2 Int)) (=> (< (colPtr e1) (colPtr e2)) (< e1 e2))))
$(\forall x_1, x_2)(colPtr(x_1) <$ $x_2 \implies x_1 < row(x_2))$	(assert (forall ((e1 Int) (e2 Int)) (=> (< (colPtr e1) e2) (< e1 (row e2)))))

3.3   Index-Array Properties as Universally Quantified Assertions

In this section, we describe such index array properties that can be formulated as universally quantified assertions.

- **Functional Consistency**: If two inputs to a function are equal then the function will return equivalent results.

$$(\forall x_1, x_2)(x_1 = x_2 \Rightarrow f(x_1) = f(x_2))$$

- **Domain and range of index arrays**: We assume the input domain and output range of the index arrays are known and can be expressed as follows:

$$(\forall x)(p \leq x \leq q \Rightarrow LB_{range} \leq f(x) <= UB_{range}).$$

- **Monotonic index arrays**: In several different sparse matrix formats, it is common to see index arrays that are monotonic. There are four variations of the monotonicity property:

  <code>Increasing:</code> $(\forall x_1, x_2)(x_1 \leq x_2 \Rightarrow f(x_1) \leq f(x_2))$.
  <code>Strictly Increasing:</code> $(\forall x_1, x_2)(x_1 < x_2 \iff f(x_1) < f(x_2))$.
  <code>Decreasing:</code> $(\forall x_1, x_2)(x_1 \geq x_2 \Rightarrow f(x_1) \geq f(x_2))$.
  <code>Strictly Decreasing:</code> $(\forall x_1, x_2)(x_1 > x_2 \iff f(x_1) > f(x_2))$.

  For instance the `colPtr` in Fig. 3 is monotonically strictly increasing since it stores the starting point of nonzero row indices in `row` and values in `val`, and computation always operates on matrices that have nonzeros in main diagonal, therefore we have $(\forall x_1, x_2)(x_1 < x_2 \iff colPtr(x_1) < colPtr(x_2))$.

- **Injective index arrays**: An index array is injective if none of its values are the same. Index arrays that have strict monotonicity, also have injectivity property. Strict monotonicity is a more informative property. Consequently, in our experimental evaluations, we only utilize strict monotonicity for index arrays that poses them. Note, in the kernels that we have looked for parallelism, we have not come across any index array that only poses injectivity, that is why injectivity property does not show up in our results.

  <code>Injectivity:</code> $(\forall x_1, x_2)(x_1 \neq x_2 \Rightarrow f(x_1) \neq f(x_2))$.

- **Periodic injective/monotonic index arrays**: Some index arrays are monotonic or injective in intervals.

  <code>Periodic Property:</code> $(\forall x_1, x_2, x_3)(x_2 \bowtie x_3 \wedge g(x_1) \leq x_2 < g(x_1 + 1)$
  $\wedge\, g(x_1) < x_3 < g(x_1 + 1) \Rightarrow f(x_1) \bowtie f(x_2))$.

  Where $\bowtie$ can be $\neq$, $\leq$, $<$, $\geq$, and $>$, for injectivity and different forms of monotonicity. For instance the `row` in Fig. 3 is periodically monotonically strictly increasing and it is indexed using `colPtr`. This is because `row` stores row index values of nonzeros which are unique for nonzeros in a column. Therefore, we have:

  $$(\forall x_1, x_2, x_3)(x_2 < x_3 \wedge colPtr(x_1) < x_2 < colPtr(x_1) \wedge$$
  $$colPtr(x_1) < x_3 < colPtr(x_1) \iff row(x_1) < row(x_2)).$$

- **Triangular Matrix (Triangularity)**: Some numerical computations only operate on lower or upper triangular parts of matrices. We express this property for CSC, Compressed Sparse Row (CSR), and Block CSR (BCSR) formats as following assertions, assuming `f` is the compressed index array of the format and `g` is the non-compressed one:

  <code>CSC Lower Triangularity:</code> $(\forall x_1, x_2)(f(x_1) < x_2 \iff x_1 < g(x_2))$.
  <code>CSC Upper Triangularity:</code> $(\forall x_1, x_2)(f(x_1) > x_2 \iff x_1 > g(x_2))$.
  <code>(B)CSR Lower Triangularity:</code> $(\forall x_1, x_2)(x_1 < f(x_2) \iff f(x_1) < x_2)$.
  <code>(B)CSR Upper Triangularity:</code> $(\forall x_1, x_2)(x_1 > f(x_2) \iff f(x_1) > x_2)$.

For instance the Incomplete Cholesky computation in Fig. 3 operates on lower triangular matrices. Considering the `colPtr` compresses the column index arrays in CSC format, and `row` stores row indices explicitly, we have:

$$(\forall x_1, x_2)(colPtr(x_1) < x_2 \implies x_1 < row(x_2))$$

This indicates that the integer value of row indices of nonzeros in columns after column x_1 are greater than the integer value of (column index) x_1.

4 Impact on Finding Full Parallelism

In this section, we study the effect of utilizing index array properties for finding fully parallel loops in number of popular numerical sparse computations. Section 4.1 presents the suite of numerical kernels that we compiled to evaluate our approach, and discusses the automatic driver that utilizes index array properties for finding full parallelism. Section 4.2 presents results for finding fully parallel loops in each benchmark, we also indicate what kind of index array properties were needed to prove that a loop is parallel. We also parallelized the parallel loops found in two of the kernels by hand using simple OpenMP parallel loop pragma. Section 4.3 reports the performance results for hand parallelized kernels while comparing performance to serial versions' performance, and discusses the implications of this results. Following public git repository hosts this paper's artifact, and includes instructions on how to reproduce the evaluation results: https://github.com/CompOpt4Apps/Artifact-SparseLoopParallelism

The driver depends on CHiLL compiler [1], IEGenLib library [22], and Z3 SMT solver. CHiLL is a source-to-source compiler framework for composing and applying high level loop transformations. IEGenLib is a library for manipulating integer sets/relations that contain uninterpreted function symbols.

4.1 Sparse Computation Benchmark Suite and Methodology

Table 1 lists the numerical sparse codes that we have used to evaluate usefulness of utilizing index array properties. The benchmark suite includes the fundamental blocks in several applications: (1) The Cholesky factorization, Incomplete Cholesky0, and sparse triangular solver, which are commonly used in direct solvers and as preconditioners in iterative solvers; (2) sparse matrix vector multiplication and Gauss-Seidel methods, often used in iterative solvers.

We specify user-defined properties about index arrays in JSON files for each code. The driver for finding parallel loops uses CHiLL to extract the dependences for different loops in a code that would include loops in different levels and locations of an (im)perfectly nested loop. Then, it converts extracted dependences one at a time alongside related user defined assertions to an input file for Z3, and queries Z3 whether the constraints are satisfiable. If all the dependences of a loop are unsatisfiable we say that loop is parallel.

SMT solvers like Z3 use numerous heuristics to detect unsatisfiable set of constraints quickly. In our experience, Z3 can return with answer for any of

Table 1. The code benchmarks that we apply our data dependence analysis on, with formatting and source.

Algorithm name	Format	Source
Forward solve	CSC	[7]
Forward solve	CSR	[25]
Gauss-Seidel solver	CSR	MKL [26]
Gauss-Seidel solver	BCSR	MKL [26]
Sparse MV Multiply	CSR	Common
Incomplete Cholesky	CSC(R)	[2]
Static Left Cholesky	CSC	[7]

Table 2. Input Matrices for parallelized codes from [8]. Sorted in order of Number of Nonzeros per Column

Matrix	Columns	Nonzeros	$\frac{NNZ}{COL}$
G3_circuit	1,585,478	7,660,826	5
af_shell3	504,855	17,562,051	35
bmwcra_1	148,770	10,641,602	72
crankseg_2	63,838	14,148,858	222
nd24k	72,000	28,715,634	399

unsatisfiable (unsat) dependencies in our benchmark suite in less than 1 s. It also quickly comes back with the answer satisfiable (sat) for some of the dependences. However, for dependences that there is not enough constraints to determine them either as sat or unsat, it could run for a long time while deriving new (not helpful) constraints from universally quantified assertions. Therefore, we use a 2 s timeout so if Z3 could not detect a single dependence as sat or unsat, it would return **unknown** after timeout. In such case, we conservatively consider the dependence satisfiable.

It takes about 34, 18, and 18 s respectively to determine outer most loops of Incomplete Cholesky, Static Cholesky, and Gauss-Seidel BCSR, are not parallel. The dependence analysis of all other loops in all benchmarks takes less than 2.5 s. The reason why it takes more for those mentioned three loops is that there are lots of dependences to check for them, some of which exhausts the 2-s timeout we specified for Z3.

We hand parallelized some of the parallel loops that we found in our benchmarks to study the pragmatic impact of our methods, the results are presented in Sect. 4.3. We ran our experiment on a machine with an Intel(R) Core(TM) i7-6900K CPU, 32 GB of 3000 MHz DDR4 memory, and Ubuntu 16.04 OS. The CPU has 8 cores, therefore we record performance for 2, 4, and 8 OpenMP threads while the hyper-threading is disabled. We report mean value of 5 runs, though there were no significant variation between runs. All codes are compiled with GCC 5.4.0 with -O3 flag enabled.

Table 2 lists set of five matrices from the University of Florida sparse matrix collection [8] that we used as input to our experiments. The matrices are listed in increasing ordered of average nonzeros per column. Generally speaking, the loops that we are parallelizing usually operate on different nonzeros in a column (or row). Therefore, one can expect the parallelization result getting better for matrices with more nonzero per columns (rows).

4.2 Finding Loop Parallelism

Since we want to study effect of using different index array properties, as well as using all available properties, we have look into what set of index array properties can help us prove a loop to be parallel. We listed 6 properties in Sect. 3.3. Of those properties, we do not need to specify functional consistency for a SMT solver, since it considers it inherently for any uninterpreted function symbol. We also just specify domain and range properties while considering effect of any combination of properties. Additionally, all the injective index arrays in our benchmarks also have monotonically strictly increasing property.

Table 3. Table lists loops found in our benchmarks, whether they are statically parallel, and whether we needed index array properties to prove them parallel. The third column, ``Static Par?'', is indicating whether the loop can be considered statically parallel, if the loop would require reduction for parallelization it is noted as Reduction. Although, we are not doing dependence analysis for finding reduction operations at this time. The fourth column indicates whether we have found the loop parallel. The fifth column lists what index array property were necessary to detect the loop as parallel, while `Linear` indicates that we did not need any, functional consistency would be used by Z3 for all cases. The shortened names, Mono , PerMono , Tri stand for monotonicity, periodic monotonicity, and triangularity properties respectively

Algorithm	Loop	Static Par?	Detected?	Helps to prove parallel
Forward Solve CSC	j	No	–	–
	p	Yes	Yes	Tri + PerMono
Forward Solve CSR	i	No	–	–
	j	Reduction	–	–
Gauss-Seidel CSR	i	No	–	–
	j	Reduction	–	–
Gauss-Seidel BCSR	i	No	–	–
	$ii1$	Yes	Yes	Linear
	j	Reduction	–	–
	$jj1$	Reduction	–	–
	$ii2$	Yes	Yes	Linear
	$ii3$	Yes	Yes	Linear
	$jj2$	Reduction	–	–
	$ii4$	Yes	Yes	Linear
Sparse MV Multiply	i	Yes	Yes	Linear
	j	Reduction	–	–
Incomplete Cholesky	i	No	–	–
	$m - 4$ (line 4)	Yes	Yes	Linear
	$m - 7$ (line 7)	Yes	Yes	Tri + Mono + PerMono
	k	Yes	Yes	Tri + Mono
	l	Yes	Yes	PerMono
Static Left Cholesky	$colNo$	No	–	–
	$nzNo$	Yes	Yes	PerMono
	i	No	–	–
	l	Yes	Yes	PerMono
	j	Yes	Yes	PerMono

Table 3 presents the result of finding parallel loops while utilizing index array properties in our benchmark suite. The second column in the table lists all the unique loops in each kernel by loop's iterator name. The third column indicates whether considering the algorithmic property of the computation the loop can be statically considered parallel. And, the last column indicates what information has helped us prove the loop as parallel. The Linear keyword indicates that all the dependences of the loop can be proved unsatisfiable just by looking at their linear constraints and we would not need using index array property.

The main observation from analyzing Table 3 are: (1) The index array properties are very helpful for finding parallel loops in three codes, namely Forward Solve CSC, Incomplete Cholesky, and Static Left Cholesky; (2) We find all the loops that are parallel considering whether nature of an algorithm allows a loop to be parallel, except for loops that require parallelization with reduction, which was explained earlier; (3) All the three none-trivial index array properties that we have formulated, including Periodic Monotonicity and Triangularity that were not look at in previous works, are being helpful.

4.3   Performance Impact

Results presented in this section will indicate our dependence analysis can indeed improve performance of serial implementations of some of the sparse kernels in our benchmarks. This could be useful in practice, since to the best of our knowledge, library implementations of parallel sparse computations are not common, and we could not find any open source, parallel libraries for our benchmark computation. At this time, there is no generic code generator that can generate transformed code for our sparse benchmarks. Consequently, we only hand parallelized the parallel loops that our analysis founds in Forward Solve CSC and Incomplete Cholesky, simply by using OpenMP parallel pragma's without any further optimization. The parallel loop in Forward Solve computation only has one subtraction and one multiplication operations, hence it is memory-bound. As could be expected, our experiment results showed that parallelization overhead only slow downs the Forward Solve CSC compared to serial version. Nonetheless, we get considerable performance gain by parallelizing Incomplete Cholesky even without any enabling transformation like tiling.

Table 3 shows that our analysis detects 4 loops as fully parallel in Incomplete Cholesky. Nonetheless, we have experimented with parallelizing two of those loops, namely m-7 (line 7 in Fig. 3) and k. Fig. 5 presents relative performance of parallelizing m-7 and k. The result show steady increase in performance gain for parallel version over serial as we increase the number of threads compared. Parallelizing loop m-7 gives us performance gain of 1.3–3.5× in 4 out of 5 while utilizing 8 threads, For G3_circuit matrix parallelization overhead makes parallel version slower than sequential version since it has very few nonzeros per columns. Parallelizing the k loop has worse results compared to m-7 loop for three of the matrices, but has better results for two of the matrices. This could be attributed to sparsity structure of matrices that can effect parallel load balancing.

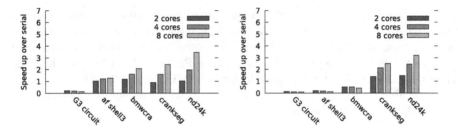

(a) Performance of parallelized m-7-loop.   (b) Performance of parallelized k-loop.

Fig. 5. Incomplete Cholesky loop parallelization performance. The serial absolute execution time in order from top are: 1.9, 11.1, 18.1, 202.6, and 725.4 s.

5   Related Work

Several previous works have looked into usefulness of index array properties for improving data dependence analysis. Nonetheless, it seem that index array properties have not been taken advantage of in production compilers. In this section, we describe what properties each previous work has look into, how they have derived them, and what impact index array properties had on their results.

5.1   Initial Observation of Index Array Property Utility

McKinley [12] studied how using assertions about index arrays can improve dependence testing precision at compile-time. She observed and discussed 5 common assertions about index arrays that included, injectivity $(index(I) \neq index(J), I \neq J)$, monotonically non-decreasing $(index(I) \leq index(I + 1))$, monotonically increasing $(index(I) < index(I+1))$, monotonically non-increasing $(index(I) \geq index(I+1))$, and monotonically decreasing $(index(I) > index(I+1))$. We usually refer to later four properties simply as monotonicity. Author then discussed how these properties can effect founding flow, anti, or output independence in some common memory access patterns. The report discussed two loops in MDG from PERFECT club where using monotonicity is necessary to detected the loop as parallel in compile-time. Automating the approach of utilizing index arrays was left as future work.

5.2   Exact Data Dependence Analysis

Pugh and Wonnacott [16] presented a constraint based data dependence analysis that was able to handle nonlinear data access including index arrays. They represented affine parts of the dependences with Presburger Formulas while representing index arrays as uninterpreted function symbols. Authors used Ackerman Reduction procedure that can be applied to Presburger formulas with uninterpreted function calls [20]. By using that procedure they inherently utilized functional consistency for index arrays. Their framework could also come up with sufficient constraints to prove the dependences unsatisfiable for some of codes that earlier methods could not. Although, solving those constraints required methods that were not discussed or implemented for that work. Authors used their methods to do dependence analysis for PERFECT CLUB benchmarks. They were able to directly find parallel loops in MDG and ARC2D, one in each, and were able to find sufficient conditions for showing one parallel loops in each of TRFD, and ARC2D benchmarks.

5.3   Automating the detection of properties

Lin and Padua [11] looked into two types of irregular array accesses, single-index, and indirect (index array) accesses. The single-index was defined for array index expressions, and included: Consecutively written accesses, and stack accesses. They also formulated tests for detecting 5 index array properties: monotonicity, injectiveness, closed-form distance (CFD), closed-form value (CFV), and closed-form bound (CFB). The closed-formed properties are defined when either difference of two consecutive values (CFD), or all values (CFV), or upper or lower bound (CFB), of an index array can be defined with a closed-form expression over loop iterators. Analyzing benchmarks from PERFECT club, this work showed following usefulness for those properties: CFV and CFD each separately helped to find one parallel in TRFD and DYFESM benchmarks respectively, and CFB helped privatization analysis in two loops inside BDNA and P3M.

5.4   Combining with More General Dependence Analysis

Hybrid analysis (HA) presented over several works is an approach to do general data dependence analysis of generic array accesses for optimization purposes [13,15,18,19]. It gathers dependence constraints with inter-procedural analysis, and represents the gathered summary sets with an intermediate representation called Unified Set Representation (USR). The USRs can include uninterpreted function calls to represent index arrays. HA formulates flow, anti, and output independence with USRs, and uses them for for finding full parallelism, private arrays, and reduction operations. HA also formulates the monotonicity and injectivity properties directly for array access expressions, which could have index arrays, and uses them in facilitation of different dependence analysis. Hybrid analysis works successfully find many parallel loops in PERFECT CLUB and SPEC benchmarks, however, the usefulness of index array properties is not exactly clear in their results, partially because they define the properties for array indexing expression and not index array, and partially because they usually just differentiate between finding a loop parallel either in compile-time or runtime. Nonetheless, their results implies that they do get similar results, for finding parallel loops and analyzing privatization in MDG, BDNA, TRFD, and DYFESM, as McKinley [12], and Lin and Padua [11].

5.5   Other Uses for Index Array Properties

Unlike other works that were either doing general dependence analysis or finding full parallelism, Venkat et al. [23] used index array properties in wavefront parallelization. They were trying to partially parallelize outer most loops in two numerical sparse computation, namely Gauss-Seidel, and Incomplete LU0. And, since the index array values would not be available until runtime, they were using runtime inspectors to generate dependence graph of loop iterations, which could be used to generate wavefronts of iterations, which can be run in parallel. One problem that they addressed was that if one naively generates runtime inspectors for all the compile-time extracted dependence, the overhead of runtime inspection would make parallelization useless. Instead, they used index array properties for two purposes, for one they used them to prove as many dependence as unsatisfiable at compile-time, then they also used index array properties to derive new equality constraints in remaining dependences that made their runtime inspectors faster. They formulated and used two index arrays properties for Incomplete LU0 namely monotonicity, and correlated monotonicity (a relation between two related index arrays in this code). They also formulated and used monotonicity property for index arrays in Gauss-Seidel computation. In follow-on work, Mohammadi et al. [21] formulated these constraints with universally quantified constraints and instantiated them to ISL [24].

6   Conclusion

In this paper, we showed how properties about index arrays in sparse matrix computation can be formulated with universally quantified assertions and automatically utilized in compile-time dependence analysis. Although, previous works have looked into usefulness of index array properties, to our knowledge, none of them has formulated or utilized all the properties formulated in this paper for dependence analysis. Particularly, we are not aware of any previous work that would describe triangularity and periodic monotonicity properties. Our results showed index array properties can help us find several parallel loops in our benchmarks that would have not been possible without them, at least not without runtime analysis. We also discussed results of parallelization for two of the codes in our benchmark where detected parallel loops by our framework had been hand-parallelized. The results showed 1.3–3.5× performance gain for parallelized Incomplete Cholesky over its sequential version.

References

1. Ctop research group webpage at utah (2018). http://ctop.cs.utah.edu/ctop/
2. Sparselib++ homepage (2018). https://math.nist.gov/sparselib++/
3. Z3 git homepage (2018). https://github.com/Z3Prover/z3/wiki
4. Barrett, C., Fontaine, P., Tinelli, C.: The Satisfiability Modulo Theories Library (SMT-LIB) (2016). www.SMT-LIB.org

5. Barthou, D., Collard, J.F., Feautrier, P.: Fuzzy array dataflow analysis. J. Parallel Distrib. Comput. **40**(2), 210–226 (1997)

6. Bradley, A.R., Manna, Z., Sipma, H.B.: What's decidable about arrays? In: Emerson, E.A., Namjoshi, K.S. (eds.) VMCAI 2006. LNCS, vol. 3855, pp. 427–442. Springer, Heidelberg (2005). https://doi.org/10.1007/11609773_28

7. Cheshmi, K., Kamil, S., Strout, M.M., Dehnavi, M.M.: Sympiler: transforming sparse matrix codes by decoupling symbolic analysis. In: Proceedings of the International Conference for High Performance Computing, Networking, Storage and Analysis, SC 2017, pp. 13:1–13:13. ACM, New York (2017). https://doi.org/10.1145/3126908.3126936

8. Davis, T.A., Hu, Y.: The university of Florida sparse matrix collection. ACM Trans. Math. Softw. (TOMS) **38**(1), 1:1–1:25 (2011). https://doi.org/10.1145/2049662.2049663. Article no. 1. http://doi.acm.org/10.1145/2049662.2049663

9. Ge, Y., de Moura, L.: Complete instantiation for quantified formulas in satisfiabiliby modulo theories. In: Bouajjani, A., Maler, O. (eds.) CAV 2009. LNCS, vol. 5643, pp. 306–320. Springer, Heidelberg (2009). https://doi.org/10.1007/978-3-642-02658-4_25

10. Habermehl, P., Iosif, R., Vojnar, T.: What else is decidable about integer arrays? In: Amadio, R. (ed.) FoSSaCS 2008. LNCS, vol. 4962, pp. 474–489. Springer, Heidelberg (2008). https://doi.org/10.1007/978-3-540-78499-9_33

11. Lin, Y., Padua, D.: Compiler analysis of irregular memory accesses. In: Proceedings of the ACM SIGPLAN Conference on Programming Language Design and Implementation, vol. 35, pp. 157–168. ACM, New York, May 2000

12. McKinley, K.: Dependence analysis of arrays subscriptecl by index arrays. Technical report. TR91187, Rice University (1991)

13. Oancea, C.E., Rauchwerger, L.: Logical inference techniques for loop parallelization. In: Proceedings of the 33rd ACM SIGPLAN Conference on Programming Language Design and Implementation, PLDI 2012. ACM, New York (2012)

14. Oancea, C.E., Rauchwerger, L.: A hybrid approach to proving memory reference monotonicity. In: Rajopadhye, S., Mills Strout, M. (eds.) LCPC 2011. LNCS, vol. 7146, pp. 61–75. Springer, Heidelberg (2013). https://doi.org/10.1007/978-3-642-36036-7_5

15. Paek, Y., Hoeflinger, J., Padua, D.: Simplification of array access patterns for compiler optimizations. In: Proceedings of the ACM SIGPLAN 1998 Conference on Programming Language Design and Implementation, PLDI 1998, pp. 60–71. ACM, New York (1998)

16. Pugh, W., Wonnacott, D.: Nonlinear array dependence analysis. In: Third Workshop on Languages, Compilers, and Run-Time Systems for Scalable Computers, Troy, New York, May 1995

17. Pugh, W., Wonnacott, D.: Constraint-based array dependence analysis. ACM Trans. Program. Lang. Syst. **20**(3), 635–678 (1998)

18. Rus, S.: Hybrid analysis of memory references and its application to automatic parallelization. Ph.D. thesis, Texas A&M (2006)

19. Rus, S., Hoeflinger, J., Rauchwerger, L.: Hybrid analysis: static & dynamic memory reference analysis. Int. J. Parallel Program. **31**(4), 251–283 (2003)

20. Shostak, R.E.: A practical decision procedure for arithmetic with function symbols. J. ACM **26**(2), 351–360 (1979). https://doi.org/10.1145/322123.322137

21. Soltan Mohammadi, M., et al.: Sparse matrix code dependence analysis simplification at compile time. ArXiv e-prints, July 2018

22. Strout, M.M., LaMielle, A., Carter, L., Ferrante, J., Kreaseck, B., Olschanowsky, C.: An approach for code generation in the sparse polyhedral framework. Parallel Comput. **53**(C), 32–57 (2016)
23. Venkat, A., et al.: Automating wavefront parallelization for sparse matrix computations. In: Proceedings of the International Conference for High Performance Computing, Networking, Storage and Analysis, SC 2016, pp. 41:1–41:12 (2016)
24. Verdoolaege, S.: Integer Set Library: Manual (2018). http://isl.gforge.inria.fr
25. Vuduc, R., Kamil, S., Hsu, J., Nishtala, R., Demmel, J.W., Yelick, K.A.: Automatic performance tuning and analysis of sparse triangular solve. ICS (2002)
26. Wang, E., et al.: Intel math kernel library. High-Performance Computing on the Intel® Xeon Phi™, pp. 167–188. Springer, Cham (2014). https://doi.org/10.1007/978-3-319-06486-4_7

Optimized Sound and Complete
Data Race Detection in Structured
Parallel Programs

Kyle Storey, Jacob Powell, Ben Ogles, Joshua Hooker, Peter Aldous⬤,
and Eric Mercer(✉)⬤

Brigham Young University, Provo, UT 84601, USA
kyle.r.storey@gmail.com, s.jacob.powell@gmail.com,
benjaminogles@gmail.com, joshua.d.hooker@gmail.com,
{aldous,egm}@cs.byu.edu

Abstract. Task parallel programs that are free of data race are guaranteed to be deterministic, serializable, and free of deadlock. Techniques for verification of data race freedom vary in both accuracy and asymptotic complexity. One work is particularly well suited to task parallel programs with isolation and lightweight threads. It uses the Java Pathfinder model checker to reason about different schedules and proves the presence or absence of data race in a program on a fixed input. However, it uses a direct and inefficient transitive closure on the happens-before relation to reason about data race. This paper presents Zipper, an alternative to this naïve algorithm, which identifies the presence or absence of data race in asymptotically superior time. Zipper is optimized for lightweight threads and, in the presence of many threads, has superior time complexity to leading vector clock algorithms. This paper includes an empirical study of Zipper and a comparison against the naïve computation graph algorithm, demonstrating the superior performance it achieves.

1 Introduction

Correctness in task parallel programs is only guaranteed if the programs are free of data race. A data race is a pair of concurrent uses of a shared memory location when at least one use writes to the location. The order in which these uses occur can change the outcome of the program, creating nondeterminism.

Structured parallelism sometimes takes the form of lightweight tasks. Languages such as Habanero Java, OpenMP, and Erlang encourage the use of new tasks for operations that can be done independently of other tasks. As a result, many programs written in this family of languages use large numbers of threads. In some cases, the number of threads cannot be statically bounded.

Data race is usually undesirable and there is much work to automatically and efficiently detect data race statically. However, static techniques often report too many false positives to be effective tools in practice. Precise data race detection

The research presented here is supported in part by the NSF under grant 1302524.

M. Hall and H. Sundar (Eds.): LCPC 2018, LNCS 11882, pp. 94–111, 2019.
https://doi.org/10.1007/978-3-030-34627-0_8

for a single input can be achieved dynamically. Many dynamic techniques use access histories (shadow memory) to track accesses to shared memory locations.

Vector clocks [12,22] are an efficient implementation of shadow memory. One analysis based on vector clocks is capable of reasoning about multiple schedules from a single trace [17]. Its complexity is linear if the number of threads and locks used is constant. Vector clocks have been extended to more efficient representations for recursively parallel programs [1,6] that yield improved empirical results. In all of these cases, the complexity of vector clock algorithms is sensitive to the number of threads used.

When programs are restricted to structured parallelism, shadow memory can reference a computation graph that encodes which events are concurrent. This allows the size of shadow memory to be independent from the number of threads in the program.

The SP-bags algorithm [11], which has been extended to task parallel languages with futures [26], detects data race by executing a program in a depth first fashion and tracking concurrent tasks. Other extensions enable locks [5] and mutual exclusion [25], but can produce false positives.

As an alternative to shadow memory, each task can maintain sets of shared memory locations they have accessed. Lu et al. [20] created TARDIS, a tool that detects data race in a computation graph by intersecting the access sets of concurrent nodes. TARDIS is more efficient for programs with many sequential events or where many accesses are made to the same shared memory location. However, TARDIS does not reason about mutual exclusion.

The computation graph analysis by Nakade et al. [24] for recursively task parallel programs can reason precisely about mutual exclusion [24]. By model checking, it is capable of proving or disproving the presence of data race over all possible schedules. Its algorithm for detecting data races in a single trace is direct, albeit naïve; it computes the transitive closure of the computation graph. This quadratic algorithm admits significant improvement.

This paper presents such an improvement in the form of Zipper, a new algorithm for detecting data races on computation graphs. Zipper maintains precision while utilizing mutual exclusion to improve the efficiency of the computation graph analysis. This algorithm is superior in asymptotic time complexity to that of vector clock implementations when the number of threads is large. It also presents an implementation of the algorithm and a comparison with the naïve computation graph algorithm. The implementation is an addition to the code base published by Nakade et al., which allows for a direct comparison of the two.

In summary, the contributions of this paper are:

- An algorithm for identifying data races in the framework of Nakade et al.,
- A discussion of the relative merits of vector clocks and this algorithm, and
- An empirical study of both the naïve computation graph algorithm and the optimized Zipper algorithm.

The structure of this paper is as follows: Sect. 2 discusses computation graphs and SP-bags. Section 3 presents the Zipper algorithm, and demonstrates the algorithm on a small graph. Section 4 contains an empirical study that compares

Zipper to the original computation graph algorithm. Section 5 details work related to this paper. Section 6 concludes.

2   Background

2.1   Programming Model

The surface syntax for the task parallel language used in this paper is based on the language used by Nakade et al. [24] and is given in Fig. 1. A program **P** is a sequence of procedures, each of which takes a single parameter l of type L. The body of a procedure is inductively defined by **s**. The expression language, e, is elided.

$$
\begin{aligned}
\mathbf{P} ::=\ & (\mathbf{proc}\ p\ (\mathbf{var}\ l : L)\ s)* \\
\mathbf{s} ::=\ & s;\ s\ \mid\ l := e\ \mid\ \mathbf{skip}\ \mid\ [\mathbf{if}\ e\ \mathbf{then}\ s\ \mathbf{else}\ s] \\
& \mid\ [\mathbf{while}\ e\ \mathbf{do}\ s]\ \mid\ \mathbf{call}\ l := p\ e\ \mid\ \mathbf{return}\ e \\
& \mid\ \mathbf{async}\ p\ e\ \mid\ [\mathbf{finish}\ s]\ \mid\ [\mathbf{isolated}\ s]
\end{aligned}
$$

Fig. 1. The surface syntax for task parallel programs.

The **async, finish,** and **isolated** have interprocedural effects that influence the shape of the computation graph. The remaining statements have their usual sequential meaning. The **async**-statement calls a procedure p asynchronously with argument e. The **finish** statement waits until all tasks initiated within its dynamic scope terminate.

This programming model disallows task passing and therefore does not capture some concurrent language constructs like futures. Futures can result in non-strict computation graphs that Zipper is not currently able to analyze. Related work for structured parallelism can reason about programming models that include futures [20,26] but cannot reason about isolation. ESP-bags can reason about isolated regions, but only when they commute [25], as discussed in Sect. 2.3.

Restrictions on task passing are not unique to this programming model. Task parallel languages usually restrict task passing in some way in order to ensure deadlock freedom. For example, Habanero Java [4] restricts futures to be declared final. Deterministic Parallel Ruby [20] requires futures to be completely independent and to deep copy their arguments. Extending Zipper to treat task passing is the subject of further research. Despite this restriction, the collection of concurrent constructs treated in this paper is sufficient to simulate a wide range of functionality common in modern task parallel languages.

2.2   Computation Graph

A Computation Graph for a task parallel program is a directed acyclic graph representing the concurrent structure of one program execution [7]. The edges in the graph encode the happens before relation [19] over the set of nodes: $\prec \subset N \times N$. There is a data race in the graph if and only if there are two nodes, n_i and n_j, such that the nodes are concurrent, $(n_i \parallel_\prec n_j \equiv n_i \not\prec n_j \wedge n_j \not\prec n_i)$, and the two nodes conflict:

$$conflict(n_i, n_j) = \begin{array}{l} \rho(n_i) \cap \omega(n_j) \neq \emptyset \vee \\ \rho(n_j) \cap \omega(n_i) \neq \emptyset \vee \\ \omega(n_i) \cap \omega(n_j) \neq \emptyset, \end{array} \tag{1}$$

where $\rho(n)$ and $\omega(n)$ are the sets of read and write accesses recorded in n.

In order to prove or disprove the presence of data race in a program that uses mutual exclusion, a model checker must be used to enumerate all reorderings of critical sections [24]. For each reordering, a different computation graph is generated that must be checked for data race. The main contribution of this paper is an algorithm that can efficiently check a computation graph for data race without reporting false positives even in the presence of mutual exclusion.

2.3   The SP-Bags Algorithm

The SP-bags algorithm can check a computation graph for data race with a single depth first traversal. ESP-bags [25] generalizes SP-bags to task parallel models similar to the one in Fig. 1. However, it can report false positives when the isolated regions in a program do not commute. To demonstrate this limitation, an example is given where it reports a race when in fact there is none.

ESP-bags maintains shadow memory for each shared memory location. The reader and writer shadow spaces record the last relevant task to read or write to the location. Similar shadow spaces exist for isolated regions. To check an access for data race, one must determine if the last task to access a location is executing concurrently with the current task. Tasks that are executing concurrently with the current task are stored in "P-bags". Serialized tasks are stored in "S-bags". Therefore, checking an access for data race reduces to checking whether the last task to access the location is in a P-bag.

When a task is created with **async** its S-bag is created containing itself. Its P-bag is empty. When it completes and returns to its parent, its S-bag and P-bag are emptied into its parent's P-bag. When a **finish** block completes the contents of its S-bag and P-bag are emptied into its parent's S-bag.

2.4   Example

The program contained in Fig. 2 represents a program with critical sections that do not commute and therefore cause ESP-bags and similar algorithms to report races when there are none. There are two isolated blocks in the program. If the isolated block in procedure *main* executes first then the shared variable x is

```
1           x := false // unwritten
2           a := false
3           proc main () {
4             finish {
5               async p
6               isolated {
7                 a := true
8               }
9               y := x
10            }
11          }
12          proc p () {
13            isolated {
14              if (!a)
15                x := true // written
16            }
17          }
```

Fig. 2. A simple example of a task parallel program.

never written. Otherwise, it is written and the isolated block in p happens before the isolated block in $main$. Because the happens before relation is transitive, the read of x in $main$ becomes ordered with the write in p and there is no race.

Table 1 shows the state of the ESP-bags algorithm as it executes the program. Only rows that contain state changes are listed. The thread that executes procedure $main$ is labeled as T_1 and the thread that executes procedure p is labeled T_2. The only finish block is labeled F_1.

Table 1. ESP-bags state through Fig. 2

Line	T_1 S	F_1 P	T_2 S	x I-Writer
0	–	–	–	–
3	T_1	–	–	–
5	T_1	–	T_2	–
15	T_1	–	T_2	T_2
17	T_1	T_2	–	T_2

The first row shows the initial state of the algorithm. The next two rows show the correct initialization of T_1 and T_2 S-bags. On line fifteen, the shared variable x is written to because of the order in which ESP-bags executes the critical sections in the program. When T_2 completes and the algorithm returns to the **finish** block that spawned it, T_2 is placed in the P-bag of F_1 signifying that it will be in parallel with all subsequent statements in the **finish** block.

This is the state that is in play when x is read outside of an isolated block on line nine. Here ESP-bags reports a race because the last isolated writer is in a P-bag. This is a false positive.

ESP-bags is an efficient algorithm, but its imprecision makes it unsuitable when false positives are unacceptable. The goal of the computation graph analysis is to precisely prove or disprove the absence of data race. As such, a comparison of the efficiency of ESP-bags with Zipper is not given in this work.

3 The Zipper Algorithm

The algorithm presented by Nakade et al. [24] checks every node against every other node. While effective, this algorithm is inefficient. This paper presents the Zipper algorithm, which is more efficient but still sound. Zipper performs a depth-first search over non-isolation edges in the computation graph, capturing serialization imposed by isolation. Section 3.1 describes the variables and algorithmic semantics. Section 3.2 presents the algorithm in several procedures. Lastly, Sect. 3.3 shows an example execution of the algorithm.

3.1 Definitions

Integers have lowercase names and collection names (arrays and sets) are capitalized. Their types are as follows:

- $Z\downarrow$, $Z\uparrow$: Array of sets of node IDs; indices correspond to isolation nodes
- $slider\downarrow$, $slider\uparrow$, $next\_branch\_id$, $next\_bag\_id$: Integer
- $Z\downarrow_\lambda$, $Z\uparrow_\lambda$, S, I: Array of sets of node IDs; indices correspond to branch IDs
- C: Array of sets of pairs of node IDs; indices correspond to branch IDs
- R: Set of node IDs
- B_λ: Array of sets of branch IDs; indices correspond to bag IDs
- B_i: Array of sets of isolation indices; indices correspond to bag IDs

Zippers encode serialization. The isolation zipper Z captures serialization with respect to isolation nodes. The "lambda" zipper Z_λ captures nodes not in the isolation zipper in a particular task.

Traversal begins at the topmost **async** node. Anytime an **async** node is visited, each branch is given a new branch ID (tracked with $next\_branch\_id$) and are queued for evaluation in arbitrary order. As the algorithm traverses downward, the visited node IDs are added to the set at the index of the branch ID in the S array. This continues until an isolation node is visited that has an outgoing isolation edge. Then, contents of the S array set for the current branch ID are emptied into the set at the index of the isolation node in the down zipper $Z\downarrow$. Once a wait node is visited on the way down, all nodes in the S array set for the current branch ID are emptied into the set at the index of the current branch ID in the down lambda zipper $Z\downarrow_\lambda$. The process is then performed again on the way up, except isolation nodes that have incoming edges are used to trigger a dump from S into $Z\uparrow$. Additionally, when an async node is hit the S set for the current branch is emptied into the up lambda zipper $Z\uparrow_\lambda$.

When an isolated node is visited, its ID is also placed into the set at the index of the current branch ID in I, creating an easily-accessible mapping of branch ID to the isolated nodes on that branch. The ready set R is used to identify which async nodes have had all children traversed; therefore after the last branch of a async node is traversed, the async node ID is placed into the set R to signify that the algorithm can continue with the wait node that corresponds with the async node, since all children have been processed. Any time an isolation node is visited on the way down, $slider\downarrow$ is set to that isolation node's index; similarly, $slider\uparrow$ is set to the index of isolation nodes seen on the way up, restricting data race checks to the fewest possible nodes.

When returning to an async node, the set in I at the current branch ID is emptied into the B_i at the current bag ID. The current branch ID is also placed into the set at the current bag ID index in B_λ. The B_i and B_λ are used to indicate nodes that are concurrent and are not serialized by an isolation edge with the current node.

On the way down a branch, each time a node is visited the p_bag_id is used to index into the B_λ and B_i sets. Each of the indices in the B_λ set at the p_bag_id index is used to index into the $Z\downarrow_\lambda$ to obtain node IDs that are possibly in parallel with the current node. Each pair of possibly parallel nodes is placed into the set located in the C array at the current branch ID. A similar process is used with B_i and $Z\downarrow$; however, only indices larger than $slider\downarrow$ that are in the set in B_i at the p_bag_id index are paired and placed in C.

On the way up the same process is followed, except $Z\uparrow$ and $Z\uparrow_\lambda$ are used, and only indices smaller than $slider\uparrow$ are used when indexing into $Z\uparrow$. Also, node pairs that are possibly in parallel are not placed in C; instead, node pairs are checked against C. A node pair discovered in both the upwards and downwards traversal is actually in parallel and is checked with *conflict*.

3.2   The Algorithm

The top level of the algorithm is the *recursive_analyze* function. Before it is invoked, several variables are declared and initialized:

```
1:  Z↓ = []
2:  Z↑ = []
3:  Z↓λ = []
4:  Z↑λ = []
5:  slider↓ = NULL
6:  slider↑ = NULL
7:  next_branch_id = 1
8:  next_bag_id = 2
9:  R = {}
10: S = []
11: I = []
12: C = []
```

13: $B_\lambda = [\emptyset, \emptyset]$
14: $B_i = [\emptyset, \emptyset]$
15: $recursive\_analyze\,(entry, 0, 0, 1)$
16: **procedure** RECURSIVE_ANALYZE$(n,\ branch\_id,\ s\_bag\_id,\ p\_bag\_id)$
17:     **if async** (n) **then**
18:         $async\_node\,(n, branch\_id, s\_bag\_id, p\_bag\_id)$
19:     **end if**
20:     **if wait** (n) **then**
21:         $wait\_node\,(n, branch\_id, s\_bag\_id, p\_bag\_id)$
22:     **end if**
23:     $other\_node\,(n, branch\_id, s\_bag\_id, p\_bag\_id)$
24: **end procedure**

   recursive_analyze relies on three helpers. *async_node* analyzes nodes with **async**-statements, *wait_node* analyzes nodes that terminate **finish**-statements, and *other_node* analyzes other nodes:

1: **procedure** ASYNC_NODE$(n,\ branch\_id,\ s\_bag\_id,\ p\_bag\_id)$
2:     $thread\_bag\_id = next\_bag\_id$
3:     $next\_bag\_id = next\_bag\_id + 1$
4:     $B_\lambda\,[thread\_bag\_id] = B_\lambda\,[p\_bag\_id]$
5:     $B_i\,[thread\_bag\_id] = B_i\,[p\_bag\_id]$
6:     $slider{\uparrow}_0 = slider{\uparrow}$
7:     $slider{\downarrow}_0 = slider{\downarrow}$
8:     $\lceil slider{\uparrow} \rceil = slider{\uparrow}$
9:     $\lfloor slider{\downarrow} \rfloor = slider{\downarrow}$
10:     **for** $n' \in succs\,(n)$ **do**
11:         $slider{\uparrow} = slider{\uparrow}_0$
12:         $slider{\downarrow} = slider{\downarrow}_0$
13:         $id = next\_branch\_id$
14:         $next\_branch\_id = next\_branch\_id + 1$
15:         $S\,[id] = \emptyset$
16:         $C\,[id] = \emptyset$
17:         $new\_bag\_id = next\_bag\_id$
18:         $next\_bag\_id = next\_bag\_id + 1$
19:         $B_\lambda\,[new\_bag\_id] = \emptyset$
20:         $B_i\,[new\_bag\_id] = \emptyset$
21:         $recursive\_analyze\,(n, next\_branch\_id, new\_bag\_id, thread\_bag\_id)$
22:         $Z{\uparrow}_\lambda\,[id] = S\,[id]$
23:         $\lceil slider{\uparrow} \rceil = min(\lceil slider{\uparrow} \rceil, slider{\uparrow})$
24:         $\lfloor slider{\downarrow} \rfloor = max(\lfloor slider{\downarrow} \rfloor, slider{\downarrow})$
25:         $B_\lambda\,[s\_bag\_id] = B_\lambda\,[s\_bag\_id] \cup \{id\}$
26:         $B_i\,[s\_bag\_id] = B_i\,[s\_bag\_id] \cup I\,[id]$
27:         $B_\lambda\,[thread\_bag\_id] = B_\lambda\,[thread\_bag\_id] \cup \{id\}$
28:         $B_i\,[thread\_bag\_id] = B_i\,[thread\_bag\_id] \cup I\,[id]$
29:     **end for**
30:     $slider{\downarrow} = \lfloor slider{\downarrow} \rfloor$

```
31:      R = R ∪ {n}
32:      j = get_join(n)
33:      recursive_analyze (j, branch_id, s_bag_id, p_bag_id)
34:      slider↑= ⌈slider↑⌉
35:      return
36: end procedure
 1: procedure WAIT_NODE(n, branch_id, s_bag_id, p_bag_id)
 2:      a = get_async (n)
 3:      if a ∈ R then
 4:          c = get_child (n)
 5:          recursive analyze (c, branch_id, s_bag_id, p_bag_id)
 6:          return
 7:      end if
 8:      Z↓_λ [branch_id] = Z↓_λ[branch_id] ∪ S[branch_id]
 9:      S [branch_id] = ∅
10:      return
11: end procedure
 1: procedure OTHER_NODE(n, branch_id, s_bag_id, p_bag_id)
 2:      S [branch_id] = S [branch_id] ∪ {n}
 3:      if isolated (n) then
 4:          i = isoindex (n)
 5:          slider↓ = i
 6:          if hasOutgoingEdge (n) then
 7:              Z↓ [i] = Z↓ [i] ∪ S [branch_id]
 8:              S [branch_id] = ∅
 9:              I [branch_id] = I [branch_id] ∪ {i}
10:          end if
11:      end if
12:      checkDown (n, branch_id, p_bag_id)
13:      c = get_child (n)
14:      recursive analyze (c, branch_id, s_bag_id, p_bag_id)
15:      checkUp (n, branch_id, p_bag_id)
16:      S [branch_id] = S [branch_id] ∪ {n}
17:      if isolated (n) then
18:          i = isoindex (n)
19:          slider↑ = i
20:          if hasIncomingEdge (n) then
21:              Z↑ [i] = Z↑ [i] ∪ S [branch_id]
22:              S [branch_id] = ∅
23:              I [branch_id] = I [branch_id] ∪ {i}
24:          end if
25:      end if
26: end procedure
```

Lastly, *checkDown* and *checkUp* are used for identifying data races:

```
1: procedure checkDown(n, branch_id, p_bag_id)
2:     for branch_id' ∈ B_λ [p_bag_id] do
3:         for n' ∈ Z↓_λ [branch_id'] do
4:             C[branch_id] = C[branch_id] ∪ {(n, n')}
5:         end for
6:     end for
7:     for i ∈ isoindex (branch_id) do
8:         if i <= slider↓ then continue
9:         end if
10:        for n' ∈ Z↓ [i] do
11:            C[branch_id] = C[branch_id] ∪ {(n, n')}
12:        end for
13:    end for
14: end procedure
```

```
1: procedure checkUp(n, branch_id, p_bag_id)
2:     for branch_id' ∈ B_λ [p_bag_id] do
3:         for n' ∈ Z↑_λ [branch_id'] do
4:             if ((n, n') ∈ C[branch_id]) ∧ conflicts (n, n') then reportRace()
5:             end if
6:         end for
7:     end for
8:     for i ∈ isoindex (branch_id) do
9:         if i <= slider↑ then continue
10:        end if
11:        for n' ∈ Z↑ [i] do
12:            if ((n, n') ∈ C[branch_id]) ∧ conflicts (n, n') then reportRace()
13:            end if
14:        end for
15:    end for
16: end procedure
```

3.3 Zipper Example

Figure 3 is a computation graph that serves to illustrate the Zipper algorithm, each step of the algorithm is given in Table 2. The Node column in Table 2 represents the visited nodes, in traversal order. The other columns refer to the global variables and their values at each step. For brevity, empty sets in the $Z\downarrow$, $Z\uparrow$, $Z\downarrow_\lambda$, and $Z\uparrow_\lambda$ arrays are omitted and nonempty sets are preceded by their index. Additionally, the S column shows the set at the current branch ID rather than the entire S array.

At node a in Fig. 3 all variables are initialized to empty; ASYNC_NODE is then called, which calls RECURSIVE_ANALYZE on line 21. Node b is then visited in OTHER_NODE, and added to the S set at the current branch ID. Then, node b is checked for conflicts at line 12 in OTHER_NODE, however, the B_i and B_λ

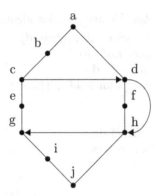

Fig. 3. An example computation graph

at p_bag_id are empty, so no operation takes place. This is true for the entirety of the first branch; data race checks are performed while traversing the second branch. It then recursively visits its child node, c. Node c calls OTHER_NODE and is an isolated node, therefore $slider\downarrow$ is set to the index of c (0), on line 5. Node c is also added to S which is emptied into $Z\downarrow$ at index 0 on lines 7 and 8. Recursion continues until node g. The slider is set to the index of g, but S is not emptied because the isolation edge is not outgoing as shown on line 6 in OTHER_NODE. Execution continues to node i until the WAIT_NODE j is visited and WAIT_NODE is called.

Table 2. Step-by-step Zipper algorithm

Node	$Z\downarrow$	$Z\uparrow$	$Z\downarrow_\lambda$	$Z\uparrow_\lambda$	$slider\downarrow$	$slider\uparrow$	S
a	[]	[]	[]	[]	–	–	{}
b	[]	[]	[]	[]	–	–	{b}
c	[0 : {c, b}]	[]	[]	[]	0	–	{b, c}
e	[0 : {c, b}]	[]	[]	[]	0	–	{e}
g	[0 : {c, b}]	[]	[]	[]	3	–	{e, g}
i	[0 : {c, b}]	[]	[]	[]	3	–	{e, g, i}
j	[0 : {c, b}]	[]	[1 : {e, g, i}]	[]	3	–	{}
i	[0 : {c, b}]	[]	[1 : {e, g, i}]	[]	3	–	{i}
g	[0 : {c, b}]	[3 : {i, g}]	[1 : {e, g, i}]	[]	3	3	{i, g}
e	[0 : {c, b}]	[3 : {i, g}]	[1 : {e, g, i}]	[]	3	3	{e}
c	[0 : {c, b}]	[3 : {i, g}]	[1 : {e, g, i}]	[]	3	0	{e, c}
b	[0 : {c, b}]	[3 : {i, g}]	[1 : {e, g, i}]	[]	3	0	{e, c, b}
a	[0 : {c, b}]	[3 : {i, g}]	[1 : {e, g, i}]	[1 : {e, c, b}]	–	–	{}
d	[0 : {c, b}, 1 : {d}]	[3 : {i, g}]	[1 : {e, g, i}]	[1 : {e, c, b}]	1	–	{d}
f	[0 : {c, b}, 1 : {d}]	[3 : {i, g}]	[1 : {e, g, i}]	[1 : {e, c, b}]	1	–	{f}
h	[0 : {c, b}, 1 : {d}, 2 : {f, h}]	[3 : {i, g}]	[1 : {e, g, i}]	[1 : {e, c, b}]	2	–	{f, h}
j	[0 : {c, b}, 1 : {d}, 2 : {f, h}]	[3 : {i, g}]	[1 : {e, g, i}]	[1 : {e, c, b}]	2	–	{}
h	[0 : {c, b}, 1 : {d}, 2 : {f, h}]	[2 : {h}, 3 : {i, g}]	[1 : {e, g, i}]	[1 : {e, c, b}]	2	2	{h}
f	[0 : {c, b}, 1 : {d}, 2 : {f, h}]	[2 : {h}, 3 : {i, g}]	[1 : {e, g, i}]	[1 : {e, c, b}]	2	2	{f}
d	[0 : {c, b}, 1 : {d}, 2 : {f, h}]	[1 : {f, d}, 2 : {h}, 3 : {i, g}]	[1 : {e, g, i}]	[1 : {e, c, b}]	2	1	{f, d}
a	[0 : {c, b}, 1 : {d}, 2 : {f, h}]	[1 : {f, d}, 2 : {h}, 3 : {i, g}]	[1 : {e, g, i}]	[1 : {e, c, b}]	–	–	{}

In WAIT_NODE the S set is emptied into $Z\downarrow_\lambda$ at the current branch ID on lines 8 and 9. Node i is placed in S on line 2 in OTHER_NODE, then recursion returns to node g. The S set is then emptied into $Z\uparrow$ at index 3 (the index of g) on lines 21 and 22. Execution continues in a similar fashion until it arrives at a. Take note that since the execution is returning up the first branch, the S set is not emptied at node c, since it has an outgoing edge (S empties on the way down on isolation nodes with outgoing edges and on the way up with incoming edges). It is important to note that c and b are in $Z\uparrow_\lambda$ at the branch index. Then a recursive call is made to traverse the second branch in the same manner as the first branch, except data race checks will be performed. The data race checks are not in the table, but are shown in the algorithm in CHECKDOWN and CHECKUP and described in Sect. 3.

4   Implementation and Results

4.1   Methods

The implementation of Zipper is an addition to the implementation provided by Nakade et al. [24] in their paper. The original implementation is available at https://jpf.byu.edu/jpf-hj/. The benchmarks referenced in their paper, which are available as part of the same repository, provide a rich comparison of the two algorithms.

The results of the comparison of the two analyses are included in Table 3. In the table, the *Benchmark* column contains the name of the program used. The *Nodes* column contains the number of nodes in a computation graph. The *Isolation* and *Race* columns indicate, respectively, whether or not isolation and data race are present. The *CG (ms)* and *Zipper (ms)* columns contain the execution time for the respective analyses in milliseconds. Lastly, $\frac{Zipper}{CG}$ is the ratio of the two time measurements.

The experimental results measure the time taken to model check over all possible isolation schedules and reason about each resulting computation graph. All experiments were run on an Intel(R) Xeon(R) Gold 5120 CPU with 8 GB RAM.

4.2   Analysis

Zipper performed better on every benchmark (except for DoAll2OrigNo) whose computation graph had more than 37 nodes. For all of the benchmarks with 37 nodes or fewer, the Zipper analysis performed slower except for IsolatedBlockNo and PrimeNumCounter. In all of these smaller cases, the analyses' execution time was virtually identical. As expected, the degree to which Zipper outperforms the computation graph analysis grows with the number of nodes.

While the size of the computation graph is the strongest predictor of relative runtime performance between the two analyses, other factors contribute to performance. For example, DoAll1OrigNo and DoAll2OrigNo produce computation graphs with identical structure. However, they differ in both number and

Table 3. Comparison of the computation graph and Zipper analyses

Benchmark	Nodes	Isolation	Race	CG (ms)	Zipper (ms)	$\frac{Zipper}{CG}$
ClumpedAcess	11	Y	–	4	14	3.5
PrimitiveArrayNoRace	11	–	–	1	12	12
PrimitiveArrayRace	11	–	Y	1	8	8
SimpleSimpleSimple	11	–	Y	1	14	14
SimpleSimpleSimple2	11	–	Y	1	7	7
VectorAdd	11	–	–	5	18	3.6
DataRaceIsolateSimple	13	Y	Y	10	17	1.7
DoubleBranchExample	13	Y	–	1	7	7
DataRaceIsolateSimple1	15	Y	Y	5	22	4.4
ForallWithIterable	17	–	–	4	11	2.75
IsolatedBlockNo	19	Y	–	9	2	0.2222
Add	23	–	–	18	28	1.5555
PrimeNumCounter	23	Y	–	34	22	0.6470
PrimeNumCounterForAll	27	Y	–	39	44	1.1282
ScalarMultiply	27	–	–	37	41	1.108
TwoDimArrays	27	–	–	22	40	1.8181
ReciprocalArraySumFutures	37	–	–	32	72	2.25
IntegerCounterIsolated	43	Y	–	774	697	0.9005
PrimeNumCounterForAsync	43	Y	–	138	103	0.7463
Antidep1VarYes	45	–	Y	1271	54	0.0424
Antidep2OrigYes	45	–	Y	1234	58	0.0470
ReciprocalArraySum	53	–	–	1801	51	0.0283
PipelineWithFutures	62	–	–	61	53	0.8688
DoAll1OrigNo	207	–	–	650	372	0.5723
DoAll2OrigNo	207	–	–	47287	49534	1.0475
Antidep1OrigYes	2005	–	Y	247736	58215	0.2349
Antidep2VarYes	2005	–	Y	246561	7003	0.0284

placement of shared variable reads and writes in their respective nodes. As a result, the Zipper analysis executes in half the time that the computation graph analysis does on DoAll1OrigNo. On the other hand, the two analyses take about the same amount of time when analyzing DoAll2OrigNo.

The key difference between the Zipper algorithm and the CG algorithm is in the work done to identify the nodes that need to be checked for data race. The Zipper algorithm is able to identify the nodes that execute in parallel much more quickly than the CG algorithm. If there is a large number of reads and writes in proportion to the number of nodes, the Zipper algorithm performs comparably to the CG algorithm, since they both spend a majority of the time checking conflicting nodes for data race in the same way. Conversely, if there are relatively few reads and writes in proportion to the number of nodes, identifying the nodes that need to be checked becomes much more significant in the analysis time. This makes Zipper more suitable for recursively parallel programs or any task parallel programs that utilize many light weight threads. The Zipper algorithm identifies the nodes that need to be checked much quicker than CG and therefore the overall time is reduced.

4.3   Comparison with TARDIS, SP-Bags and Vector Clocks

Like SP-bags and TARDIS, the Zipper algorithm operates as a depth first traversal of a computation graph that represents a single execution of the program. Zipper tracks reads and writes to shared memory locations in a set for each task and intersects these sets to check for race. However, Zipper does not union access sets and therefore performs more intersect operations than TARDIS. Unlike TARDIS and SP-bags, Zipper can reason about mutual exclusion and includes the scheduled order of isolated regions to reduce the number of intersect operations necessary to check a graph for race.

The vector clock algorithm by Kini et al. [17] checks a program execution for data race by comparing the vector clock of shared memory locations after they are accessed with the current thread's vector clock in order to ensure that the last thread to access the same location is not concurrent with the current thread. The vector clocks are updated after access events and synchronization events.

The vector clock algorithm takes $O(N(L+T^2))$ time to analyze a trace where N is the number of events in the trace, L is the number of locks used and T is the number of threads. In the programming model used in this paper L is always one. It is linear in the length of the trace for programs that use a small, bounded number of locks and threads.

It takes $O(M(T + I))$ time for Zipper to analyze a computation graph and compute the pairs of nodes that are parallel with each other. M is the number of nodes, T is the number of branches in the computation graph and I is the number of isolated regions. Zipper must take the intersection of the access sets for $O(M^2)$ pairs containing K events. This makes the total complexity of Zipper $O(M(T + I) + M^2K)$.

When a program repeats many accesses to the same shared memory locations M and K can be much smaller than N, as TARDIS shows. In this case, Zipper is more efficient than vector clocks and can scale to larger programs. In addition, it may be possible to apply the ideas of TARDIS to Zipper in order to achieve a linear number of intersect and union operations.

5   Related Work

This work is an improvement upon the computation graph analysis by Nakade et al. [24]. Lu et al. [20] implement a similar analysis based on access sets in their tool TARDIS. TARDIS only requires a linear number of intersect and union operations to detect data race in a computation graph but does not support mutual exclusion.

Feng and Leiserson's SP-bags algorithm [11] is a sound and complete data race detection algorithm for a single program execution but it can only reason about a subset of task-parallel programs that do not use locks. Work has been done to apply SP-bags to other task-parallel models with the use of futures [26], async and finish constructs and isolation [25] with limitations discussed in Sect. 2. Defined in [5] the ALL-SETS and BRELLY algorithms extend SP-bags to handle locks and enforce lock disciplines but can also report false positives when the execution order of critical sections change the control flow of the program being verified. Other SP-bags implementations use parallelization to increase performance [2].

Mellor-Crummey [23] uses thread labels to determine whether two nodes in a graph are concurrent and gives a labeling scheme that bounds the length of labels to be proportional to the nesting level of parallel constructs. This work however, does not treat critical sections at all.

Many algorithms for detecting data race are based on vector clocks that map events to timestamps such that the partial order relation on the events is preserved over the set of timestamps. The complexity of vector clocks algorithm is sensitive to the number of threads used in a program. Fidge [12] modifies vector clocks to support dynamic creation and deletion of threads. Christiaens and Bosschere [6] developed vector clocks that grow and shrink dynamically as threads are created and destroyed. Flanagan et al. [13] replace vector clocks with more lightweight "epoch" structures where possible. Audenaert [1] presents clock trees that are also more suitable for programs with many threads. The time taken in a typical operation on a clock tree is linear with respect to the level of nested parallelism in the program. Kini et al. [17] present a vector clock algorithm that runs in linear time with respect to the number of events in the analyzed execution assuming the number of threads and the number of locks used is constant. This assumption also fails in programs that use large numbers of lightweight threads.

This work relies on structured parallelism to reduce the cost of precise dynamic analysis. Structured parallelism is strict in how threads are created and joined, for example, a locking protocol leads to static, dynamic, or hybrid lock-set analyses for data race detection that are often more efficient than approaches to unstructured parallelism [9,10,28]. Unstructured parallelism defines no protocol for when and where threads can be created or join together. Data race detection in unstructured parallelism typically relies on static analysis to approximate parallelism and memory accesses [16,18,27] and then improves precision with dynamic analysis [3,8,14]. Other approaches reason about threads individually [15,21]. The work in this paper relies heavily on structured parallelism and it is hard to directly compare to these more general approaches.

6   Conclusion

The computation graph analysis presented by Nakade et al. [24] is well suited to task parallel programs with isolation and lightweight threads. However, its admittedly direct algorithm for identifying data races is inefficient. The Zipper algorithm achieves the same soundness and completeness as does the direct algorithm with significantly improved asymptotic time complexity and empirical performance. In programs with many threads, its time complexity is superior to that of vector clock implementations. This improved algorithm affords improved efficiency to the computation graph analysis, enabling it to prove the presence or absence of data race in larger and more complex task parallel programs.

References

1. Audenaert, K.: Clock trees: Logical clocks for programs with nested parallelism. IEEE Trans. Softw. Eng. **23**(10), 646–658 (1997)
2. Bender, M.A., Fineman, J.T., Gilbert, S., Leiserson, C.E.: On-the-fly maintenance of series-parallel relationships in fork-join multithreaded programs. In: Proceedings of the Sixteenth Annual ACM Symposium on Parallelism in Algorithms and Architectures, SPAA 2004, pp. 133–144. ACM, New York (2004). https://doi.org/10.1145/1007912.1007933
3. Brat, G., Visser, W.: Combining static analysis and model checking for software analysis. In: Proceedings 16th Annual International Conference on Automated Software Engineering (ASE 2001). IEEE Computer Society (2001). https://doi.org/10.1109/ase.2001.989812
4. Cavé, V., Zhao, J., Shirako, J., Sarkar, V.: Habanero-Java: the new adventures of old X10, August 2011
5. Cheng, G.I., Feng, M., Leiserson, C.E., Randall, K.H., Stark, A.F.: Detecting data races in CILK programs that use locks. In: Proceedings of the Tenth Annual ACM Symposium on Parallel Algorithms and Architectures, SPAA 1998, pp. 298–309. ACM, New York (1998). https://doi.org/10.1145/277651.277696
6. Christiaens, M., De Bosschere, K.: Accordion clocks: logical clocks for data race detection. In: Sakellariou, R., Gurd, J., Freeman, L., Keane, J. (eds.) Euro-Par 2001. LNCS, vol. 2150, pp. 494–503. Springer, Heidelberg (2001). https://doi.org/10.1007/3-540-44681-8_73
7. Dennis, J.B., Gao, G.R., Sarkar, V.: Determinacy and repeatability of parallel program schemata. In: Data-Flow Execution Models for Extreme Scale Computing (DFM), pp. 1–9. IEEE (2012)
8. Dimitrov, D., Raychev, V., Vechev, M., Koskinen, E.: Commutativity race detection. SIGPLAN Not. **49**(6), 305–315 (2014)
9. Elmas, T., Qadeer, S., Tasiran, S.: Goldilocks: a race and transaction-aware Java runtime. In: Proceedings of the 28th ACM SIGPLAN Conference on Programming Language Design and Implementation, PLDI 2007, pp. 245–255. ACM, New York (2007). https://doi.org/10.1145/1250734.1250762
10. Engler, D., Ashcraft, K.: RacerX: effective, static detection of race conditions and deadlocks. In: Proceedings of the Nineteenth ACM Symposium on Operating Systems Principles, SOSP 2003 pp. 237–252. ACM, New York (2003). https://doi.org/10.1145/945445.945468

11. Feng, M., Leiserson, C.E.: Efficient detection of determinacy races in CILK programs. Theory Comput. Syst. **32**(3), 301–326 (1999). https://doi.org/10.1007/s002240000120

12. Fidge, C.J.: Partial orders for parallel debugging. In: Proceedings of the 1988 ACM SIGPLAN and SIGOPS Workshop on Parallel and Distributed Debugging, PADD 1988, pp. 183–194. ACM, New York (1988). https://doi.org/10.1145/68210.69233

13. Flanagan, C., Freund, S.N.: FastTrack: efficient and precise dynamic race detection. In: Proceedings of the 30th ACM SIGPLAN Conference on Programming Language Design and Implementation, PLDI 2009, pp. 121–133. ACM, New York (2009). https://doi.org/10.1145/1542476.1542490

14. Godefroid, P.: Model checking for programming languages using VeriSoft. In: Proceedings of the 24th ACM SIGPLAN-SIGACT Symposium on Principles of Programming Languages, pp. 174–186 (1997)

15. Gotsman, A., Berdine, J., Cook, B., Sagiv, M.: Thread-modular shape analysis. SIGPLAN Not. **42**(6), 266–277 (2007)

16. Kahlon, V., Sinha, N., Kruus, E., Zhang, Y.: Static data race detection for concurrent programs with asynchronous calls. In: Proceedings of the 7th Joint Meeting of the European Software Engineering Conference and the ACM SIGSOFT Symposium on the Foundations of Software Engineering, pp. 13–22 (2009)

17. Kini, D., Mathur, U., Viswanathan, M.: Dynamic race prediction in linear time. In: ACM SIGPLAN Notices, vol. 52, pp. 157–170. ACM (2017)

18. Kulikov, S., Shafiei, N., Van Breugel, F., Visser, W.: Detecting data races with Java PathFinder (2010). http://nastaran.ca/files/race.pdf

19. Lamport, L.: Time, clocks, and the ordering of events in a distributed system. Commun. ACM **21**(7), 558–565 (1978)

20. Lu, L., Ji, W., Scott, M.L.: Dynamic enforcement of determinism in a parallel scripting language. SIGPLAN Not. **49**(6), 519–529 (2014). https://doi.org/10.1145/2666356.2594300

21. Malkis, A., Podelski, A., Rybalchenko, A.: Precise thread-modular verification. In: Nielson, H.R., Filé, G. (eds.) SAS 2007. LNCS, vol. 4634, pp. 218–232. Springer, Heidelberg (2007). https://doi.org/10.1007/978-3-540-74061-2_14

22. Mattern, F., et al.: Virtual time and global states of distributed systems. Parallel Distrib. Algorithms **1**(23), 215–226 (1989)

23. Mellor-Crummey, J.: On-the-fly detection of data races for programs with nested fork-join parallelism. In: Proceedings of the 1991 ACM/IEEE Conference on Supercomputing, Supercomputing 1991, pp. 24–33. ACM, New York (1991). https://doi.org/10.1145/125826.125861

24. Nakade, R., Mercer, E., Aldous, P., McCarthy, J.: Model-checking task parallel programs for data-race. In: Dutle, A., Muñoz, C., Narkawicz, A. (eds.) NFM 2018. LNCS, vol. 10811, pp. 367–382. Springer, Cham (2018). https://doi.org/10.1007/978-3-319-77935-5_25

25. Raman, R., Zhao, J., Sarkar, V., Vechev, M., Yahav, E.: Efficient data race detection for async-finish parallelism. In: Barringer, H., Falcone, Y., Finkbeiner, B., Havelund, K., Lee, I., Pace, G., Roşu, G., Sokolsky, O., Tillmann, N. (eds.) RV 2010. LNCS, vol. 6418, pp. 368–383. Springer, Heidelberg (2010). https://doi.org/10.1007/978-3-642-16612-9_28

26. Surendran, R., Sarkar, V.: Dynamic determinacy race detection for task parallelism with futures. In: Falcone, Y., Sánchez, C. (eds.) RV 2016. LNCS, vol. 10012, pp. 368–385. Springer, Cham (2016). https://doi.org/10.1007/978-3-319-46982-9_23

27. Vechev, M., Yahav, E., Raman, R., Sarkar, V.: Automatic verification of determinism for structured parallel programs. In: Cousot, R., Martel, M. (eds.) SAS 2010. LNCS, vol. 6337, pp. 455–471. Springer, Heidelberg (2010). https://doi.org/10.1007/978-3-642-15769-1_28

28. Voung, J.W., Jhala, R., Lerner, S.: RELAY: static race detection on millions of lines of code. In: Proceedings of the 6th Joint Meeting of the European Software Engineering Conference and the ACM SIGSOFT Symposium on the Foundations of Software Engineering, ESEC-FSE 2007, pp. 205–214. ACM, New York (2007). https://doi.org/10.1145/1287624.1287654

Compiler Optimizations for Parallel Programs

Johannes Doerfert$^{(\boxtimes)}$ and Hal Finkel

Argonne Leadership Computing Facility, Argonne National Laboratory,
Argonne, IL 60439, USA
{jdoerfert,hfinkel}@anl.gov

Abstract. This paper outlines a research and development program to enhance modern compiler technology, and the LLVM compiler infrastructure specifically, to directly optimize parallel-programming-model constructs. The goal is to produce higher-quality code, and moreover, to remove abstraction penalties generally associated with such constructs. We believe that such abstraction penalties are increasing in importance due to C++ parallel-algorithms libraries and other performance-portability-motivated programming methods.

In addition, we will discuss when, and more importantly when not, explicit parallelism-awareness is necessary within the compiler in order to enable the desired optimization capabilities.

Keywords: Parallel programming · LLVM · OpenMP · Compiler optimizations · Intermediate representation · Programming models

1 Introduction

Parallel programming, and often heterogeneous programming, is becoming a ubiquitous part of writing high-performance applications for modern architectures. This raises the question how compilers have to adapt to this new reality. To this end, we have to look at several important trends that are intersecting at the present time:

- Parallel processing, and heterogeneous architectures, have become a common reality across much of modern computing technology. Everything from mobile devices to supercomputers offer multiple cores and heterogeneous accelerators.
- Parallel programming models are nowadays commonly used. This includes source-language directives, e.g., OpenMP [6], and OpenACC, and data-parallel languages, e.g., CUDA, and OpenCL [17]. While this additional semantic information should tend to the compiler, the low-level encoding of parallelism in the otherwise sequential compiler intermediate languages generally prevent analyses and optimizations to cross the barrier between sequential and parallel code.

M. Hall and H. Sundar (Eds.): LCPC 2018, LNCS 11882, pp. 112–119, 2019.
https://doi.org/10.1007/978-3-030-34627-0_9

– The use of parallel libraries, including the new parallel C++ STL, but also libraries such as Thrust [4], Kokkos [8], and RAJA [10], is increasing. These libraries provide a way to cleanly integrate parallel and heterogeneous programming constructs into software-engineering practices and, in addition, provides performance-portability benefits.

The result of these trends is that parallel, and heterogeneous, programming is becoming important for a larger class of applications, and moreover, the potential for compiler optimizations in this space increases as well. Because of directives and other language constructs, the compiler can understand the parallel/heterogeneous semantics. At the same time, the level of abstraction is rising thanks to high-level parallel-programming libraries and other performance-portability techniques. To write modular and clean code, a key aspect in modern software-engineering efforts, the description of parallelism is often separated from the actual algorithm. This separation, and other aspects of the aforementioned abstraction, add penalties to the overall performance of the application. It is therefore clear what needs to be done: The compiler should exploit available information to perform optimizations that mitigate common abstraction penalties and aid the programmer's effort to write maintainable, high-performance code.

The work we present here takes place in the context of the LLVM compiler infrastructure [13]. Currently, there are various research groups and companies exploring options to enhance the existing LLVM intermediate representation (LLVM-IR) with parallelism/heterogeneity-aware optimizations. Given that there are already several proposals that show promising results [7,12,15,20], we will primarily focus on a different question, namely: *For what purposes do we require parallelism-aware extensions to the existing code base and when are more general abstractions better suited to enable the desired optimizations?*

To answer this question we will first review some of the fundamental constructs provided by parallel programming models in Sect. 2. Our focus will be on the "default representation" in the LLVM compiler toolchain and the reasons abstraction penalties occur when these constructs are used. In this context, we elaborate direct consequences of the internal representation as well as additional penalties that arise from otherwise-reasonable uses of modularity, e.g., through parallel libraries. In Sect. 3 we show how the right abstraction can enable classical compiler optimizations to mitigate abstraction penalties with only marginal changes to their implementation. The limits of existing (sequential) optimization techniques and the need for a specific representation of parallelism in the compiler is afterwards discussed in Sect. 4. We also provide a brief introduction into related work in Sect. 5 before we finish with a conclusion and remarks for future research in Sect. 6.

2   Compiler Representation of Parallel Constructs

Most compilers for non-explicitly-parallel languages are designed with sequential program execution in mind. The LLVM compiler toolchain, on which our work is build, is no exception. When parallelism is present in the input program, e.g., through directive-based language extensions like OpenMP or the (transitive) use of parallel libraries such as pthreads, a layer of indirection in the internal program representation is used to ensure the separation of parallel and sequential program parts. Without this separation, existing optimizations which were written with sequential program execution in mind, and are consequently unaware of the parallel semantics, will probably miscompile the code. While there are certainly differences in the way this code separation is implemented for parallel libraries and programming models, the general structure is always the same:

- The parallel code is placed into a separate function (or a similar abstraction).
- A runtime-library call is placed at the original location of the parallel code.
- The arguments of the call include the address of the newly-created function as well as a way to access captured variables, e.g., through pointers.

```
#pragma omp parallel for
for (int i = 0; i < N; i++)
{/* Use i, read In, write Out */}
```

(a) Generic parallel loop.

```
int v = ...
#pragma omp task
{/* Use v, read In, write Out */}
```

(b) Generic parallel task.

```
static void body_fn(int i,
        float** In, float** Out);

omp_parallel_for(0, N, &body_fn,
            &In, &Out);
```

(c) The loop in part 1a after lowering.

```
static void task_fn(int *v,
        float** In, float** Out);

task = omp_alloc_task(&task_fn, &v,
            &In, &Out);
omp_add_task(task);
```

(d) The task in part 1b after lowering.

Fig. 1. OpenMP constructs (top) and their representation in LLVM (bottom).

In Fig. 1 we illustrate this process through examples that depict the lowering of OpenMP constructs[1] as performed by LLVM's C/C++ front-end Clang. The example in Fig. 1a features a generic parallel loop. During the lowering to the LLVM intermediate representation (LLVM-IR) its body is outlined into the function body_fn and the loop is replaced by a runtime library call as shown in Fig. 1c. Depending on the capture declarations, the variables used in the parallel function are either passed "by-value" (for firstprivate) or as shown, "by-reference" (if unspecified or explicitly declared as shared). Depending on the runtime, variables might be passed directly (as shown) or in a compound object. The latter, which is commonly known from the pthread_create method but also employed by various parallel libraries, is similar to the way OpenMP tasks

---

[1] It is important to note that we use OpenMP only to improve readability. The same situation arises for various other parallel programming models and library solutions.

are handled. The lowered version of the generic task shown in Fig. 1b is illustrated in Fig. 1d. The most important conceptual difference between these two examples is the point at which the parallel code is invoked. In the first example the parallel function was directly called, while in the second example a closure is built and execution is potentially delayed.

Confronted only with a low-level encoding of parallelism through runtime-library calls, a compiler can generally not conclude anything about the interaction of the sequential code in the caller with the parallel code in the outlined function. This includes alias information on the pointer values available at the call site and also argument usage information that can be derived from the parallel function. As an example, for the latter we could assume that the compiler determines both the In pointer and its address, which might be captured by the runtime calls or the parallel functions (body_fn and task_fn) are only read. However, even if that is determined for these parallel functions, the information could not be used at the call sites, e.g., to pass the value of the In pointer directly. From a compiler perspective, the problem with the current encoding of parallelism is less related to the actual parallel execution but stems mainly from the indirection through a function pointer and the runtime-library call. While the uncertainty that is induced by this separation is also the reason we can actually compile parallel programs with compilers that are generally unaware of parallel semantics, the information that is lost will often prevent optimizations in both the caller as well as the parallel function [7].

3   Reuse of Parallelism-Unaware Optimizations

To allow classical, parallelism-unaware optimizations to transform parallel code we need to describe the semantics of the low-level parallelism encoding from a sequential standpoint. To this end, we could state that the omp_parallel_for function in Fig. 1c will invoke its third argument exactly N times, with some value between 0 and N-1 passed as i, and the addresses of the pointers In and Out. Similarly, omp_add_task would eventually result in the invocation of the "task function" stored in the closure. Even if we omit the number of invocations and the value ranges for varying arguments like i, this description already suffices to perform important transformations using only existing optimization passes.

As an example we can consider function argument promotion, an optimization that tries to communicate an argument that is only read and not captured "by-value" instead of "by-reference". In the context of OpenMP this transformation would correspond to a declaration change for that variable from shared to firstprivate. As LLVM already has an implementation for argument promotion, it would be optimal if we could reuse it in this context. Similarly, we want to reuse the analyses that propagate information derived for the arguments of a function to the call site and vise versa. The latter allows for example transformations based on the fact that a pointer argument is only passed through to the transitively invoked parallel function and there only read and not captured.

To perform these kind of optimizations with the existing code base, we introduce *transitive call sites* to LLVM. Similar to the already available, and ubiquitously used, *direct call site* abstraction, transitive call sites allow the user to query information on the callee, caller, arguments, and parameters of a call, without explicitly dealing with the underlying instruction. We currently use manual annotations to identify transitive call sites, thus we mark functions that might invoke one of their function pointer arguments later on. The annotation also describes which arguments to the initial callee are only forwarded to the transitive callee, hence not captured or otherwise inspected. Given this information, which we plan to automatically derive in the future, we can create the transitive call abstractions that relate the initial caller with the transitively called function.

While we are still in the development stage we already have two analyses passes that act on transitive call site information. The first propagates information on the parameters to transitive call sites. If all call sites are known, the second analysis will propagate globally veritable information from arguments to the corresponding parameters in the callee. In addition, we also enabled argument promotion to work with transitive call sites. This change required us to modify less than 50 lines of code, thus less than 5% of the total size.

Even with this minimal investment we already achieve speedups similar to the ones presented by Doerfert and Finkel [7], thus more than 10% improvement for the cfd and srad benchmark from the Rodinia suite [5].

While our initial results are already promising and we strongly believe other existing interprocedural optimizations can be similarly easy generalized to transitive call sites, there still is the closure abstraction that has to be overcome. In fact, most parallel runtimes employ at least argument aggregation, e.g., as known from `pthread_create` function. For lowered OpenMP tasks (ref. Fig. 1d) the closure even contains the parallel function pointer. To cope with these additional complications we are looking into different possible extensions of our work, including interprocedural memory tracking.

4   The Need for Parallelism-Awareness

Classically, compilers are written with a sequential execution model in mind. If we want to reuse existing analysis and optimization capabilities for parallel programs, we therefore have to rephrase our problems to match the original sequential mindset. While this is certainly possible for many low-level optimizations, this approach is infeasible for transformations that have to explicitly deal with the parallel semantic. Thus, if we want the compiler to optimize parallel task granularity, eliminate explicit and implicit barriers, or determine cutoff values for parallel execution, we will need to introduce new analyses and transformations.

Most of the currently ongoing work in this area (that we are aware of) is in part considering new optimizations to explicitly alter parallel program execution. However, this effort is often mixed with concerns about the reuse of existing scalar analyses and transformations through the embedding of parallel code into the sequential CFG [12,15,20]. While this is can certainly lead to good solutions, they might be more complex and less focused on their main task, namely to perform explicit parallelism-aware transformations. Especially if we assume we can continue to introduce abstractions that allow the reuse of existing scalar optimizations for parallel programs, it seems non-essential to keep such "reuse" as a requirement in the design of a parallelism-aware compiler extension.

Going forward, we will explore how these ideas can be employed in the heterogeneous setting. Currently, for example, when Clang targets GPUs using OpenMP offloading, the frontend itself decides on the code-generation strategy and generates multiple LLVM modules at this early stage in the pipeline (a module for the host code and modules for each accelerator target). So-called "late outlining" approaches have been discussed that will delay this module splitting and allow for compiler optimizations to take place across the host/accelerator boundary prior to that point. These may be important because, for example, deciding how to map OpenMP code onto a GPU kernel might depend on what OpenMP features are actually used in that kernel (and that may not be known until after inlining and/or other inter-procedural analyses, plus analysis-enabling optimizations, are employed). How to best adapt the compiler's internal representation to enable this kind of functionality is yet unknown.

5   Related Work

Various techniques have been proposed to enable compiler optimizations for parallel programs. Most of them involve some native embedding of parallelism that allows or simplifies the use of existing transformations [11,12,15, 16,18–21]. In addition, there is a vast body of research on explicitly parallelism-aware optimizations [1–3,7,9,14].

In contrast to these efforts, we put our focus on simple abstractions that facilitate the reuse of existing analyses and optimizations. We believe that such abstractions are, when applicable, superior to most parallelism-representation schemes. We base this assessment on the required implementation effort for the already proposed approaches, but also the fact that any change to the compiler's internal program representation induces a non-trivial cost as potential interactions with existing analysis and transformation have to be checked.

6   Conclusion and Future Work

We believe our initial result show that certain optimizations for parallel programs are well within reach of a parallelism-unaware compiler. We will continue to explore the use of transitive call sites and we also plan to investigate new abstractions to facilitate the optimization of scalar and parallel programs alike.

Since our work is still in a prototype state, we refrained from a dedicated evaluation. However, our initial results for the cfd and srad benchmark are already on a par with the improvements reported by Doerfert and Finkel [7]. We consequently believe that new abstractions, and increased use of the existing one, will eventually lead to similar results on various benchmarks.

To facilitate the adaption of this work, and to create an incentive for further refinement, we already proposed parts of our implementation to the LLVM community. While a verdict on the integration was not yet reached, we hope that our minimal intrusive proposal will foster the development of optimizations that cross the current optimization barrier between sequential and parallel code.

Acknowledgments. This research was supported by the Exascale Computing Project (17-SC-20-SC), a collaborative effort of two U.S. Department of Energy organizations (Office of Science and the National Nuclear Security Administration) responsible for the planning and preparation of a capable exascale ecosystem, including software, applications, hardware, advanced system engineering, and early testbed platforms, in support of the nation's exascale computing imperative.

References

1. Agarwal, S., Barik, R., Sarkar, V., Shyamasundar, R.K.: May-happen-in-parallel analysis of X10 programs. In: Proceedings of the 12th ACM SIGPLAN Symposium on Principles and Practice of Parallel Programming, PPOPP 2007, San Jose, California, USA, 14–17 March 2007, pp. 183–193 (2007). https://doi.org/10.1145/1229428.1229471
2. Barik, R., Sarkar, V.: Interprocedural load elimination for dynamic optimization of parallel programs. In: PACT 2009, Proceedings of the 18th International Conference on Parallel Architectures and Compilation Techniques, Raleigh, North Carolina, USA, 12–16 September 2009, pp. 41–52 (2009). https://doi.org/10.1109/PACT.2009.32
3. Barik, R., Zhao, J., Sarkar, V.: Interprocedural strength reduction of critical sections in explicitly-parallel programs. In: Proceedings of the 22nd International Conference on Parallel Architectures and Compilation Techniques, Edinburgh, UK, 7–11 September 2013, pp. 29–40 (2013). https://doi.org/10.1109/PACT.2013.6618801
4. Bell, N., Hoberock, J.: Thrust: a productivity-oriented library for CUDA. In: GPU Computing Gems Jade Edition, pp. 359–371. Elsevier (2011)
5. Che, S., et al.: Rodinia: a benchmark suite for heterogeneous computing. In: Proceedings of the 2009 IEEE International Symposium on Workload Characterization, IISWC 2009, Austin, TX, USA, 4–6 October 2009, pp. 44–54 (2009). https://doi.org/10.1109/IISWC.2009.5306797
6. Dagum, L., Menon, R.: Openmp: an industry standard API for shared-memory programming. IEEE Comput. Sci. Eng. **5**(1), 46–55 (1998)
7. Doerfert, J., Finkel, H.: Compiler Optimizations for OpenMP. In: Proceedings of Evolving OpenMP for Evolving Architectures - 14th International Workshop on OpenMP, IWOMP 2018, Barcelona, Spain, 26–28 September 2018, pp. 113–127 (2018). https://doi.org/10.1007/978-3-319-98521-3_8
8. Edwards, H.C., Trott, C.R., Sunderland, D.: Kokkos: enabling manycore performance portability through polymorphic memory access patterns. J. Parallel Distrib. Comput. **74**(12), 3202–3216 (2014)
9. Grunwald, D., Srinivasan, H.: Data flow equations for explicitly parallel programs. In: Proceedings of the Fourth ACM SIGPLAN Symposium on Principles and Practice of Parallel Programming (PPOPP), San Diego, California, USA, 19–22 May 1993, pp. 159–168 (1993). https://doi.org/10.1145/155332.155349

10. Hornung, R.D., Keasler, J.A.: The raja portability layer: overview and status. Technical report, Lawrence Livermore National Laboratory (LLNL), Livermore, CA, USA (2014)
11. Jordan, H., Pellegrini, S., Thoman, P., Kofler, K., Fahringer, T.: INSPIRE: the insieme parallel intermediate representation. In: Proceedings of the 22nd International Conference on Parallel Architectures and Compilation Techniques, Edinburgh, UK, 7–11 September 2013, pp. 7–17 (2013). https://doi.org/10.1109/PACT. 2013.6618799
12. Khaldi, D., Jouvelot, P., Irigoin, F., Ancourt, C., Chapman, B.M.: LLVM parallel intermediate representation: design and evaluation using OpenSHMEM communications. In: Proceedings of the Second Workshop on the LLVM Compiler Infrastructure in HPC, LLVM 2015, Austin, Texas, USA, 15 November 2015, pp. 2:1–2:8 (2015). https://doi.org/10.1145/2833157.2833158
13. Lattner, C., Adve, V.S.: LLVM: a compilation framework for lifelong program analysis & transformation. In: 2nd IEEE/ACM International Symposium on Code Generation and Optimization (CGO 2004), San Jose, CA, USA, 20–24 March 2004, pp. 75–88 (2004). https://doi.org/10.1109/CGO.2004.1281665
14. Moll, S., Doerfert, J., Hack, S.: Input space splitting for OpenCL. In: Proceedings of the 25th International Conference on Compiler Construction, CC 2016, Barcelona, Spain, 12–18 March 2016, pp. 251–260 (2016). https://doi.org/10.1145/2892208. 2892217
15. Schardl, T.B., Moses, W.S., Leiserson, C.E.: Tapir: embedding fork-join parallelism into LLVM's intermediate representation. In: Proceedings of the 22nd ACM SIGPLAN Symposium on Principles and Practice of Parallel Programming, Austin, TX, USA, 4–8 February 2017, pp. 249–265 (2017). http://dl.acm.org/citation.cfm? id=3018758
16. Stelle, G., Moses, W.S., Olivier, S.L., McCormick, P.: OpenMPIR: implementing OpenMP tasks with Tapir. In: Proceedings of the Fourth Workshop on the LLVM Compiler Infrastructure in HPC, LLVM-HPC@SC 2017, Denver, CO, USA, 13 November 2017, pp. 3:1–3:12 (2017). https://doi.org/10.1145/3148173.3148186
17. Stone, J.E., Gohara, D., Shi, G.: OpenCL: a parallel programming standard for heterogeneous computing systems. Comput. Sci. Eng. 12(3), 66–73 (2010). https:// doi.org/10.1109/MCSE.2010.69
18. Tian, X., Girkar, M., Bik, A.J.C., Saito, H.: Practical compiler techniques on efficient multithreaded code generation for OpenMP programs. Comput. J. 48(5), 588–601 (2005). https://doi.org/10.1093/comjnl/bxh109
19. Tian, X., Girkar, M., Shah, S., Armstrong, D., Su, E., Petersen, P.: Compiler and runtime support for running OpenMP programs on Pentium-and Itanium-architectures. In: Eighth International Workshop on High-Level Parallel Programming Models and Supportive Environments (HIPS 2003), Nice, France, 22–22 April 2003, pp. 47–55 (2003). https://doi.org/10.1109/HIPS.2003.1196494
20. Tian, X., et al.: LLVM framework and IR extensions for parallelization, SIMD vectorization and offloading. In: Third Workshop on the LLVM Compiler Infrastructure in HPC, LLVM-HPC@SC 2016, Salt Lake City, UT, USA, 14 November 2016, pp. 21–31 (2016). https://doi.org/10.1109/LLVM-HPC.2016.008
21. Zhao, J., Sarkar, V.: Intermediate language extensions for parallelism. In: Conference on Systems, Programming, and Applications: Software for Humanity, SPLASH 2011, Proceedings of the Compilation of the Co-located Workshops, DSM 2011, TMC 2011, AGERE! 2011, AOOPES 2011, NEAT 2011, and VMIL 2011, Portland, OR, USA, 22–27 October 2011, pp. 329–340 (2011). https://doi.org/10. 1145/2095050.2095103

MATE, a Unified Model for Communication-Tolerant Scientific Applications

Sergio M. Martin[1]([✉])[iD] and Scott B. Baden[1,2][iD]

[1] University of California San Diego, La Jolla, CA 92093, USA
`sergiom@eng.ucsd.edu`
[2] Lawrence Berkeley National Laboratory, Berkeley, CA 94720, USA
`baden@lbl.gov`

Abstract. We present *MATE*, a model for developing communication-tolerant scientific applications. MATE employs a combination of mechanisms to reduce or hide the cost of network and intra-node data movement. While previous approaches have been proposed to reduce both sources of communication overhead separately, the contribution of MATE is demonstrating the symbiotic effect of reducing both forms of data movement taken together. Furthermore, MATE provides these benefits within a single unified model, as opposed to hybrid (*e.g.*, *MPI+X*) approaches. We demonstrate MATE's effectiveness in reducing the cost of communication in three scientific computing motifs on up to 32k cores of the NERSC Cori Phase I supercomputer.

Keywords: Scientific computing · Communication-Tolerance · SPMD

1 Introduction

The advent of many-core processors and the fast-approaching age of Exascale computing have rendered the challenge of developing scalable scientific applications too complex for domain-area experts to tackle without the help of an HPC expert. Of the many hurdles involved in this endeavor, coping with the ever-growing cost of communication is perhaps the most daunting as existing programming models lack adequate support. Our research tackles the two primary sources of overhead: *network communication* and *intra-node data motion*.

Reducing the cost of network communication data motion involves primarily overlapping computation with communication[1]. This technique requires a manual restructuring of a program to enable processors to continue computing sections of the code that are independent of incoming data, *e.g.*, via *split-phase* coding [26]. These modifications, however, require significant domain-specific

---

[1] Other approaches include communication reordering [27], concurrency optimizations [16], and communication avoiding algorithms [13].

© Springer Nature Switzerland AG 2019
M. Hall and H. Sundar (Eds.): LCPC 2018, LNCS 11882, pp. 120–137, 2019.
https://doi.org/10.1007/978-3-030-34627-0_10

refactoring of the source code that may prove to be impractical in large applications and will entangle application logic with implementation policy.

Reducing the cost of intra-node data motion involves replacing message exchanges among processes on the same node with communication via shared memory bypass. An optimal approach is to employ two communication models in the same application, one for inter-node communication (*e.g.,* MPI [1]) and another for intra-node communication (*e.g.,* OpenMP [2], MPI-SHM [19]). This solution poses two difficulties: (1) it entangles communication and synchronization logic, and (2) it exposes inefficiencies in the interaction between the two models (*e.g.,* threads synchronize before issuing MPI calls).

To address these shortcomings, we have developed *MATE*, a programming model that reduces both sources of communication overhead in scientific applications while requiring minimal intervention inside application source code. MATE provides hierarchical decomposition and dependency-driven semantics that support communication reducing performance programming within a single unified model. By providing a unified model, MATE exposes its communication-reducing benefits while avoiding the complexity of combining two programming interfaces. We have implemented MATE as a programming framework comprising an annotation model, a source code translator, and a runtime system library.

The rest of this paper is organized as follows: Sect. 2 introduces MATE's hierarchical decomposition and code scheduling model, Sect. 3 describes the mechanisms MATE employs to reduce the cost of communication, Sect. 4 provides implementation details, Sect. 5 presents our experimental results, Sect. 6 discusses previous and related work, and Sect. 7 discusses conclusions and future research directions.

2   The MATE Model

The MATE model re-interprets an application by introducing (1) a *hierarchical rank decomposition*, and (2) a *code scheduling* logic. Together, these two features enable the programmer to alter program semantics to reduce the cost of communication. To explain our model, we use a stencil method example that computes the solution to a partial differential equation on a n-dimensional grid. The application splits the grid into rectangular subgrids, each assigned to a different rank. Figure 1 (top) shows the pseudo-code representation for the solver.

Each rank obtains a unique rank identifier and rank count (*lines 1–2*), and then iterate (*line 4*) on the solution by: (*line 5*) issuing receive requests for boundary cells, (*line 6*) sweeping the subgrid with a stencil operator and swapping grid pointers, (*line 7*) packing non-contiguous boundary cells, (*line 8*) sending buffered data to neighbor ranks, (*line 9*) waiting for communication to finish, and (*line 10*) unpacking boundary cells into non-contiguous ghost cells.

MATE supports a hierarchical model with multiple levels of workload decomposition and locality. At the first level, MATE distributes the workload onto a set of processes. A *MATE Process* represents a grouping of ranks that share a common *virtual address* space. At the second level, each process is further distributed among multiple local *MATE Ranks*. Unlike MPI ranks, MATE ranks

```
1   MPI_Comm_size(MPI_COMM_WORLD, &nRanks);
2   MPI_Comm_rank(MPI_COMM_WORLD, &myRank);
3
4   for (int i = 0; i < Iterations; i++) {
5     for (n in Neighbors) MPI_Irecv(recvBuf(n)←n);
6     Compute_and_Swap();
7     for (n in Neighbors) MPI_Pack(bCells→sendBuf(n));
8     for (n in Neighbors) MPI_Isend(sendBuf(n)→n);
9     MPI_Waitall(MPIRequests);
10    for (n in Neighbors) MPI_Unpack(gCells←recvBuf(n));
11  }
```

```
1   Mate_local_rank_id(&localRankId);
2   Mate_global_process_id(&myProcessId);
3   Mate_local_rank_count(&localRankCount);
4   Mate_global_process_count(&globalProcessCount);
5
6   for(n in Neighbors) if(Mate_isLocal(n)) Mate_AddLocalNeighbor(n);
7
8   #pragma mate graph
9   for(int i = 0; i < Iterations; i++) {
10    #pragma mate region(request) depends(unpack*)
11      for(n in Neighbors) if(!Mate_isLocal(n)) MPI_Irecv(recvBuf(n)←n);
12    #pragma mate region(compute) depends(pack*, unpack*, compute*@)
13      Compute_and_Swap();
14    #pragma mate region(pack) depends(compute, send*)
15      for(n in Neighbors) if(!Mate_isLocal(n)) MPI_Pack(bCells→sndBuf(n));
16    #pragma mate region(send) depends(pack)
17      for(n in Neighbors) if(!Mate_isLocal(n)) MPI_Isend(sendBuf(n)→n);
18    #pragma mate region(unpack) depends(compute, request)
19      for(n in Neighbors) if(!Mate_isLocal(n)) MPI_Unpack(gCells←rcvBuf(n));
20  }
```

Fig. 1. Simplified pseudo-code of (*top*) a structured grid stencil solver, and (*bottom*) the same solver with added MATE directives and API calls.

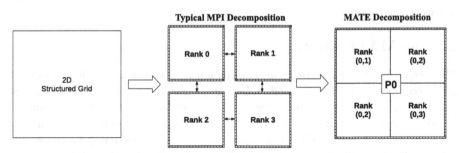

Fig. 2. MPI vs. MATE's decomposition of a 2D grid on 4 cores.

living in the same MATE process share the same address space and can communicate through shared memory.

To identify a rank, MATE uses a *process-level* and *local-level* identifier pair, as shown in Fig. 2. That is, a MATE rank is identified by combining its parent MATE process identifier, and a unique local identifier within the process. Figure 1 (*bottom*) shows how to query a rank's local id (*line 1*) and (*line 2*) process id, (*line 3*) the local rank count, and (*line 4*) the MATE process count.

Under the MATE model, local ranks communicate by either (1) making direct memory to memory copies, or (2) by exchanging local pointers to their data. Thus, in the MATE version of our example, ranks belonging to the same process do not exchange data via messages since they can communicate through shared memory. MATE provides a guard, *Mate_isLocal()*, to test rank locality. In our example (*lines 11, 15, 17, 19*), ranks exchange data only if the neighboring rank belongs to a different MATE process (*i.e. Mate_isLocal(n)* returns *false*). The test for locality compares the process id's of the caller rank and the *n* rank.

MATE supports a third level of decomposition that is orthogonal to the process-rank organization, called *regions*. MATE regions split a program into a logical grouping of contiguous code statements. MATE schedules regions independently, guided by a dependency graph defined statically by the programmer via *#pragma mate region (name)* directives. Lines *10–19* show how MATE directives split the original code into separate regions. Figure 3 shows the dependency graph corresponding to the code in Fig. 1 (*bottom*).

Programmers define dependencies among regions explicitly by appending a *depends(region1, region2,...)* clause. Every region name included in the *depends* clause will create a new region-to-region dependency. As in traditional dataflow [10,18], the order in which regions execute is determined by the flow of data in a dependency graph. A rank will not execute the statements enclosed by a *region* directive until it has previously executed all the regions in the *depends* clause. For example, the *send* (line *16*) region will not execute until after executing the *pack* region. The statements inside a region will execute in order.

MATE annotations enable programmers to express cross-iteration dependencies inside a *for* loop, by appending the '***' modifier to regions in the *depends* clause. This modifier tells the scheduler that the dependency will be satisfied if the region has executed in the previous iteration. In our example (*line 10*), the *request* region will not issue new MPI requests until the *unpack* region from the previous iteration has finished unpacking the receive buffers. Wherever the '***' is not specified, then the dependency refers to the current iteration. Lastly, this modifier is ignored during the first iteration to avoid deadlocks.

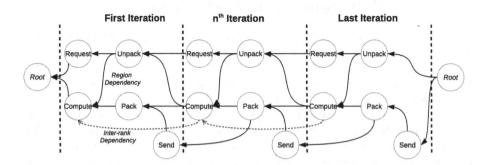

Fig. 3. Code Region Dependency from the example in Fig. 1 (*bottom*). Solid arrows represent region dependencies and dotted arrows represent inter-rank dependencies

Since MATE's hierarchical model enables the use of shared memory, MATE applications require means for local synchronization. For this purpose, our model exposes *inter-rank* dependencies, in which a code region of one given task depends upon the execution of a code region from another local rank. Programmers define inter-rank dependencies by appending a '@' modifier to a region in the *depends* clause. This modifier instructs the runtime system that all neighbor ranks should execute the depended region before the current rank can execute this region. Ranks call the *Mate_AddLocalNeighbor(localId)* function (*line 6*), to indicate which other local ranks are also their neighbors. This distinction is important since not all local ranks are neighbors (*i.e.* share a common boundary).

In our example, (*line 12*), the *compute* region will not execute until the *compute* region from all neighbor ranks have finished, guaranteeing that no *read-after-write* violations will occur by updating boundary data that has not yet been used by neighbors in the previous iteration.

Communication requests (*e.g., MPI_Irecv, MPI_Isend*) issued during the execution of a region need to complete before dependent regions are issued. In our example, all the *MPI_Irecv* requests instantiated during the execution of *request* will have finished before MATE issues the *unpack* region for execution.

MATE supports incremental development where only part of the application need be annotated. To execute un-annotated code, MATE implicitly defines a *root* region that represents the whole program outside user-defined regions. Upon finding a *#pragma mate graph* directive, the *root* region yields execution until all regions inside the graph finish, and then resumes execution.

As mentioned previously, MATE enables the program to reorder code blocks, altering program semantics. The programmer is responsible for ensuring that their annotations preserve correctness. For example, incorrect dependency annotations could induce a deadlock or execute code using stale data. Furthermore, to avoid incorrect behavior, annotated *for* loop iterators (*e.g., i*) should only be accessed at the *for*'s increment ($i++$). MATE does not currently support nested *graph* blocks. Lastly, reordering could affect numerical results, for example, in computing convergence criteria.

3   Communication-Reducing Mechanisms

To reduce the cost of network and intra-node communication, MATE employs a combination of mechanisms. *Domain overdecomposition* [21] or *virtualization* [23] is a well-known technique for hiding the cost of network communication by overlapping computation with communication. An overdecomposed SPMD application splits the workload into a number of ranks larger than the number of cores, pipelining the execution of a rank while another waits for communication.

Although the MPI specification provides few restrictions on how an MPI library is implemented, its most widely used implementations [5–9] instantiate each rank as a separate process. Since these libraries delegate process scheduling to the operating system (which is unaware of communication), overdecomposition will cause destructive interference for core usage. Therefore, MPI applications run best when they employ no more processes than available cores.

Figure 5 (*top*) shows the execution of a typical MPI iterative solver under the *Bulk-Synchronous model* [38], where every core alternates between periods of performing actual computation, and waiting periods. Since they do not overlap communication with computation, these solvers incur the full cost of communication. On the other hand, user-level runtime systems, such as MATE, can instantiate more ranks while avoiding destructive interference since they do not depend on the OS scheduler. Figure 4 (*top*) shows the 2D grid from Fig. 2 overdecomposed into 16 subgrids. This configuration represents an *overdecomposition factor* of four, assuming four available cores. Figure 5 (*Middle*) shows how MATE swaps ranks as they suspend to wait for data, achieving overlap.

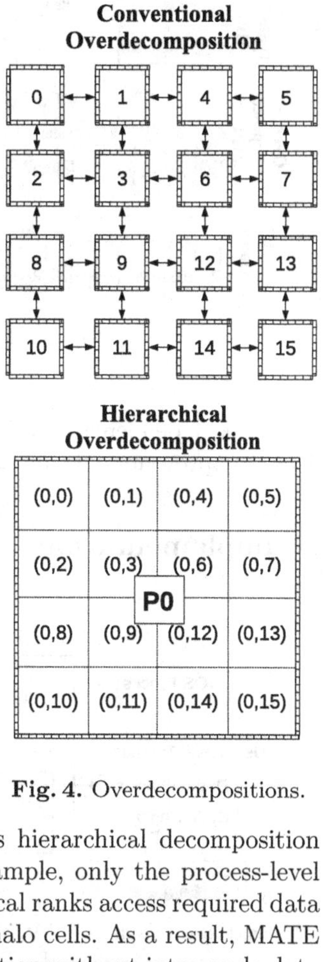

Although effective in overlapping communication and computation, overdecomposition leads to an increase in internal data motion overhead due to a higher surface-to-volume ratio in exchange buffers, as shown in Fig. 4 (*top*). This increase in boundary surface exacerbates both data motion and packing overhead costs and can reverse the benefits obtained from overlap. We show these overheads as spurious computation time.

Fig. 4. Overdecompositions.

The MATE model avoids this problem via its hierarchical decomposition model as illustrated in Fig. 4 (*bottom*). In the example, only the process-level boundary requires exchanging, while neighboring local ranks access required data via shared memory without the need to exchange halo cells. As a result, MATE enables applications to benefit from overdecomposition without intra-node data copying overheads, as shown in Fig. 5 (*bottom*). Furthermore, cores can execute any of the 16 ranks in the process at any given time, maximizing concurrency.

MATE regions enable concurrency within a rank by dividing it into groups of code statements that execute in a partial order. Regions increase the amount of available parallelism among computation and communication operations. This principle is similar to that used in *instruction-level-parallel* processors [37], in which instructions execute as sub-instructions that can be pipelined in several execution ports simultaneously, and also to large grain dataflow [11].

MATE's code region semantics provide an additional optimization: they enable local tasks to use lightweight synchronization. Since neighboring local tasks can execute on the same address space without exchanging messages, they require a synchronization mechanism to prevent them from violating loop-carried dependencies on their boundary elements. Whereas a process-wide barrier would achieve this effect, it would also reduce opportunities for overlap. However, with

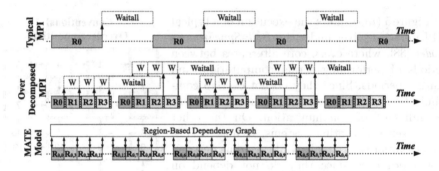

Fig. 5. Hypothetical core usage timelines.

inter-rank dependencies, MATE exposes a fine-grained synchronization mechanism that prevents data hazards, maximizing concurrency among local ranks.

4   Implementation

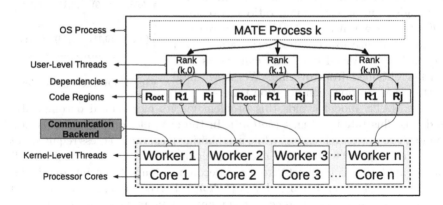

Fig. 6. Decomposition model and implementation of a MATE process.

MATE applications execute as a set of processes distributed across the system. A MATE process contains (1) a pool of MATE regions, (2) a set of local MATE ranks, and (3) a pool of MATE workers, as shown in Fig. 6.

A MATE Region is the sole atomic scheduling unit in MATE. Regions can exist in three possible states: *wait*, *ready*, or *exec*. A region is in the *wait* state if at least one of its dependencies is unsatisfied. Once all of its dependencies are satisfied, it transitions to the *ready* state, and then to *exec* during execution. We developed a source-to-source translator, using the ROSE compiler framework [22], to parse MATE annotations and inject calls to the MATE runtime system's

API to create regions and dependencies dynamically and to provide scheduling logic to support out-of-order region execution.

A MATE Rank is a C++ object comprising an array of MATE regions, and one *user-level thread*, re-entrant functions that can yield/resume at any point. Once a rank resumes execution, it will not yield until all its *ready* regions have executed. Conversely, a MATE rank will not execute until at least one of its regions is ready. Although several regions in a given rank may be ready, only one of them can execute at a time to preserve stack integrity.

MATE Workers are kernel-level threads mapped to a single processor core whose goal is to execute MATE ranks. A MATE worker will execute a rank by resuming its user-level thread, only if at least one of its regions is in the *ready* state. After the rank yields execution, a MATE worker will search for the next available rank. In case no ranks are available, the worker polls for incoming message requests. Only one MATE worker can poll MPI requests at any given time to prevent concurrency hazards.

To provide communication-aware scheduling, MATE intercepts communication requests and performs two operations: (1) it issues an MPI request with encoded MATE local/process ids in the *tag* field, and (2) creates a new dependency between the request and every region that depends on the currently executing region. This linkage guarantees that dependent regions will wait until requests have finished before becoming *ready*.

MATE currently supports latency hiding only for 2-sided operations. While many MPI collectives are supported, they are not optimized for overlap, as they do not contribute a significant overhead in our test cases. However, it is possible to implement overlap-enabled collectives that take advantage of MATE for applications with frequent collective calls as future research. Though MATE does not currently support user-defined MPI groups and communicators, we do not rule out their implementation. Finally, our translator can only process annotations from C/C++ source. However, since the MATE model is language-neutral, we could support other languages (ROSE supports Fortran).

5   Experimental Results

For our computational testbed, we used *Cori*, a Cray XC40 supercomputer [3] located at the *National Energy Research Scientific Computing Center* (NERSC) [31]. We used the Cori Phase I partition, comprising 2,388 compute nodes, each equipped with two sockets, each populated with a 2.3 GHz 16-core Intel Xeon E5-2698v3 "Haswell" processor and 128 GB of DRAM. We used Cray's PrgEnv-intel/6.0.4 and cray-mpich/7.7.0 modules and the Intel compiler version 18.0.1.163 with -O3 optimization (includes auto-vectorization). To ensure proper optimizations for the Haswell CPU, we employed the craype-haswell and craype-hugepages2M modules. Other environment modules and settings were the NERSC default. None of our test cases benefit from hyperthreading.

5.1 Test Case I: Jacobi3D

Our first test case is *Jacobi3D*, a stencil method that
solves the 3D Poisson equation subject to Dirich-
let boundary conditions using Jacobi's method. The
computation iterates over a grid using a 13-point central difference [39] stencil that updates each element
of the grid with the average of its a central point
and 4 points per axis in a 2-point deep straight line
(see Fig. 7).

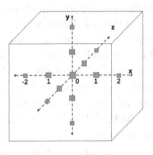

Fig. 7. 13-Point stencil.

We study six variants of the Jacobi3D solver: (1)
Flat-MPI establishes the performance baseline and
does not attempt to overlap communication with
computation. We optimized this code for cache locality with a 2D blocking over
its non-contiguous Y and Z axes. (2) *Olap-MPI* improves the baseline code with
a split-phase strategy that divides the rank's grid into smaller tiles. As soon as
it finishes computing a tile, *Olap-MPI* initiates its boundary exchange requests
and continues to the next tile, overlapping communication with computation. (3)
MPI+OpenMP provides a 2-level decomposition (similar to MATE's) in which
multiple OpenMP threads share the work assigned to a single process, and thus
do not explicitly move data on-node but does not overlap communication with
computation. (4) *OD-Only* represents MATE with overdecomposition as the sole
mechanism for hiding the cost of communication and does not use a hierarchical
decomposition. (5) *Toucan* employs hierarchical overdecomposition but anno-
tates the code with the fixed 3-region syntax prescribed in *Toucan* Model [30]
without inter-rank dependencies. (6) The *MATE* variant applies all the optimizations described in Sect. 2 and uses the region graph from Fig. 3.

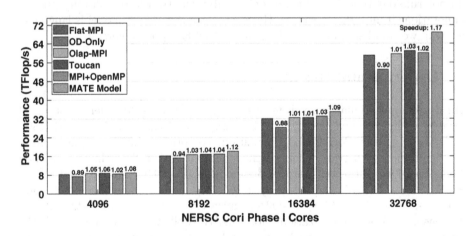

Fig. 8. Strong Scaling results for Jacobi3D on 128 to 1024 nodes of Cori Phase I. The
number above each bar represents the speedup relative to the baseline variant.

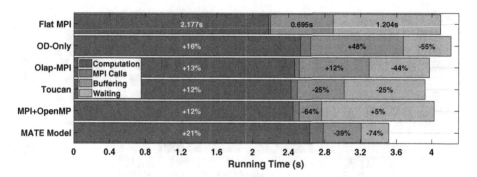

Fig. 9. Execution breakdown for Jacobi3D on 32768 cores.

We performed a strong scaling study over a range of 128 to 1024 nodes (4K to 32K cores; 43% of all available nodes), with 100 solver iterations on a grid of $n = 4096^3$ cells. At 512 nodes, the grid consumes 1.3% of node memory per variable, which is representative of a structured adaptive mesh solver for solving combustion problems[2]. We ran each variant three times (we measured $\leq 1\%$ variation in running time between runs) and report the best outcome. MPI variants ran with one process per core. We determined experimentally that the best configuration for MPI+OpenMP was 4 processes × 8 threads per node. For MATE variants, we used 4 processes × 8 threads × 64 ranks per node. Figure 8 shows the results of our study in *TFlop/s*. The *MATE* variant was able to outperform all the variants, yielding a 1.17x speedup on 32768 cores.

To evaluate how each variant affects the solver's performance, we analyzed their mean running time breakdown on 1024 nodes. Figure 9 shows this breakdown where: *Computation* represents the solver kernel time; *MPI Calls* is time spent issuing *MPI* requests; *Buffering* is the time spent packing/unpacking buffers, and; *Waiting* is the time spent waiting on network communication. We indicate time taken per operation for the base *Flat-MPI* variant, and the % of time differential of each variant, compared to *Flat-MPI*.

Results show that MATE was able to reduce a large amount of the network communication (74%) on 32768 cores, compared to *Flat-MPI*. We observed similar communication reductions at smaller scales. We also see that, while the overdecomposition only (*OD-Only*) variant reduces 55% of network communication time, its benefits diminish due to a notable increase (48%) in the costs of intra-node data motion and thus fails to produce any speedup, illustrating the importance of employing a hierarchical model. On the other hand, the strategy used in *Olap-MPI* succeeded in reducing the communication time with a smaller impact on its intra-node data motion costs.

All our variants suffered an increase in computation time. This increase comes from a loss in cache efficiency due to lack of prefetching. In the Flat-MPI variant, the side effect of buffer unpacking is to prefetch grid data before

---

[2] Sam Williams, private conversation, 2018.

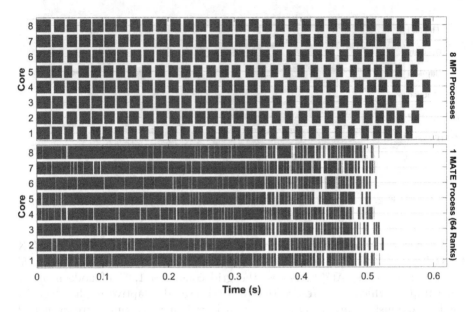

Fig. 10. Core Timelines. **(Top)** Flat-MPI (8 Ranks), **(Bottom)** MATE (64 Ranks). (Color figure online)

executing the kernel, which will help speed it up. In turn, the kernel smoother will improve cache locality of buffer packing. We used the *Performance Application Programming Interface* (PAPI) [36] to activate hardware counters in the Haswell processor during the main loop of the solver and found that absolute number of L2 and L3 cache misses increased by 8% in the computational kernel due when we disabled packing/unpacking operations.

Notably, *MATE* suffered from a higher increase in computation costs (21%). We attribute this effect to a disruption of cache locality from dividing the grid into smaller subgrids. Every time a rank resumes, it reloads its data back into cache lines, producing an excess in cache misses. This effect also explains why buffer packing cost in MPI+OpenMP shrinks by a more significant amount than MATE: 64% vs. 39%.

Threading variants suffer from an additional cost from MPI call overheads. In MATE, workers serialize the injection of MPI messages due to threading concurrency limitations in the Cray-MPI library, producing periods of busy-waiting that extend the rank's occupancy in the core. The *MPI+OpenMP* variant suffers from this limitation as well as it also relies on multi-threading but to a lesser extent since it does not employ overdecomposition. These results demonstrate that MATE can improve performance by hiding communication, even though there is a loss of cache locality in computation and message serialization.

To gain insight into why the MATE variant was able to hide a large portion of the network communication time, we plotted the activity of 8 cores during the execution of a short run (30 iterations). Figure 10 shows core usage timelines of the (*top*) Flat MPI and (*bottom*) MATE variants at 1024 nodes (32768 cores). These timelines show how cores fluctuate between busy time executing a rank (*dark blue*) and idle time waiting for network communication (*white*).

Since Flat-MPI assigns every MPI rank to an MPI process, mapped to a single core, it cannot perform any useful work while a rank is waiting. The wide white-space segments in between computation segments in the figure show that this variant suffers from the full cost of communication. On the other hand, the MATE variant keeps cores busy by executing ranks while others communicate. Indeed, the figure shows minimal white space separation between computation segments. Furthermore, since a MATE process manages a pool of 64 ranks and 8 threads, it maximizes parallelism by allowing ranks to execute in any cores.

5.2 Test Case II: Cannon's Algorithm

Cannon's algorithm [15] is a parallel algorithm for computing the product of two dense square matrices $C = A \times B$ in a series of $\sqrt{p}$ steps, where p is the number of ranks. Each rank owns a square sub-block of C and local sub-blocks of A and B. Each step rotates sub-blocks A and B along rows and columns of the 2D processor geometry and computes a partial matrix product using *dgemm* to update its local portion of C ($C+ = A \times B$), as shown in Fig. 11 (*top*).

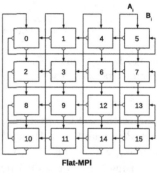

In this experiment, we show that MATE improves over a manually optimized MPI variant. We consider three code variants: the *Flat-MPI* variant establishes the performance baseline, and it does not attempt to overlap communication with computation, while; the *Olap-MPI* is a manually optimized version that overlaps communication with computation by employing additional buffers to exchange the rank's A and B submatrices for the next step while computing the current.

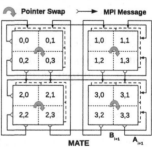

Fig. 11. Cannon variants.

The *MATE* variant adds a hierarchical decomposition to the overlapping strategy. This variant divides the input matrices into $m_0{}^2$ level 0 submatrices, and then subdivides these submatrices into $m_1{}^2$ level 1 submatrices, where $m_0{}^2$ is the number of MATE processes and $m_1{}^2$ is the number of local ranks. Local ranks declare inter-rank dependencies only with local ranks in the same row and columns. Each level 1 rank calculates a level 1 matrix multiplication and then rotates shared pointers among local neighboring ranks residing in the same level 0 submatrix, avoiding explicit intra-process data movement. This step is repeated m_0 times until the current iteration's value of C at a process-level completes.

Rank residing in the process boundary then send their level 0 part of the local A and B matrices to neighboring MATE processes (Fig. 11, *bottom*).

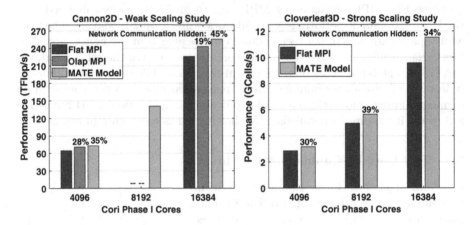

Fig. 12. Left: Cannon2D, weak scaling. **Right:** Cloverleaf3D, strong scaling results. The numbers above each bar represent % of communication hidden.

Since the 2D Cannon algorithm requires that p be a perfect square, we ran the MPI variants on 4K and 16K cores. The MATE variant provided added flexibility, via MATE's support for overdecomposition, enabling us to run on 8K cores using 2 MATE ranks per core (for 4K and 16K cores, the MATE variant ran with 4 MATE ranks per core). We performed a weak scaling study, starting with a matrix size of $n = 24576^2$. Figure 12 (*left*) shows results for 4K, 8K, and 16K cores. On 16K cores, MATE was able to reduce 45% of the communication cost on 4K cores, yielding a 1.13x speedup. MATE's results exceeded that of the manually optimized variant which yielded a 19% communication reduction.

5.3   Test Case III: Cloverleaf3D

Cloverleaf3D [4] is a Lagrangian-Eulerian hydrodynamics benchmark. It solves the compressible Euler equations on a 3D Cartesian grid using an explicit, second-order accurate stencil method. The grid is divided into volume cells containing energy, density, pressure, and velocity variables. The computation in CloverLeaf divides into different kernels that sweep over the entire grid and updates one or multiple variables based on a kernel-specific stencil.

Cloverleaf3D exchanges boundary cells at different points of the solver kernel among 26 nearest neighbors. The exchange routine uses a 3-stage approach to reaching corner neighbors. First, ranks pack and exchange boundary face information across the x-axis, including edges and corners. After unpacking the incoming x-axis face, ranks pack and exchange face information across the y-axis. This step is repeated for the z-axis face as well, allowing corner information to reach neighbors at a 3-deep Manhattan distance. Given the complexity of this code, it was not reasonable to employ an overlapping strategy manually.

Although Cloverleaf3D is programmed entirely in Fortran, we were able to apply the MATE model by manually introducing calls to the MATE runtime, instead of translation assisted by annotations. In the MATE variant, local ranks do not exchange messages. Instead, each rank copies its boundary cells onto their neighbors' ghost cell space directly (*i.e.,* via *memcpy*), avoiding message packing, unpacking and exchange costs. Although this does not avoid intra-node data motion entirely, it reduces the data motion costs considerably. Nevertheless, we limited MATE to 4 ranks per core since finer decompositions did increase buffering costs, unacceptably offsetting the benefits of improving overlap.

We performed a strong scaling study, keeping the number of elements fixed at 1024^3. We report performance as the number of cells processed per second (inverse of the *time per cell* metric provided in the original code). Figure 12 (*right*) shows results on 4K, 8K, and 16K cores. At 16K cores MATE was able to reduce communication by 34% and yielded a 1.19x speedup, with similar results at smaller scales. This result shows that MATE, through minimal modifications, can reduce the cost of communication even in applications that are too complex for manual restructuring.

6   Related Work

The MATE model is the successor of our previous project, *Toucan* [30]. Like MATE, Toucan relies on overdecomposition and a dependency graph-driven task parallel program. However, MATE makes three significant contributions. First, it generalizes Toucan's dependence model. Whereas Toucan provides a fixed set of region types, MATE admits user-defined region types. Second, MATE introduces a hierarchical locality-based decomposition model, which substantially enhances the benefit of overdecomposition. Third, MATE adds inter-rank dependencies, which enable efficient local synchronization without process-wide barriers that impede the advance of ranks that are otherwise ready to continue.

Many parallel programming models have been proposed to reduce the cost of communication. Source-to-source translation, as employed in Toucan and MATE, is also used in *Bamboo* [32]. Although Bamboo supports dependency-driven execution, it employs static inlining which causes code bloating and does not support recursive code nor a hierarchical decomposition.

In *FPMPI* [25], MPI ranks run as user-level threads (ULT), rather than OS processes. By using ULTs, ranks are no longer tied to the kernel scheduler and are instead scheduled by a user-level runtime system that enables overdecomposition. *MPI+ULT* models [14,28] describe how these mechanisms can be used to overlap communication with computation. *AMPI* [20] is implemented on top of Charm++ [24] which uses overdecomposition (virtualization) to support load balancing. Our experiments using AMPI on stencil methods revealed that it was unable to hide communication. Furthermore, none of these approaches combine overdecomposition with a locality-based decomposition model which we have found beneficial in hiding communication.

Hybrid MPI models, *aka "MPI+X"*, use MPI to handle network communication, and then drop into a threading or shared memory library to avoid moving data explicitly on-node. The widely used *MPI+OpenMP* [17] approach offers the benefits of shared memory but requires a meticulous interaction between both communication models. Additionally, programmers need to be careful when using local synchronization mechanisms (*e.g.*, omp barrier) that can stall threads that are otherwise ready to continue, punishing performance. Another approach, the *MPI+MPI* [19] model, extends the MPI interface with shared memory capabilities that facilitate local shared memory access through shared objects (called *windows*), which preserve portability since only the MPI interface is required. MATE, on the other hand, enables shared memory among local ranks with a simple interface. Similarly, work has been performed to instantiate MPI ranks themselves as kernel-level threads, providing native shared memory access [35].

MPI/SMPSs [29] integrates the MPI model with *SMPSs* [34], a task-based dependency model now used in *OpenMP Tasking* [33]. MPI/SMPSs provides a directive-based interface to describe input/output dependencies across functions that can contain MPI code. MATE's interface is similar: programmers can use these dependencies to build a valid MPI program that executes based on data/execution dependencies. However, there is no support for overdecomposition; the programmer has to implement this capability themselves.

7   Conclusions

We introduced MATE, a new approach to developing distributed scientific applications that integrates communication-reducing mechanisms into a single, unified model, providing a benefit that is greater than the sum of the parts. MATE supports hierarchical decomposition and locality models that enable efficient overdecomposition, a technique that enhances communication/computation overlap, while preventing an increase in (and even reducing) intra-node data motion without the need for a hybrid execution model. Results with two stencil methods and with matrix-matrix multiplication show that MATE can realize a noticeable reduction in communication cost on large-scale experiments. MATE's ability to hide network communication with the help of overdecomposition, while managing intra-node data motion costs, provides a novel way to manage excessive communication costs on upcoming exascale systems. Future research directions include: extending the MATE model to handle heterogeneous systems (*e.g.*, GPU) and PGAS languages (*e.g.*, UPC++ [12]).

Acknowledgments. This research was supported by the Advanced Scientific Computing Research office of the U.S. Department of Energy under contracts No. DE-FC02-12ER26118 and DE-FG02-88ER25053. It was also supported in part by the Fulbright Foreign Student Program grant from the U.S. Department of State. Scott Baden dedicates his contributions to this paper to the memory of William Miles Tubbiola (1934–2018).

References

1. https://www.mpi-forum.org/
2. https://www.openmp.org/
3. http://www.nersc.gov/users/computational-systems/cori/configuration/
4. http://uk-mac.github.io/CloverLeaf3D/
5. Cray MPI. https://pubs.cray.com/
6. Intel MPI library. https://software.intel.com/en-us/intel-mpi-library
7. MPICH library. http://www.mpich.org/
8. MVAPICH library. http://mvapich.cse.ohio-state.edu/
9. Open MPI library. https://www.open-mpi.org/
10. Arvind, K., Nikhil, R.S.: Executing a program on the MIT tagged-token dataflow architecture. IEEE Trans. Comput. **39**(3), 300–318 (1990). https://doi.org/10.1109/12.48862
11. Babb, R.G.: Parallel processing with large-grain data flow technique. Computer **17**(7), 55–61 (1984)
12. Bachan, J., et al.: The UPC++ PGAS library for exascale computing: extended abstract. In: PAW17: Second Annual PGAS Applications Workshop, p. 4. ACM, New York, 12–17 November 2017. https://doi.org/10.1145/3144779.3169108
13. Ballard, G., Carson, E., Demmel, J., Hoemmen, M., Knight, N., Schwartz, O.: Communication lower bounds and optimal algorithms for numerical linear algebra. Acta Numerica **23**, 1–155 (2014)
14. Barrett, R.F., Stark, D.T., Vaughan, C.T., Grant, R.E., Olivier, S.L., Pedretti, K.T.: Toward an evolutionary task parallel integrated MPI + X programming model. In: Proceedings of the Sixth International Workshop on Programming Models and Applications for Multicores and Manycores, PMAM 2015, pp. 30–39. ACM, New York (2015). https://doi.org/10.1145/2712386.2712388
15. Cannon, L.E.: A Cellular computer to implement the Kalman filter algorithm. Ph.D. thesis, Bozeman, MT, USA (1969). aAI7010025
16. Chaimov, N., Ibrahim, K.Z., Williams, S., Iancu, C.: Exploiting communication concurrency on high performance computing systems. In: Proceedings of the Sixth International Workshop on Programming Models and Applications for Multicores and Manycores, PMAM 2015, pp. 132–143. ACM, New York (2015). https://doi.org/10.1145/2712386.2712394
17. Debudaj-Grabysz, A., Rabenseifner, R.: Nesting OpenMP in MPI to implement a hybrid communication method of parallel simulated annealing on a cluster of SMP nodes. In: Di Martino, B., Kranzlmüller, D., Dongarra, J. (eds.) EuroPVM/MPI 2005. LNCS, vol. 3666, pp. 18–27. Springer, Heidelberg (2005). https://doi.org/10.1007/11557265_8
18. Dennis, J.: Data flow supercomputers. IEEE Comput. **13**(11), 48–56 (1980)
19. Hoefler, T., et al.: MPI + MPI: a new hybrid approach to parallel programming with MPI plus shared memory. Computing **95**, 1121–1136 (2013). https://doi.org/10.1007/s00607-013-0324-2
20. Huang, C., Lawlor, O., Kalé, L.V.: Adaptive MPI. In: Rauchwerger, L. (ed.) LCPC 2003. LNCS, vol. 2958, pp. 306–322. Springer, Heidelberg (2004). https://doi.org/10.1007/978-3-540-24644-2_20
21. Iancu, C., Hofmeyr, S., Blagojević, F., Zheng, Y.: Oversubscription on multi-core processors. In: 2010 IEEE International Symposium on Parallel Distributed Processing (IPDPS), pp. 1–11 (April 2010). https://doi.org/10.1109/IPDPS.2010.5470434

22. Quinlan, D.: ROSE: compiler support for object-oriented frameworks. Parallel Process. Lett. **10**, 215–226 (2000)
23. Kalé, L.V.: The virtualization approach to parallel programming: runtime optimizations and the state of the art. In: Los Alamos Computer Science Institute Symposium-LACSI (2002)
24. Kale, L.V., Krishnan, S.: CHARM++: a portable concurrent object oriented system based on C++. In: Proceedings of the Eighth Annual Conference on Object-oriented Programming Systems, Languages, and Applications, OOPSLA 1993, pp. 91–108. ACM, New York (1993). https://doi.org/10.1145/165854.165874
25. Kamal, H., Wagner, A.: FG-MPI: fine-grain MPI for multicore and clusters. In: 2010 IEEE International Symposium on Parallel Distributed Processing, Workshops and Phd Forum (IPDPSW), pp. 1–8, April 2010. https://doi.org/10.1109/IPDPSW.2010.5470773
26. Krishnamurthy, A., et al.: Parallel programming in split-C. In: Proceedings of the 1993 ACM/IEEE Conference on Supercomputing, Supercomputing 1993, pp. 262–273. ACM, New York (1993). https://doi.org/10.1145/169627.169724
27. Lavrijsen, W., Iancu, C.: Application level reordering of remote direct memory access operations. In: 2017 IEEE International Parallel and Distributed Processing Symposium (IPDPS), pp. 988–997, May 2017. https://doi.org/10.1109/IPDPS.2017.98
28. Lu, H., Seo, S., Balaji, P.: MPI+ULT: overlapping communication and computation with user-level threads. In: 2015 IEEE 17th International Conference on High Performance Computing and Communications, 2015 IEEE 7th International Symposium on Cyberspace Safety and Security, and 2015 IEEE 12th International Conference on Embedded Software and Systems, pp. 444–454, August 2015. https://doi.org/10.1109/HPCC-CSS-ICESS.2015.82
29. Marjanović, V., Labarta, J., Ayguadé, E., Valero, M.: Overlapping communication and computation by using a hybrid MPI/SMPSS approach. In: Proceedings of the 24th ACM International Conference on Supercomputing, ICS 2010, pp. 5–16. ACM, New York (2010). https://doi.org/10.1145/1810085.1810091
30. Martin, S.M., Berger, M.J., Baden, S.B.: Toucan - a translator for communication tolerant MPI applications. In: 2017 IEEE International Parallel and Distributed Processing Symposium (IPDPS), pp. 998–1007, May 2017. https://doi.org/10.1109/IPDPS.2017.44
31. NERSC: National Energy Research Scientific Computing Center. http://www.nersc.gov
32. Nguyen, T., Cicotti, P., Bylaska, E., Quinlan, D., Baden, S.B.: Bamboo - translating MPI applications to a latency-tolerant, data-driven form. In: 2012 International Conference for High Performance Computing, Networking, Storage and Analysis (SC), pp. 1–11, November 2012. https://doi.org/10.1109/SC.2012.23
33. OpenMP, ARB: OpenMP 4.0 specification (2013)
34. Perez, J.M., Badia, R.M., Labarta, J.: A dependency-aware task-based programming environment for multi-core architectures. In: 2008 IEEE International Conference on Cluster Computing, pp. 142–151, September 2008. https://doi.org/10.1109/CLUSTR.2008.4663765
35. Tang, H., Yang, T.: Optimizing threaded MPI execution on SMP clusters. In: Proceedings of the 15th International Conference on Supercomputing, ICS 2001, pp. 381–392. ACM, New York (2001). https://doi.org/10.1145/377792.377895

36. Terpstra, D., Jagode, H., You, H., Dongarra, J.: Collecting performance data with PAPI-C. In: Müller, M.S., Resch, M.M., Schulz, A., Nagel, W.E. (eds.) Tools for High Performance Computing 2009, pp. 157–173. Springer, Heidelberg (2010). https://doi.org/10.1007/978-3-642-11261-4_11
37. Tomasulo, R.M.: An efficient algorithm for exploiting multiple arithmetic units. IBM J. Res. Dev. **11**(1), 25–33 (1967). https://doi.org/10.1147/rd.111.0025
38. Valiant, L.G.: A bridging model for parallel computation. Commun. ACM **33**(8), 103–111 (1990). https://doi.org/10.1145/79173.79181
39. Zhang, Q., Johansen, H., Colella, P.: A fourth-order accurate finite-volume method with structured adaptive mesh refinement for solving the advection-diffusion equation. SIAM J. Sci. Comput. **34**(2), B179–B201 (2012). https://doi.org/10.1137/110820105

GASNet-EX: A High-Performance, Portable Communication Library for Exascale

Dan Bonachea$^{(\boxtimes)}$ and Paul H. Hargrove

Computational Research Division, Lawrence Berkeley National Laboratory,
Berkeley, CA 94720, USA
{DOBonachea,PHHargrove}@lbl.gov
https://gasnet.lbl.gov

Abstract. Partitioned Global Address Space (PGAS) models, typified by languages such as Unified Parallel C (UPC) and Co-Array Fortran, expose one-sided communication as a key building block for High Performance Computing (HPC) applications. Architectural trends in supercomputing make such programming models increasingly attractive, and newer, more sophisticated models such as UPC++, Legion and Chapel that rely upon similar communication paradigms are gaining popularity. GASNet-EX is a portable, open-source, high-performance communication library designed to efficiently support the networking requirements of PGAS runtime systems and other alternative models in future exascale machines. The library is an evolution of the popular GASNet communication system, building upon over 15 years of lessons learned. We describe and evaluate several features and enhancements that have been introduced to address the needs of modern client systems. Microbenchmark results demonstrate the RMA performance of GASNet-EX is competitive with several MPI-3 implementations on current HPC systems.

Keywords: HPC · PGAS · RMA · Active Messages · Middleware

1 Introduction

1.1 Background on GASNet-1

The GASNet project began in 2002 [14] as an effort to provide a common, open-source HPC communication API tailored for use as a compilation target by Partitioned Global Address Space (PGAS) languages, notably including UPC [75], Titanium [38], and Co-Array Fortran [65]. Communication behavior in these models is often characterized by one-sided, remote-memory-access (RMA) communication (i.e., Puts and Gets operating on physically distributed memory), and sensitivity to the latency and overheads of fine-grained communication. The initial GASNet API (hereafter referred to as GASNet-1) offers two primary modes of communication: (1) a one-sided RMA interface that exposes the RDMA

M. Hall and H. Sundar (Eds.): LCPC 2018, LNCS 11882, pp. 138–158, 2019.
https://doi.org/10.1007/978-3-030-34627-0_11

capabilities of network hardware, enabling their use to directly implement PGAS Put/Get operations on user data structures, and (2) a streamlined Active Message (AM) [30] interface to provide extensibility and efficient management of the client's parallel runtime system.

Design goals for the GASNet communication system included: network-independence (insulating long-lived clients from low-level hardware details and changes), language-independence (leaving details of the PGAS system such as global pointer representation and allocation strategy to the client), robust multi-threading support (efficiently allowing a variety of client threading models on multi-core architectures), and widespread portability. The GASNet development effort has focused on providing a high-performance, production-quality communication layer tailored for the needs of PGAS systems.

The GASNet API [17] has become the *de-facto* communication standard targeted by portable PGAS system implementations developed by many institutions. Current and historical GASNet clients include: LBNL UPC++ [3,4,79], Berkeley UPC [22], GCC/UPC [46], Clang UPC [45], Cray Chapel [19], Stanford Legion [6], Titanium [78], Rice Co-Array Fortran [26], OpenUH Co-Array Fortran [29], OpenCoarrays in GCC Fortran [32], OpenSHMEM Reference implementation [70], Omni XcalableMP [57], and several miscellaneous projects [10,18,20,27,51,52,71]. Some of these clients implement models that fall outside the traditional PGAS definition, showing that the applicability of GASNet exceeds the original goals. The services provided and the match to modern hardware capabilities make GASNet an excellent communication substrate for implementing a wide variety of models.

GASNet uses the term "conduit" to refer to any complete implementation of the GASNet API which targets a specific network device or lower-level networking layer. GASNet conduits have been written that target a variety of past and current vendor-proprietary or hardware-specific networking interfaces, including: OpenFabrics Verbs/VAPI for InfiniBand [37,42], Mellanox MXM for Infini-Band [53], Cray GNI for Gemini and Aries fabrics [1,36,41], Intel PSM2 for Omni-Path [9,44], IBM PAMI for BlueGene/Q (and others) [49], IBM DCMF for BlueGene/P [50,63], IBM LAPI for SP Colony/Federation [40], Cray Portals for XT3/XT4 [16], SHMEM for the Cray X1 [8] and SGI Altix [28], Quadrics elan3/elan4 for QsNetI/II [69], Myricom GM for Myrinet [7,11], and Dolphin SISCI [73]. There are also GASNet conduits implemented over portable network APIs that enable deployment on early systems or those lacking HPC networking hardware. These include: udp-conduit (for any network with a TCP/IP stack, such as Ethernet) mpi-conduit (for any system providing MPI 1.1 [55] or newer), ofi-conduit (targeting the portable libfabric API [35]), portals4-conduit (for Sandia Portals 4 [5]), and smp-conduit (for single-node systems, such as laptops).

Most of the conduits described above were authored by members of our group, but several conduits have been contributed by a relevant vendor or external group. Additionally, some projects have developed forks of GASNet (for instance to target non-public network APIs), including MVAPICH2-X [47] and others [48,77]. GASNet's implementation is designed so that authors of new conduits only need to port a minimal core (consisting of a few job management routines and the AM interfaces) to achieve full functionality. We provide reference implementations of all other interfaces, which can be incrementally replaced with higher-performing native versions. The GASNet implementation is written in standard C and is very portable across architectures and operating systems. Over the years, it has been ported to a diverse range of systems, encompassing over 10 compiler families, 15 operating systems and dozens of architectures – see [33] for details.

1.2   Philosophy of GASNet-EX Improvements

GASNet-EX is the next generation of the GASNet-1 communication system, continuing our commitment to provide portable, high-performance, production-quality, open-source software. The GASNet-EX upgrade is being done over the next several years as part of the U.S. Department of Energy's Exascale Computing Program (ECP). The GASNet interfaces are being redesigned to accommodate the emerging needs of exascale supercomputing, providing communication services to a variety of programming models on current and future HPC architectures. This work builds on fifteen years of lessons learned with GASNet-1, and is informed and motivated by the evolving needs of distributed runtime systems.

The end of Moore's Law scaling for serial processor performance has led to increasing levels of on-die parallelism, lighter-weight cores, and deeper on-node memory hierarchies; these trends are expected to continue in future HPC architectures. We expect future runtime systems and applications will migrate away from bulk-synchronous parallel algorithms and increasingly adopt approaches with looser inter-node synchronization, using aggressively asynchronous communication such as in UPC++ [3] or dynamic tasking features available in systems such as Chapel [19], Legion [6] and X10 [21]. This motivates a communication system interface that enables the client to adapt to the dynamic behavior of the system, for example adjusting the communication schedule on-the-fly based on network backpressure. There is also motivation to improve the efficiency of memory buffer behavior in the communication system, for example providing finer-grained control over buffer lifetime and exposing mechanisms to reduce in-memory payload copying. Modern HPC networks often include hardware support for offloading various communication-related tasks from the host processor, such as packing/unpacking of non-contiguous communication buffers, performing atomic memory updates initiated by remote peers, and orchestrating collective communications (e.g., reductions and barriers). Interfaces are being added in GASNet-EX that allow clients to express these high-level patterns in ways that can take advantage of such hardware support where available. Finally, there is a need for improved system abstractions to enable interoperability in hybrid programs, allow finer-grained or thread-level partitioning of communication work, and ensure all parts of the communication system scale efficiently to millions of ranks.

2 Design of GASNet-EX

2.1 Overview of Improvements

The GASNet interface is being redesigned and extended in a number of ways to meet the needs of exascale runtime systems. Most of the functionality and abstractions from GASNet-1 are still present, but have been generalized in several ways. (The GASNet-EX distribution notably includes a backwards-compatibility layer to enable incremental migration of current GASNet-1 client software to GASNet-EX). In GASNet-1, initialization was monolithic and assumed a single client/endpoint/segment per process. In GASNet-EX, initialization becomes more incremental and includes an object model where the Client, registered memory Segments and communication Endpoints are all managed separately and explicitly. This design has already enabled several interface improvements, and enables clients to naturally express more complicated use cases. For example, AM handler registration is now per-Endpoint and can be performed incrementally, improving client modularity. The Endpoint abstraction allows for multiple isolated communication contexts to co-exist within a process, for example enabling GASNet-EX Active Messages to target specific threads within a remote process. GASNet-EX adds APIs to scalably query and manage hierarchical process layouts and memory Segments residing in inter-process shared memory.

Here is the signature for a representative non-blocking RMA Put operation in GASNet to demonstrate some of the changes:

```
gasnet_handle_t     /* GASNet-1 */
gasnet_put_nb(gasnet_node_t node, void *dest_addr,
             void *src_addr, size_t nbytes);


gex_Event_t         /* GASNet-EX */
gex_RMA_PutNB(gex_TM_t tm, gex_Rank_t rank,
             gex_Addr_t dest_addr,
             void *src_addr, size_t nbytes,
             gex_Event_t *lc_opt, gex_Flags_t flags);
```

In both cases the contiguous source payload is indicated by a base address and size, but everything else has changed. In GASNet-1, the destination process of every point-to-point operation was indicated using an integer node id. In GASNet-EX a destination Endpoint is named via a team (TM) and rank id pair – improving client composability, and enabling Endpoints to be dynamically added to the system for various purposes. The team argument names not only an ordered set of Endpoints, but also the local representative Endpoint and its containing Client. This object hierarchy can be traversed by client code, which can query various attributes and even set client-owned context attributes.

In the GASNet-1 API, the remote target for the RMA Put is specified using a virtual address. The GASNet-EX API still allows this, but additionally enables offset-based addressing into a memory Segment bound to the destination Endpoint – potentially improving scalability of client metadata, and enabling future work in binding of memory Segments to non-DRAM device memory. GASNet-EX adds a flags argument to most functions for extensibility, allowing the semantics and performance characteristics of many calls to be modified by passing appropriate flags (e.g., passing assertions about the argument values that can obviate the need for more expensive dynamic checking).

GASNet-1 non-blocking operations return a monolithic handle used for later synchronization. This concept has been generalized to GASNet-EX Events, which can have sub-Events representing intermediate steps that occur before completion of an entire operation, enabling clients to explicitly respond to such state changes. For example, the RMA Put has an argument for specifying the local completion behavior of the source memory (i.e. the two options in GASNet-1 being stall upon injection or delay until remote completion). GASNet-EX allows the operation to generate a sub-Event, so the client initiating the Put can independently track both local and remote completion of the same operation.

All figures in the remainder of Sect. 2 are reproduced (with permission) from our technical report [36] and show the performance of GASNet-EX aries-conduit on Cray XC40 systems (Cray Aries network) – see the report for full methodological details (omitted from this paper due to space constraints).

2.2 Local Completion Control

As mentioned above, GASNet-EX adds sub-Events into the generalization of the GASNet-1 handle abstraction, and "local completion" is one of the uses for this new concept. With the new option to independently track local completion, a client can free or reuse a source buffer as soon as it is safe to do so without the cost of blocking for local completion in the injection call (the only mechanism available in GASNet-1 for separating local and remote completion). This provides an increase in time available for overlap of communication with computation, or with additional communication. To evaluate the effects of this enhancement, we measured the bandwidth achieved by a microbenchmark where the client issues a series of non-blocking Puts but requests each injection to stall for local completion before return. Figure 1 shows this benchmark can be improved by as much as 32% through the separation of local completion from operation completion.

2.3 Immediate-Mode Communication Injection

Both GASNet APIs permit "non-blocking" communication injection operations to block temporarily (stall) when resources are not readily available to initiate the requested communication. This backpressure behavior arises fundamentally from a design principle prohibiting unbounded buffering within our GASNet implementation. However, a client of GASNet-EX can use the new flags argument to request "immediate mode" injection, wherein an operation that determines it would stall will instead be cancelled and return a distinguishing value. This enables the client to dynamically respond to the resource congestion along that path in a client-specific manner; for example rescheduling the operation for later

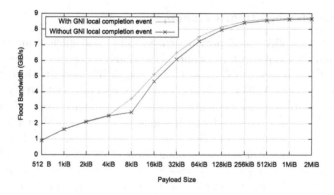

Fig. 1. Non-bulk Put flood bandwidth on Cray Aries with and without use of a local completion event at the GNI level.

retry or electing to attempt communication with a *different*, less-congested peer (as one might do when implementing a work-stealing task scheduler).

The effect of stalling can be especially evident in communications using AMs destined to a peer which is not actively entering the GASNet library (an "inattentive" peer). Our investigation found that exposing backpressure in the Active Message APIs can reduce running time by as much as 97% on a synthetic benchmark simulating communication with inattentive peers. This is illustrated in Fig. 2 which shows the reduction in overall communication time obtained by using immediate-mode AM injection to dynamically adjust the communication schedule in response to backpressure, as compared to three static schedules that stall on backpressure.

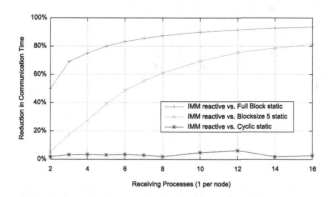

Fig. 2. Reduced communication delays using immediate-mode Active Messages.

2.4   Active Message Improvements

Inclusion of AMs in GASNet-1 provides extensibility and efficient management of the client's parallel runtime, for instance UPC shared-heap management or locks. More recent GASNet clients such as Cray Chapel [19] and Stanford Legion [6] make heavy use of GASNet AMs for moving computation to data. GASNet-EX introduces several improvements to the AM interfaces, primarily related to efficient use of memory and reduced in-memory copies. GASNet-EX AM calls provide for immediate-mode injection and local-completion control, as described previously. These are notable improvements over GASNet-1, where AM injection calls unconditionally block until the message is guaranteed to enter the network, and return only after local completion of the payload. While GASNet-1 has APIs to query the maximum AM payload for distinct classes of message, GASNet-EX refines the precision of these queries; this enables the client to, for instance, take advantage of space otherwise occupied by unused arguments, or to send significantly larger payloads when the destination is reachable through shared memory.

In addition to these incremental improvements, GASNet-EX adds an entirely new family of AM interfaces known as "Negotiated-Payload" AMs (NP-AM). The new NP-AM feature utilizes a split-phase send that, among other new capabilities, allows GASNet-EX to provide a network-level buffer into which the client directly writes its outgoing payload. In clients that construct payloads dynamically (for instance combining a header with data from a higher layer) this eliminates an in-memory copy often required to concatenate the AM header and to move the payload into memory registered with the network. Our measurements show that this use of NP-AM to reduce memory copies in the critical path improves measured bandwidth on an AM ping-pong benchmark by as much as 14% relative to the traditional "Fixed-Payload" AMs in GASNet-1, as illustrated by the upper (red) series in Fig. 3.

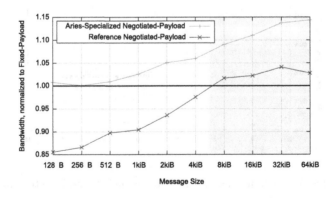

Fig. 3. NP-AM speedup of ping-pong test with dynamically generated payload. (Color figure online)

2.5   Remote Atomics

Remote atomics are a new feature in GASNet-EX, providing non-blocking interfaces to perform a rich set of operations atomically on several data types in distributed memory. The semantic design for GASNet-EX remote atomics is derived from that used in UPC 1.3 [75], where operations are performed with respect to an "atomic domain". An atomic domain is constructed (outside the critical path) by specifying a data type and a set of atomic operations, and is later used to initiate any of the given operations on data of the given type. Use of atomic domains allows for selection of the fastest-available implementation that can *correctly* provide the set of atomic operations needed concurrently by the application. This is important because in general one cannot mix atomics offloaded to a NIC with others implemented using the host CPU concurrently to the same target location, due to coherency problems on many modern systems. Atomic domains address this by selecting NIC offload implementations if and only if the entire set of operations given at domain creation can be coherently offloaded, and a CPU-based implementation otherwise. Optional flags to atomic domain construction can guide algorithm selection in application-specific ways, for example to favor the performance of accesses across the network, or trade it off for improved performance of updates from shared-memory peers.

Our measurements show there is significant advantage to offloading of atomic operations to the network hardware support provided by Cray Aries, as compared to a network-independent reference implementation, such as one a client author could write using AMs. The latency of a 64-bit fetch-and-add was reduced by 70% on a point-to-point test, and a hot-spot test was shown to scale robustly as illustrated in Fig. 4. Future work to offload atomic operations to InfiniBand network hardware is expected to yield qualitatively similar results.

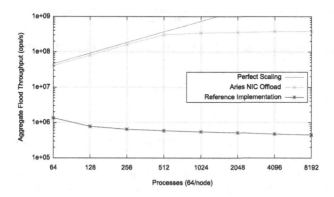

Fig. 4. Scaling of a remote atomics hot-spot test on the Cray Aries network.

2.6   Non-contiguous RMA

A set of extensions to GASNet-1 were proposed in [12] to support non-contiguous
RMA operations. These types of operations may be generated by optimizations
performed by UPC and CAF compilers, or can be used by application authors
or distributed array libraries to express transfer of multidimensional array sections. The extensions are jointly referred to as "VIS" and include "Vector",
"Indexed" and "Strided" APIs for Put and Get, differing in the generality (and
thus size) of the metadata used to describe the source and destination regions.
The Strided design for multidimensional array sections was influenced by that of
ARMCI [62]. While GASNet-1 fully implemented the VIS extensions, they were
never included in the formal specification. GASNet-EX incorporates the VIS
APIs (no longer considered extensions) with updates to express local-completion
control and immediate-mode injection. The implementation of VIS in GASNet-
EX leverages new EX features (most notably the Active Message enhancements)
to improve performance relative to GASNet-1. Figure 5 demonstrates the band-
width improvement of a microbenchmark measuring a representative 3-d Strided
Put operation, implemented inside GASNet-EX using traditional AM or NP-
AM, relative to the bandwidth achieved by the GASNet-1 VIS implementation.

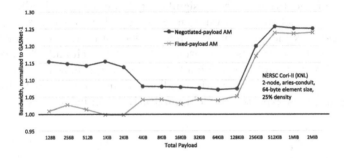

Fig. 5. Improved Strided Put performance, relative to GASNet-1.

2.7   Collective Communication

As illustrated in Sect. 2.1, point-to-point communication in GASNet-EX uses a
(team, rank) pair to identify the peer, whereas GASNet-1 took only a rank.
In addition to this role in point-to-point communication, teams name the par-
ticipants in collective communications operations. As with VIS, collectives were
implemented in GASNet-1 [64] but never appeared in a formal specification.
GASNet-EX adds specification and implementation of collective operations, with
key improvements over the APIs implemented in GASNet-1. GASNet-EX collectives are always non-blocking, using the same Event type as all other asynchronous operations, whereas GASNet-1 has a distinct type and APIs for tracking completion of collectives. The use of the general Event infrastructure enables

local-completion control for collectives. Finally, the GASNet-EX reduction operation includes type information, lacking from GASNet-1, which is critical to enabling network hardware offload.

2.8 Design Improvements for Scalability

One of the primary motivations behind the redesign of GASNet is to improve scalability of both the implementation and client-facing APIs—a necessary step towards achieving exascale performance on upcoming systems, which are expected to reach millions of cores. Several GASNet-1 APIs were designed without sufficient allowance for such extreme-scale systems, and GASNet-EX replaces these with more scalable alternatives. For example, the GASNet-1 function to query segment information writes to a client-allocated array with entries for *every* process in the job, imposing a non-scalable requirement on both the client and library. GASNet-EX instead provides a query to retrieve information about a *selected* peer, consuming only a small constant amount of memory and enabling implementations that discover peer information on-demand at scale. There are also new scalable queries for processes to discover information regarding co-located peers within a hierarchical system.

GASNet-EX API extensions to use offset-based addressing in RMA calls (Sect. 2.1) will enable client runtimes supporting symmetric heap features to eliminate non-scalable base address tables. Immediate-mode injection (Sect. 2.3) improves support for asynchrony, strengthening latency tolerance and enabling dynamic adjustment to congestion and load imbalance that become more prevalent at scale. The redesigned GASNet-EX teams interface (Sect. 2.7) includes scalable rank translation queries designed to keep non-scalable tables out of client data structures. Enhancements enabling NIC hardware offload of collectives (Sect. 2.7) and remote atomics (Sect. 2.5) are expected to become increasingly important at extreme scale.

3 RMA Microbenchmarks

Both the specification and implementation of GASNet-EX are still evolving. However, as described in the previous section, the new features are already capable of delivering measurable benefits for use cases of interest. These new features have *not* come at the cost of GASNet-1's core competencies in RMA and AM. This section presents microbenchmarks measuring the RMA performance of GASNet-EX on four systems, demonstrating that it remains competitive with MPI-3 RMA. Application-level benchmarks would introduce overheads specific to the client runtime, and are outside the scope of this paper.

Our measurements attempt to reproduce the experience of a non-expert end-user. On three vendor-integrated systems using environment modules, we have used the default modules with only one exception to be described below. On a commodity InfiniBand cluster we have used the compiler pre-installed as /usr/bin/gcc. When building software (including GASNet-EX and all microbenchmarks) we followed the instructions without the application of any expert knowledge. No configuration settings, environment variables, or similar means were used to improve the performance of GASNet-EX or MPI[1]. We benchmarked GASNet-EX version 2018.9.0 using two tests selected from those provided with the source code distribution. For MPI-3 benchmarking we have selected the publicly available Intel MPI Benchmarks [43] (IMB), version v2018.1.

3.1 Description of the Systems

The first two systems are the partitions of the Cray XC40 [23,31] system at NERSC [61], known as "Cori". Both use a Cray Aries [1] network, but they have distinct node types: "Cori-I" [59] nodes each have two Intel Xeon E5-2698v3 16-core "Haswell" processors and "Cori-II" [60] nodes each have a single Intel Xeon Phi 7250 "KNL" processor with 272 hardware threads. All tests on the Cori systems were compiled with the default programming environment modules: PrgEnv-intel/6.0.4, intel/18.0.1.163 and cray-mpich/7.7.0. The only non-default modules used were for CPU-specific optimization: following NERSC's user documentation, compilation of code to execute on Cori-I and Cori-II used the craype-haswell and craype-mic-knl environment modules, respectively.

The "Gomez" system at JLSE [2] is a commodity InfiniBand cluster. Each node has two Intel Xeon E7-8867v3 "Haswell-EX" CPUs and is connected to a 100Gb/s EDR InfiniBand network by a Mellanox "ConnectX-4" Host Channel Adapter (HCA). All tests on this system were compiled with the system-default GNU compilers, version 4.8.5 20150623 (Red Hat 4.8.5-16). MPI tests used MVAPICH2 [58], version 2.3.

The "Summitdev" [67] system at OLCF [66] consists of IBM S822LC [76] nodes, each with two 10-core POWER8 CPUs and connected to a 100 Gb/s EDR InfiniBand network by two Mellanox "ConnectX-4" HCAs, each with affinity to a single socket. Software compiled on this system used the default IBM XL compilers, version V13.1.6. MPI tests use the default IBM Spectrum MPI, version 10.2.0.0-20180110.

3.2 RMA Flood Bandwidth Benchmark

A "flood bandwidth" benchmark measures achievable bandwidth at a given transfer size by initiating a large number of non-blocking transfers and waiting for them all to fully complete. The reported metric is the total volume of data transferred, divided by the total elapsed time. We report uni-directional (one initiator to one target) flood bandwidths, where the passive target waits in a barrier.

---

[1] On Summitdev we set one environment variable to restrict the MPI implementation to a single rail of the dual-rail network, to provide a meaningful comparison to GASNet-EX. We recommend this configuration because use of a single rail per process can yield significant latency improvements.

For GASNet-EX we used the `testlarge` microbenchmark to measure performance of the `gex_RMA_PutNBI` and `gex_RMA_GetNBI` functions, synchronized with a final `gex_NBI_Wait`. We measured flood bandwidth of the `MPI_Put` and `MPI_Get` functions using the "Aggregate" timings from, respectively, the `Unidir_put` and `Unidir_get` tests from the `IMB-RMA` suite (these tests measure the time to issue RMA and synchronize using `MPI_Win_flush`, within a passive-target access epoch established by a `MPI_Win_lock(SHARED)` call outside the timed region – see [43] for further details). The `testlarge` benchmark reports bandwidths in units of "MiB/s" (2^{20} bytes per second), whereas `IMB-RMA` uses "MB/s" (10^6 bytes per second). Both have been converted to "GiB/s" (2^{30} bytes per second) for the plots which follow. To allow comparison between RMA and message passing, the plots which follow also report uni-directional bandwidth of `MPI_Isend`/`MPI_Irecv`, from the "Aggregate" timings of the `Uniband` test from the `IMB-MPI1` suite.

All tests ran between two compute nodes, using a single process per node. Data was collected from 16 distinct batch jobs, each running one instance of each GASNet-EX and MPI test back-to-back. Each data point plotted reports the maximum achieved bandwidth for that benchmark and transfer size. For RMA tests we used 100,000 iterations on the Aries systems, and 10,000 on the EDR InfiniBand systems. For the message passing test, we used 5,000 and 500 iterations, respectively.

In Fig. 6, "×" markers denote GASNet-EX RMA, "○" markers denote MPI-3 RMA, and "+" markers denote MPI message passing. RMA Put results are distinguished by the use of solid lines in shades of blue, while RMA Get results use dot-dashed lines in shades of red. Dashed green lines are message-passing results.

On three of the four systems, the bandwidth of GASNet-EX Put and Get are seen to rise rapidly to saturation, at payloads as small as 4 or 8KiB. All GASNet-EX saturation bandwidths are at least comparable to their MPI-3 RMA analogue. The KNL-based Cori-II system shows behavior different from the other three, and this is particularly unexpected because Cori-I and Cori-II use the same network and software versions. Doerfler et al. [25] identified the cause of the two maximum bandwidth plateaus on this system as an issue with PCIe bus latency.

3.3   RMA Latency Benchmark

We next report on the round-trip latency of GASNet-EX and MPI-3 RMA operations. These benchmarks report the mean time to fully complete a single RMA Put or Get operation, computed by timing a long sequence of blocking operations. For GASNet-EX we measured the `gex_RMA_PutBlocking` and `gex_RMA_GetBlocking` functions using the `testsmall` microbenchmark. For MPI-3 benchmarking we report the "Non-aggregate" timings from the `Unidir_put` and `Unidir_get` tests from the `IMB-RMA` suite, which are semantically equivalent to the GASNet-EX test. These are the same tests used to measure flood bandwidth, but differ by executing a sequence of `MPI_Put` (or `MPI_Get`) calls alternating with calls to `MPI_Win_flush`, whereas the "Aggregate" timings used for bandwidth have only a *single* `MPI_Win_flush` at the end.

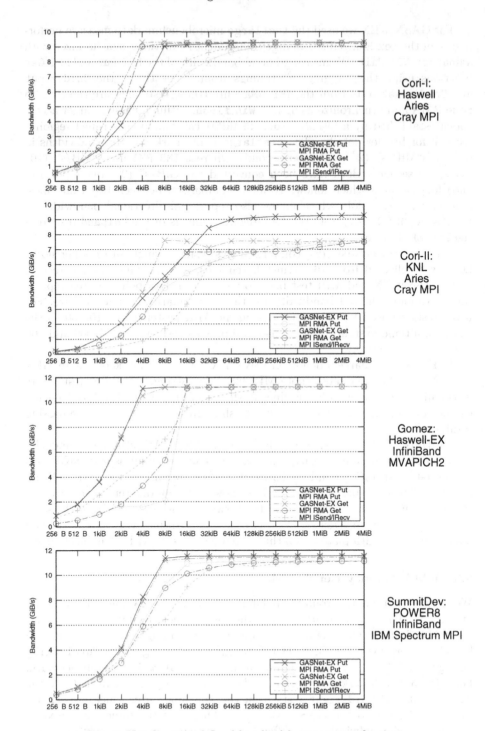

Fig. 6. Uni-directional flood bandwidth versus transfer size.

Data was collected from the same 16 batch jobs described for the flood bandwidth benchmark. Our results are summarized in Table 1, which reports the minimum latency achieved by each benchmark for the cases of blocking RMA Put and Get with 8-byte payloads. Each row includes the ratio of the corresponding GASNet-EX and MPI-3 results, which is also representative of timings over power-of-two sizes from 4 bytes to 1024 bytes (not shown). In all cases measured, GASNet-EX demonstrated comparable or improved latency relative to MPI-3 RMA.

Table 1. Round-trip latency of 8-Byte RMA accesses.

System	8-Byte RMA Put latency			8-Byte RMA Get latency		
	GASNet-EX	MPI-3 RMA	Ratio	GASNet-EX	MPI-3 RMA	Ratio
Cori-I	1.07 μs	1.20 μs	0.89	1.43 μs	1.57 μs	0.91
Cori-II	2.15 μs	3.42 μs	0.63	2.60 μs	4.06 μs	0.64
Gomez	1.41 μs	1.51 μs	0.94	1.82 μs	1.91 μs	0.95
Summitdev	1.61 μs	8.10 μs	0.20	2.10 μs	8.13 μs	0.26

4   Related Work

The GASNet library provides communication services for a wide variety of runtime clients, as discussed in Sect. 1.1. The communication requirements of these clients can be broadly summarized as including portable, high-performance RMA for one-sided data motion, and Active Messages that trigger remote code execution as a building block for higher-level distributed protocols. This section describes competing middleware efforts that provide related facilities.

At the time the GASNet project began, the most notable related effort was the RMA extensions introduced in the MPI-2 specification [54]. The widespread availability and investment in MPI implementations over the years makes MPI a politically attractive communication substrate. However as explained in [15], a number of fundamental semantic defects in the MPI-2 RMA specification made it unsuitable for practical use as communication middleware for PGAS runtimes – justifying the investment in approaches tailored to the needs of PGAS clients, such as GASNet and ARMCI [62]. Most of these defects were subsequently addressed fourteen years later in the MPI-3 specification [56]. Most importantly, the introduction of the (optional) MPI_WIN_UNIFIED memory model and dynamic MPI RMA windows made it feasible to use passive-target MPI RMA to satisfy the basic RMA communication needs of some PGAS runtimes. Section 3 demonstrates the performance of GASNet-EX RMA is competitive with that of MPI RMA in several widely used MPI-3 implementations. A number of efforts are underway to improve the behavior and performance of MPI-3 RMA implementations, for example [34,39]. During the six month interval that we performed data collection in preparation for this paper, we've observed notice-able improvement in the performance of all three MPI-RMA implementations measured. There are also efforts underway to implement some PGAS systems using MPI-3 RMA [80]. MPI-3 offers a wide variety of features that are absent from GASNet-EX, which focuses on providing AM and RMA services for parallel runtimes.

However the current MPI-3 API still lacks several features that are important to GASNet-EX's clients – most notable amongst these is Active Messages, which are critical to systems such as Berkeley UPC, UPC++, Legion, Chapel, and others. Prior work [13] has demonstrated that emulating active message func-tionality over MPI's message-passing interfaces is possible, but the performance may be prohibitively expensive relative to native implementations. ComEx [24] implements the Global Arrays PGAS library using MPI message passing and hidden progress processes operating on MPI shared memory segments (deliber-ately avoiding the MPI-RMA interface), however they admit their approach is insufficient for providing clients with Active Message functionality.

GASNet-EX and MPI-3 RMA differ in other details of relevance to PGAS clients. For example, GASNet-EX offers fine-grained control over the synchro-nization of RMA operations, whereas MPI-3 RMA notably lacks the ability to independently synchronize remote completion of concurrent Put and Accumulate operations targeting the same remote window. Atomic domains in GASNet-EX enable aggressive use of offload hardware for remote atomics, even when con-currently mixing different atomic update operations to the same target location, whereas MPI's accumulate semantics disallow this. The GASNet-EX immediate-mode injection feature introduced in Sect. 2 has no direct analogue in MPI RMA.

There are two relatively recent industry-driven efforts to provide portable, open-source HPC networking middleware to sit below parallel runtimes, similar to GASNet-EX. OpenFabrics libfabric [35,68] portably provides one-sided RMA and remote atomic operations suitable for implementing PGAS-style RMA, in addition to tag matching and messaging queues suitable for implementing message-passing APIs. There are implementations of GASNet, OpenSHMEM, MPI-3 and other models over libfabric, which in turn offers providers that run across a variety of high-performance network fabrics. Unified Communications X (UCX) [72,74] is a similar, independent effort to provide a portable net-work abstraction layer for authors of HPC middleware such as MPI and PGAS runtimes.

5   Conclusions

This paper describes GASNet-EX, a portable, open-source, high-performance, next-generation communication library designed to efficiently support the networking requirements of distributed runtime systems in future exascale machines. We presented several extensions and enhancements that GASNet-EX adds to the traditional GASNet APIs, including: independent local-completion control, immediate-mode communication injection, Active Message improvements, and remote atomic operations, as well as improved support for noncontiguous RMA, teams and collective communication. Initial evaluations of the new features and enhancements are positive, showing a potential for improved communication efficiency by reducing buffer memory size and lifetime, eliminating injection stalls, and streamlining several GASNet interfaces to maximize scalability. Finally, we presented microbenchmark results demonstrating the RMA performance of GASNet-EX is competitive with several MPI-3 implementations on modern HPC-relevant systems.

Acknowledgments. This research was funded in part by the Exascale Computing Project (17-SC-20-SC), a collaborative effort of the U.S. Department of Energy Office of Science and the National Nuclear Security Administration.

This research used resources of the National Energy Research Scientific Computing Center, a DOE Office of Science User Facility supported by the Office of Science of the U.S. Department of Energy under Contract No. DE-AC02-05CH11231.

This research used resources of the Argonne Leadership Computing Facility, which is a DOE Office of Science User Facility supported under Contract DE-AC02-06CH11357.

This research used resources of the Oak Ridge Leadership Computing Facility at the Oak Ridge National Laboratory, which is supported by the Office of Science of the U.S. Department of Energy under Contract No. DE-AC05-00OR22725.

References

1. Alverson, B., Froese, E., Kaplan, L., Roweth, D.: Cray XC series network. White Paper WP-Aries01-1112, Cray Inc., November 2012. https://www.cray.com/sites/default/files/resources/CrayXCNetwork.pdf
2. Argonne National Laboratory: Joint Laboratory for System Evaluation. http://www.jlse.anl.gov
3. Bachan, J., Baden, S.B., Bonachea, D., Hargrove, P.H., Hofmeyr, S., Jacquelin, M., Kamil, A., van Straalen, B.: UPC++ specification, v1.0 draft 8. Technical report LBNL-2001179, Lawrence Berkeley National Laboratory, September 2018. https://doi.org/10.25344/S45P4X
4. Bachan, J., Bonachea, D., Hargrove, P.H., Hofmeyr, S., Jacquelin, M., Kamil, A., van Straalen, B., Baden, S.B.: The UPC++ PGAS library for exascale computing. In: Proceedings of the Second Annual PGAS Applications Workshop, PAW17, pp. 7:1–7:4. ACM, New York (2017). https://doi.org/10.1145/3144779.3169108
5. Barrett, B.W., Brightwell, R., Hemmert, S., Pedretti, K., Wheeler, K., Underwood, K., Riesen, R., Maccabe, A.B., Hudson, T.: The Portals 4.0 network programming interface. Technical report SAND2012-10087, Sandia National Laboratories, November 2012. https://doi.org/10.2172/1088065
6. Bauer, M., Treichler, S., Slaughter, E., Aiken, A.: Legion: expressing locality and independence with logical regions. In: Proceedings of the International Conference on High Performance Computing, Networking, Storage and Analysis, SC 2012 (2012). https://doi.org/10.1109/SC.2012.71

7. Bell, C., Bonachea, D.: A new DMA registration strategy for pinning-based high performance networks. In: Proceedings of the International Parallel and Distributed Processing Symposium (IPDPS) (2003). https://doi.org/10.1109/IPDPS.2003.1213363

8. Bell, C., Chen, W., Bonachea, D., Yelick, K.: Evaluating support for global address space languages on the Cray X1. In: 19th Annual International Conference on Supercomputing (ICS), June 2004. https://doi.org/10.1145/1006209.1006236

9. Birrittella, M.S., Debbage, M., Huggahalli, R., Kunz, J., Lovett, T., Rimmer, T., Underwood, K.D., Zak, R.C.: Intel Omni-Path Architecture: enabling scalable, high performance fabrics. In: IEEE 23rd Annual Symposium on High-Performance Interconnects, pp. 1–9, August 2015. https://doi.org/10.1109/HOTI.2015.22

10. Bocchino, R.L., Adve, V.S., Chamberlain, B.L.: Software transactional memory for large scale clusters. In: Proceedings of the ACM SIGPLAN Symposium on Principles and Practice of Parallel Programming (PPoPP 2008), pp. 247–258. ACM, New York (2008). https://doi.org/10.1145/1345206.1345242

11. Boden, N.J., Cohen, D., Felderman, R.E., Kulawik, A.E., Seitz, C.L., Seizovic, J.N., Su, W.K.: Myrinet: a gigabit-per-second local area network. IEEE Micro 15(1), 29–36 (1995). https://doi.org/10.1109/40.342015

12. Bonachea, D.: Proposal for extending the UPC memory copy library functions and supporting extensions to GASNet, v2.0. Technical report LBNL-56495-v2.0, Lawrence Berkeley National Laboratory, March 2007. https://doi.org/10.2172/920052

13. Bonachea, D.: AMMPI home page. http://gasnet.lbl.gov/ammpi

14. Bonachea, D.: GASNet specification, v1.1. Technical report, UCB/CSD-02-1207, University of California, Berkeley, October 2002. https://doi.org/10.25344/S4MW28

15. Bonachea, D., Duell, J.: Problems with using MPI 1.1 and 2.0 as compilation targets for parallel language implementations. Int. J. High Perform. Comput. Netw. 1(1–3), 91–99 (2004). https://doi.org/10.1504/IJHPCN.2004.007569

16. Bonachea, D., Hargrove, P., Welcome, M., Yelick, K.: Porting GASNet to Portals: Partitioned Global Address Space (PGAS) language support for the Cray XT. In: Cray Users Group (2009). https://doi.org/10.25344/S4RP46

17. Bonachea, D., Hargrove, P.H.: GASNet specification, v1.8.1. Technical report, LBNL-2001064, Lawrence Berkeley National Laboratory, August 2017. https://doi.org/10.2172/1398512

18. Buntinas, D., Mercier, G., Gropp, W.: Design and evaluation of Nemesis, a scalable, low-latency, message-passing communication subsystem. In: Sixth IEEE International Symposium on Cluster Computing and the Grid (CCGRID 2006), vol. 1, pp. 521–530, May 2006. https://doi.org/10.1109/CCGRID.2006.31

19. Callahan, D., Chamberlain, B.L., Zima, H.P.: The Cascade High Productivity Language. In: International Workshop on High-Level Parallel Programming Models and Supportive Environments (HIPS), pp. 52–60 (2004). https://doi.org/10.1109/HIPS.2004.10002

20. Chan, C., Wang, B., Bachan, J., Macfarlane, J.: Mobiliti: scalable transportation simulation using high-performance parallel computing. In: IEEE International Conference on Intelligent Transportation Systems (ITSC), pp. 634–641 (2018). https://doi.org/10.1109/ITSC.2018.8569397

21. Charles, P., Grothoff, C., Saraswat, V., Donawa, C., Kielstra, A., Ebcioglu, K., von Praun, C., Sarkar, V.: X10: an object-oriented approach to non-uniform cluster computing. In: Proceedings of the 20th Annual ACM SIGPLAN Conference on Object-Oriented Programming, Systems, Languages, and Applications (OOPSLA 2005) (2005). https://doi.org/10.1145/1103845.1094852
22. Chen, W., Bonachea, D., Duell, J., Husband, P., Iancu, C., Yelick, K.: A performance analysis of the Berkeley UPC compiler. In: Proceedings of the 17th International Conference on Supercomputing (ICS), June 2003. https://doi.org/10.1145/782814.782825
23. Cray Inc.: Cray XC Series. https://www.cray.com/sites/default/files/Cray-XC-Series-Brochure.pdf. Accessed 17 July 2018
24. Daily, J., Vishnu, A., Palmer, B., van Dam, H., Kerbyson, D.: On the suitability of MPI as a PGAS runtime. In: 21st International Conference on High Performance Computing (HiPC), December 2014. https://doi.org/10.1109/HiPC.2014.7116712
25. Doerfler, D., Austin, B., Cook, B., Deslippe, J., Kandalla, K., Mendygral, P.: Evaluating the networking characteristics of the Cray XC-40 Intel Knights Landing-based Cori supercomputer at NERSC. Concurr. Comput. Pract. Exp. **30**(1), e4297 (2017). https://doi.org/10.1002/cpe.4297
26. Dotsenko, Y., Coarfa, C., Mellor-Crummey, J.: A multi-platform Co-array Fortran compiler. In: Proceedings of the 13th International Conference on Parallel Architecture and Compilation Techniques (PACT) (2004). https://doi.org/10.1109/PACT.2004.1342539
27. Driscoll, M.: PyGAS. http://mbdriscoll.github.io/pygas
28. Dunigan, T.H., Vetter, J.S., Worley, P.H.: Performance evaluation of the SGI Altix 3700. In: International Conference on Parallel Processing (ICPP 2005), pp. 231–240, June 2005. https://doi.org/10.1109/ICPP.2005.61
29. Eachempati, D., Jun, H.J., Chapman, B.: An open-source compiler and runtime implementation for Coarray Fortran. In: Proceedings of the Fourth Conference on Partitioned Global Address Space Programming Models (PGAS 2010), pp. 13:1–13:8. ACM (2010). https://doi.org/10.1145/2020373.2020386
30. von Eicken, T., Culler, D.E., Goldstein, S.C., Schauser, K.E.: Active Messages: a mechanism for integrated communication and computation. In: Proceedings of the 19th International Symposium on Computer Architecture, Gold Coast, Australia, pp. 256–266, May 1992. https://doi.org/10.1145/139669.140382
31. Faanes, G., Bataineh, A., Roweth, D., Court, T., Froese, E., Alverson, B., Johnson, T., Kopnick, J., Higgins, M., Reinhard, J.: Cray Cascade: a scalable HPC system based on a Dragonfly network. In: Proceedings of the International Conference on High Performance Computing, Networking, Storage and Analysis, SC 2012, Los Alamitos, CA, USA, pp. 103:1–103:9. IEEE Computer Society Press (2012). https://doi.org/10.1109/SC.2012.39
32. Fanfarillo, A., Burnus, T., Cardellini, V., Filippone, S., Nagle, D., Rouson, D.: OpenCoarrays: open-source transport layers supporting Coarray Fortran compilers. In: Proceedings of the 8th International Conference on Partitioned Global Address Space Programming Models, PGAS 2014, pp. 4:1–4:11. ACM, New York (2014). https://doi.org/10.1145/2676870.2676876
33. GASNet. http://gasnet.lbl.gov
34. Gerstenberger, R., Besta, M., Hoefler, T.: Enabling highly-scalable remote memory access programming with MPI-3 one sided. In: Proceedings of the International Conference on High Performance Computing, Networking, Storage and Analysis (SC 2013), pp. 53:1–53:12. ACM, New York (2013). https://doi.org/10.1145/2503210.2503286

35. Grun, P., Hefty, S., Sur, S., Goodell, D., Russell, R.D., Pritchard, H., Squyres, J.M.: A brief introduction to the OpenFabrics interfaces - a new network API for maximizing high performance application efficiency. In: IEEE 23rd Annual Symposium on High-Performance Interconnects, pp. 34–39, August 2015. https://doi.org/10.1109/HOTI.2015.19

36. Hargrove, P.H., Bonachea, D.: GASNet-EX performance improvements due to specialization for the Cray Aries network. Technical report. LBNL-2001134, Lawrence Berkeley National Laboratory, March 2018. https://doi.org/10.2172/1430690

37. Hargrove, P.H., Bonachea, D., Bell, C.: Experiences implementing Partitioned Global Address Space (PGAS) languages on InfiniBand. In: OpenFabrics Alliance International Workshop, April 2008. http://downloads.openfabrics.org/Media/Sonoma2008/Sonoma_2008_Wed_PGAS%20over%20IB.pdf

38. Hilfinger, P., Bonachea, D., Datta, K., Gay, D., Graham, S., Kamil, A., Liblit, B., Pike, G., Su, J., Yelick, K.: Titanium language reference manual. Technical report, UCB/EECS-2005-15.1, University of California, Berkeley, November 2001. https://doi.org/10.25344/S4H59R

39. Hjelm, N.: An evaluation of the one-sided performance in Open MPI. In: Proceedings of the 23rd European MPI Users' Group Meeting, EuroMPI 2016, pp. 184–187. ACM, New York (2016). https://doi.org/10.1145/2966884.2966890

40. IBM: LAPI programming guide. IBM Technical report SA22-7936-00 (2003)

41. Ibrahim, K.Z., Yelick, K.: On the conditions for efficient interoperability with threads: an experience with PGAS languages using Cray communication domains. In: Proceedings of the 28th ACM International Conference on Supercomputing, ICS 2014, pp. 23–32. ACM (2014). https://doi.org/10.1145/2597652.2597657

42. InfiniBand Trade Association. http://www.infinibandta.org

43. Intel Corporation: Introducing Intel®MPI Benchmarks. https://software.intel.com/en-us/articles/intel-mpi-benchmarks. Accessed 17 July 2018

44. Intel Corporation: Performance Scaled Messaging 2 (PSM2) Programmer's Guide, April 2017. Order No.: H76473-6.0

45. Intrepid Technology Inc.: Clang UPC Compiler. http://clangupc.github.io

46. Intrepid Technology Inc.: GCC/UPC Compiler. http://www.gccupc.org

47. Jose, J., Hamidouche, K., Zhang, J., Venkatesh, A., Panda, D.K.: Optimizing collective communication in UPC. In: IEEE International Parallel Distributed Processing Symposium Workshops, pp. 361–370, May 2014. https://doi.org/10.1109/IPDPSW.2014.49

48. Krasnov, A., Schultz, A., Wawrzynek, J., Gibeling, G., Droz, P.Y.: RAMP Blue: a message-passing manycore system in FPGAs. In: Proceedings of International Conference on Field Programmable Logic and Applications, pp. 54–61, August 2007. https://doi.org/10.1109/FPL.2007.4380625

49. Kumar, S., Mamidala, A.R., Faraj, D.A., Smith, B., Blocksome, M., Cernohous, B., Miller, D., Parker, J., Ratterman, J., Heidelberger, P., Chen, D., Steinmacher-Burrow, B.: PAMI: a parallel active message interface for the Blue Gene/Q supercomputer. In: 2012 IEEE 26th International Parallel and Distributed Processing Symposium, pp. 763–773, May 2012. https://doi.org/10.1109/IPDPS.2012.73

50. Kumar, S., Dozsa, G., Almasi, G., Chen, D., Giampapa, M.E., Heidelberger, P., Blocksome, M., Faraj, A., Parker, J., Ratterman, J., Smith, B., Archer, C.: The Deep Computing Messaging Framework: generalized scalable message passing on the Blue Gene/P supercomputer. In: 22nd Annual International Conference on Supercomputing (ICS), June 2008. https://doi.org/10.1145/1375527.1375544

51. Matsumiya, R., Endo, T.: Scalable RMA-based communication library featuring node-local NVMs. In: Proceedings of the IEEE High Performance Extreme Computing Conference (HPEC 2018), pp. 1–7 (2018). https://doi.org/10.1109/HPEC. 2018.8547546
52. Mattson, T.G., Cledat, R., Cavé, V., Sarkar, V., Budimlic, Z., Chatterjee, S., Fryman, J., Ganev, I., Knauerhase, R., Lee, M., Meister, B., Nickerson, B., Pepperling, N., Seshasayee, B., Tasirlar, S., Teller, J., Vrvilo, N.: The Open Community Runtime: a runtime system for extreme scale computing. In: IEEE High Performance Extreme Computing Conference (HPEC), pp. 1–7, September 2016. https://doi. org/10.1109/HPEC.2016.7761580
53. Mellanox Technologies Inc.: MellanoX Messaging Library User Manual, Rev 2.1 (2014). Document Number: 4113
54. MPI Forum: MPI-2: a message-passing interface standard. Int. J. High Perform. Comput. Appl. 12, 1–299 (1998). https://www.mpi-forum.org/docs/mpi-2.0/mpi-20.ps
55. MPI Forum: MPI: a message-passing interface standard, v1.1. Technical report, University of Tennessee, Knoxville, 12 June 1995. https://www.mpi-forum.org/docs/mpi-1.1/mpi-11.ps
56. MPI Forum: MPI: a message-passing interface standard, version 3.0. Technical report, University of Tennessee, Knoxville, 21 September 2012. https://www.mpi-forum.org/docs/mpi-3.0/mpi30-report.pdf
57. Murai, H., Nakao, M., Iwashita, H., Sato, M.: Preliminary performance evaluation of Coarray-based implementation of fiber Miniapp suite using XcalableMP PGAS language. In: Proceedings of the Second Annual PGAS Applications Workshop, PAW17, pp. 1:1–1:7. ACM (2017). https://doi.org/10.1145/3144779.3144780
58. MVAPICH: MPI over InfiniBand, Omni-Path, Ethernet/iWARP, and RoCE. http://mvapich.cse.ohio-state.edu
59. NERSC: Cori Haswell Nodes. https://doi.org/10.25344/S4859K. Accessed 17 July 2018
60. NERSC: Cori Intel Xeon Phi (KNL) Nodes. https://doi.org/10.25344/S4D012. Accessed 17 July 2018
61. NERSC: National Energy Research Scientific Computing Center. http://www.nersc.gov
62. Nieplocha, J., Carpenter, B.: ARMCI: a portable remote memory copy library for distributed array libraries and compiler run-time systems. In: Rolim, J., Mueller, F., Zomaya, A.Y., Ercal, F., Olariu, S., Ravindran, B., Gustafsson, J., Takada, H., Olsson, R., Kale, L.V., Beckman, P., Haines, M., ElGindy, H., Caromel, D., Chaumette, S., Fox, G., Pan, Y., Li, K., Yang, T., Chiola, G., Conte, G., Mancini, L.V., Méry, D., Sanders, B., Bhatt, D., Prasanna, V. (eds.) IPPS 1999. LNCS, vol. 1586, pp. 533–546. Springer, Heidelberg (1999). https://doi.org/10.1007/BFb0097937
63. Nishtala, R., Hargrove, P.H., Bonachea, D.O., Yelick, K.A.: Scaling communication-intensive applications on BlueGene/P using one-sided communication and overlap. In: Proceedings of the International Parallel and Distributed Processing Symposium (IPDPS) (2009). https://doi.org/10.1109/IPDPS.2009.5161076
64. Nishtala, R., Zheng, Y., Hargrove, P., Yelick, K.A.: Tuning collective communication for Partitioned Global Address Space programming models. Parallel Comput. 37(9), 576–591 (2011). https://doi.org/10.1016/j.parco.2011.05.006
65. Numrich, R.W., Reid, J.: Co-array Fortran for parallel programming. ACM SIGPLAN Fortran Forum 17(2), 1–31 (1998). https://doi.org/10.1145/289918.289920

66. Oak Ridge Leadership Computing Facility. https://www.olcf.ornl.gov
67. Summitdev. https://www.olcf.ornl.gov/tag/summitdev/. Accessed 17 July 2018
68. OpenFabrics Libfabric. https://ofiwg.github.io/libfabric/
69. Petrini, F., chun Feng, W., Hoisie, A., Coll, S., Frachtenberg, E.: The Quadrics network (QsNet): high-performance clustering technology. In: HOT 9 Interconnects. Symposium on High Performance Interconnects, pp. 125–130 (2001). https://doi.org/10.1109/HIS.2001.946704
70. Pophale, S., Nanjegowda, R., Curtis, T., Chapman, B., Jin, H., Poole, S., Kuehn, J.: OpenSHMEM performance and potential: a NPB experimental study. In: Proceedings of the 6th Conference on Partitioned Global Address Space Programming Models (PGAS 2012) (2012). https://www.osti.gov/biblio/1055092
71. Shah, V.B.: An interactive system for combinatorial scientific computing with an emphasis on programmer productivity. Ph.D. thesis, University of California at Santa Barbara, Santa Barbara, CA, USA (2007)
72. Shamis, P., Venkata, M.G., Lopez, M.G., Baker, M.B., Hernandez, O., Itigin, Y., Dubman, M., Shainer, G., Graham, R.L., Liss, L., Shahar, Y., Potluri, S., Rossetti, D., Becker, D., Poole, D., Lamb, C., Kumar, S., Stunkel, C., Bosilca, G., Bouteiller, A.: UCX: an open source framework for HPC network APIs and beyond. In: IEEE 23rd Annual Symposium on High-Performance Interconnects, pp. 40–43, August 2015. https://doi.org/10.1109/HOTI.2015.13
73. Su, H., Gordon, B., Oral, S., George, A.: SCI networking for shared-memory computing in UPC: blueprints of the GASNet SCI conduit. In: Proceedings of the 29th Annual IEEE International Conference on Local Computer Networks. LCN 2004, pp. 718–725. IEEE Computer Society, Washington, DC (2004). https://doi.org/10.1109/LCN.2004.107
74. UCX: Unified Communication X. http://www.openucx.org/
75. UPC Consortium: UPC Language and Library Specifications, v1.3. Technical report, LBNL-6623E, Lawrence Berkeley National Laboratory, November 2013. https://doi.org/10.2172/1134233
76. Vetter, S., Caldeira, A., Kahle, M.E., Saverimuthu, G., Vearner, K.C.: IBM Power System S822LC Technical Overview and Introduction, December 2015. IBM Form #REDP-5283-00
77. Willenberg, R., Chow, P.: A heterogeneous GASNet implementation for FPGA-accelerated computing. In: Proceedings of the 8th International Conference on Partitioned Global Address Space Programming Models, PGAS 2014, pp. 2:1–2:9. ACM, New York (2014). https://doi.org/10.1145/2676870.2676885
78. Yelick, K., Hilfinger, P., Graham, S., Bonachea, D., Su, J., Kamil, A., Datta, K., Colella, P., Wen, T.: Parallel languages and compilers: perspective from the Titanium experience. Int. J. High Perform. Comput. Appl. 21(3), 266–290 (2007). https://doi.org/10.1177/1094342007078449
79. Zheng, Y., Kamil, A., Driscoll, M.B., Shan, H., Yelick, K.: UPC++: a PGAS extension for C++. In: IEEE 28th International Parallel and Distributed Processing Symposium, pp. 1105–1114, May 2014. https://doi.org/10.1109/IPDPS.2014.115
80. Zhou, H., Mhedheb, Y., Idrees, K., Glass, C.W., Gracia, J., Fürlinger, K.: DART-MPI: an MPI-based implementation of a PGAS runtime system. In: Proceedings of the 8th International Conference on Partitioned Global Address Space Programming Models, PGAS 2014, pp. 3:1–3:11 (2014). https://doi.org/10.1145/2676870.2676875

Nested Parallelism with Algorithmic Skeletons

Alireza Majidi$^{(\boxtimes)}$, Nathan Thomas, Timmie Smith, Nancy Amato,
and Lawrence Rauchwerger

Texas A&M University, College Station, TX 77840, USA
{a.majidi,nthomas,timmie,amato,rwerger}@tamu.edu

Abstract. Nested parallelism is a natural way to express programs for hierarchical systems. It enables a compositional programming approach that can then be mapped onto the system hierarchy. In this paper, we present nested algorithm composition in the *STAPL Skeleton Library* (*SSL*) which uses a nested dataflow model as its internal representation. We show how a high level program specification using *SSL* allows for asynchronous computation and improved locality. We study both the specification and performance of the STAPL implementation of *Kripke*, a mini-app developed by Lawrence Livermore National Laboratory. *Kripke* has multiple levels of parallelism and a number of data layouts, making it an excellent test bed to exercise the effectiveness of a nested parallel programming approach. Performance results are provided for six different nesting orders of the benchmark demonstrating the flexibility and performance of nested algorithmic skeleton composition in STAPL.

Keywords: Algorithmic skeletons · Nested parallelism · Dataflow · *Kripke* mini-app · Sweep algorithm

1 Introduction

Nested parallelism is the invocation of a parallel construct from within another parallel section, and it is a natural way of expressing algorithms with a hierarchical nature. Nested parallelism presents a promising approach to address the complexities of application development on modern, high performance computing systems. However, the composition of nested parallel invocations is only beginning to find its way into parallel programming frameworks. Even when present, there is often a trade-off between expressivity and performance.

This research supported in part by NSF awards CNS-0551685, CCF-1439145, CCF-1423111, IIS-0916053, IIS-0917266, EFRI-1240483, RI-1217991, by NIH NCI R25 CA090301-11, and by DOE awards DE-NA0002376, B575363. This research used resources of the National Energy Research Scientific Computing Center, which is supported by the Office of Science of the U.S. Department of Energy under Contract No. DE-AC02-05CH11231.

© Springer Nature Switzerland AG 2019
M. Hall and H. Sundar (Eds.): LCPC 2018, LNCS 11882, pp. 159–175, 2019.
https://doi.org/10.1007/978-3-030-34627-0_12

For example, languages desiring to mimic the syntax of sequential counterparts often adopt a recursive fork-join execution model, requiring barriers between successive nested parallel sections in the program. This model is sufficient for simple parallel applications with good locality and coarse grain parallel sections. However, more complex programs will suffer from poor scalability due to unnecessary global synchronizations between nested parallel sections.

Nested parallel execution is often additionally constrained by the underlying communication primitives. Some models are effectively limited to two levels of parallelism: one across shared memory nodes using MPI and one within a node using OpenMP or a similar library. These lower level concerns become part of the higher level programming model, decreasing portability and reuse as restrictions are put both on communication between parallel sections and their placement in the system.

In [29,30], we introduced the *STAPL Skeleton Library* (SSL) which includes a set of operators that enables the composition of a sequence of algorithmic skeletons into a common parallel section. By using a dataflow model as the internal representation of skeletons in SSL, the need for global barriers is removed, allowing asynchronous execution of algorithms with fine-grain, point-to-point synchronizations between dataflow nodes which greatly improves scalability.

In this paper, we present the *nested* composition of algorithmic skeletons in SSL which leads to a nested dataflow model representation of nested parallelism in STAPL. In the following sections, we define nested skeleton composition, give examples of its use and describe how programs using it can be efficiently mapped onto the system for execution. Though the composition is static (i.e., strongly typed, recognized at compile time), the evaluation and mapping is dynamic, evaluated at runtime and executed using the asynchronous, nested parallelism support of the STAPL runtime described in [24]. Our implementation enables STAPL to support an arbitrary number of levels of nested parallelism and exploit point-to-point communication across nested sections.

We demonstrate the effectiveness of the proposed functionality by using it in the STAPL implementation of Kripke [19], a parallel transport mini-app developed at Lawrence Livermore National Laboratories. We compare our implementation with the reference MPI+OpenMP implementation.

The contributions of this paper are:

- A novel representation for nested composition of skeletons which employs point-to-point synchronizations in data flow graphs and avoid global synchronization within nested sections.
- Arbitrary levels of nested parallelism using algorithmic skeletons.
- An efficient implementation of the *Kripke* mini-app using algorithmic skeletons which shows competitive performance compared to the hand tuned reference implementation.

2   STAPL Overview

The *Standard Template Adaptive Parallel Library* (STAPL) [6] is a framework developed in C++ for parallel programming. It follows the generic design of the Standard Template Library (STL) [22], with extensions and modifications for parallelism. STAPL is a library, requiring only a C++ compiler (e.g., gcc) and established communication libraries such as MPI. An overview of its major components is presented in Fig. 1.

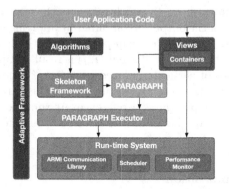

Fig. 1. The STAPL Library component diagram.

STAPL provides *parallel algorithms* and *distributed data structures* [14,28] with interfaces similar to the STL. Instead of iterators, algorithms use *views* [5] which decouple the container interfaces from the underlying storage. The *skeletons framework* [29] allows the user to express an application as a composition of simpler parallel patterns (e.g., map, reduce, scan and others). These skeletons are instantiated at runtime as task dependence graphs by the `PARAGRAPH Executor`, STAPL's data flow engine. It enforces task dependencies and is responsible for the transmission of intermediate values between tasks.

3   STAPL Skeleton Library

The STAPL Skeleton Library is the component of STAPL used to specify parallel algorithms implemented in C++. In the following sections, we discuss how common composition operations found in functional languages are provided in our library. However, we first discuss *parametric dependencies* which are a basic building block of dependence patterns in STAPL skeletons.

3.1   Parametric Dependencies

To build data flow graph representations for fundamental skeletons, we use their finest-grain dependence relations, which we refer to as *parametric dependencies* (PDs). A parametric dependency defines the relation between the input elements of a skeleton and its output as a parametric coordinate mapping and an operation. Parametric dependency specifications for *map*, *zip* and a 2D *wavefront* skeleton are provided below in Eqs. 1, 2 and 3, respectively:

$$zip\_pd_{<1>}(\oslash) = map\_pd(\oslash) \equiv \{i \mapsto i, \oslash\} \tag{1}$$

$$zip\text{-}pd_{<k>}(\oplus) \equiv \{< \underbrace{i, \ldots, i}_{k} > \mapsto < i >, \oplus)\} \tag{2}$$

$$wavefront\_pd_{2D}(\oplus) \equiv \{(i, j-1), (i-1, j) \mapsto (i, j), \oplus\} \tag{3}$$

For the *zip-pd* shown in Eq. 2, which is general form of the *map-pd* (Eq. 1), the value of element i of the output is computed by applying the $\oplus$ work-function (unary work-function $\oslash$ in case of *map-pd*), on the ith element of the inputs. For the *wavefront-pd*, the value of element (i, j) is result of applying the $\oplus$ work-function on the values of elements indexed by $(i - 1, j)$ and $(i, j - 1)$. There is an assumption that work-functions are functional, the only exception is when an argument is passed explicitly as a reference. At runtime, *PDs* are expanded to generate data flow graph nodes by the *elem* composition operator, which we describe next.

3.2 Skeleton Composition

Elem. *Elem* is the most basic operator employed to build skeletons. It expands the given parametric dependence over the domain of each input passed to the skeleton at run-time. The graph generated by the expansion of *PDs* is encapsulated by skeleton *ports*. A *port* provides an interface to access the inputs/outputs passed to/from skeletons. *Ports* play an important role as they allow the sending and receiving of data between skeletons without exposing the internal representation of skeletons (data-flow graph). For instance, the *zip* and *wavefront* skeletons are built by applying the *elem* operator to *zip-pd* and *wavefront-pd*, respectively:

$$zip_{<k>}(\oplus) = elem(zip\_pd_{<k>}(\oplus)) \tag{4}$$

$$wavefront_{2D}(\oplus) = elem(wavefront\_pd_{2D}(\oplus)) \tag{5}$$

Figure 2 shows the *ports* and data-flow graph generated for zip (2a) and wavefront (2b) skeletons using the *elem* operator.

Compose. *Function composition*, denoted by $h = f \circ g$, is the ability to create a new function of h by applying f to the input of h and then passing the output to g and then returning the result of that function invocation. The equivalent of the "$\circ$" is the *compose* operator in the STAPL skeleton library:

$$Skeleton2 = compose(Skeleton0, Skeleton1) \tag{6}$$

As shown in Fig. 3(a), *compose* connects the ports of skeletons passed to it as an argument in a functional composition manner. In this example, the input port of *sk0* is connected to the input port of *sk2* and the *sk1* output port will be the output port of the *sk2*. Finally, the output port of the *sk0* will be connected to the input port of *sk1*. Encapsulation of the data-flow graph representation of skeletons behind their *ports* makes it possible to access the output of skeletons

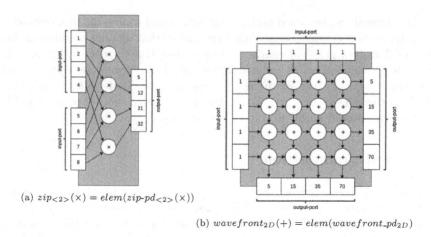

(a) $zip_{<2>}(\times) = elem(zip\text{-}pd_{<2>}(\times))$

(b) $wavefront_{2D}(+) = elem(wavefront\_pd_{2D})$

Fig. 2. Building *zip* and *wavefront* skeletons and their corresponding ports using *elem* operator.

without having any knowledge about the shape of the graph and still allows communication between graph nodes belonging to different skeletons without bulk synchronization between skeleton executions (the point-to-point synchronization shown in Fig. 3(a) with black arrows).

Repeat. The *repeat* operator takes a skeleton as an argument and composes it in a functional manner with itself some number of times. This allows the expression of many skeletons which require tree-based or multilevel data-flow graph, such as *reduce* or *scan*. In Fig. 3(b) the *reduce* skeleton is defined by applying the *repeat* operator on one level of the *reduce* skeleton, which is implemented by utilizing the *elem* operator and the reduce parametric dependency.

$$reduce(\otimes) = repeat(elem(reduce\_pd(\otimes))) \qquad (7)$$

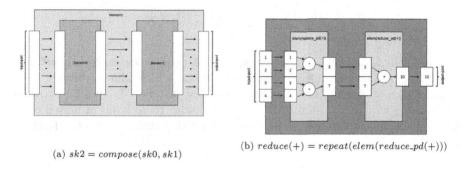

(a) $sk2 = compose(sk0, sk1)$

(b) $reduce(+) = repeat(elem(reduce\_pd(+)))$

Fig. 3.

These operators are closed under composition and enable the programmer to succinctly express complex algorithms in a manner that remains readily translatable to a data-flow graph at runtime for execution. Due to space limitations, we have only provided an overview of existing operators. More details about these operators as well as other components of our skeleton framework are presented in [29]. In the next section, we discuss the nested composition operator and its use to specify nested parallelism in STAPL programs.

4 Nested Composition

Algorithmic skeletons are rooted in the functional programming paradigm, where functions are treated as first-class citizens and are the primary means of building programs. In functional languages, functions are high-order functions, meaning they should be able to accept another function as an argument. Similarly, in our skeleton framework skeletons can receive other skeletons as arguments. This forms the basis for nested skeleton composition which in turn forms the basis of nested parallel algorithm specification in STAPL.

4.1 Specification

An ideal specification of skeletons should be oblivious of any nested composition. Consider specification of the map function in *Haskell* in Eq. 8. Except for specifying the type of the work-function $(a \rightarrow b)$ for *map*, no additional detail is provided about whether the argument is a simple user-defined function or another skeleton made by composition operators in the language.

$$map :: (a \rightarrow b) \rightarrow [a] \rightarrow [b] \tag{8}$$

Skeleton specifications in SSL follow the same approach. Equation 9 shows that the general parametric dependency definition doesn't consider any difference between a regular user-defined operator and an algorithmic skeleton as a work-function specified by $\oplus$.

$$pd(\oplus) \equiv \{(\underbrace{i_0, \ldots, i_k}_{\text{inputs}}) \mapsto (i), \oplus)\} \tag{9}$$

This general specification of parametric dependencies makes algorithmic skeletons in SSL closed under nesting compositions, which allows arbitrary specification of nested composition of skeletons. For instance, Listing 1.1 shows a small kernel written in SSL utilizing a skeleton with three levels of nested composition which is functionally composed with another skeleton with two levels of nesting.

Listing 1.1. Example of skeletons nested composition in SSL

```
// simple reduce skeleton
auto reduce_sk     = reduce(plus());

// 2 level skeletons nesting
auto map_sk        = map(reduce_sk);

// 3 level skeletons nestings
auto wavefront_sk = wavefront(map_sk);

// function composition of 3 level skeleton nesting
// with 2 level skeleton nesting
auto new_skeleton = compose(wavefront_sk, zip(zip(plus())))
```

Note that inputs to a nested skeleton need to reflect the algorithmic hierarchy. Specifically, a skeleton with n levels of nesting compositions need input views with n levels of addressing.

4.2   Execution

As mentioned earlier, there is uniform treatment in the framework of skeletons specified with or without nested composition. However, during evaluation and execution of a skeleton, we internally specialize the implementation based on whether the work-function passed to a skeleton is sequential or another algorithmic skeleton. In this section, we use a $wavefront_{2D}(zip(+))$ skeleton with two levels of parallelism, where a $zip(+)$ skeleton is passed as work-function of $wavefront_{2D}$ skeleton, to show how nested parallel execution is realized in the STAPL skeleton framework.

As shown in Eq. 3, the $wavefront$ skeleton is specified by applying the *elem* operator to *wavefront-pd*. At run-time the *elem* operator traverses the domain of its input ports and uses the parametric dependency passed to it to spawn nodes, adding them to the underlying data-flow engine (**PARAGRAPH**).

The *parametric dependency* determines the corresponding inputs of each node and the work-function which will be applied to its inputs during execution. As shown in Fig. 4, applying the *elem* operator on *wavefront-pd* spawned 4 nodes (2×2) with the *wavefront* pattern.

Up until this point everything about data-flow graph initialization is the same, regardless of whether the work-function of the node is an algorithmic skeleton or a simple sequential operator. At this point, however, we take a different path based on the type of work-function presented to the skeleton. If the work-function is a sequential operator, we add the node with its corresponding dependency information to the **PARAGRAPH**. In the presence of a nested skeleton, before adding the node to the **PARAGRAPH**, we tag the node to tell the **PARAGRAPH** to initialize a nested parallel section for execution of this node with its own instance of a nested **PARAGRAPH**. Creation of nested sections in STAPL is discussed in detail in [24].

In our example where the work-function is a $zip(+)$ skeleton we create a nested parallel section for each of the nodes in the data-flow graph of the *wavefront* skeleton at execution time, which is shown by dashed line in section of Fig. 4. At each nested section, as soon as the inputs to each node of the $zip(+)$ skeleton are ready, the PARAGRAPH starts the execution of that node and sends its corresponding output to its consumer without waiting at a barrier at the end of each nested section for completion of other tasks. The manner in which the input and output port of $zip(+)$ skeletons are connected to each other and also how the input port and output port of the *wavefront* skeleton are connected to each node is determined by the *wavefront* dependence pattern, shown by bigger arrows in Fig. 4.

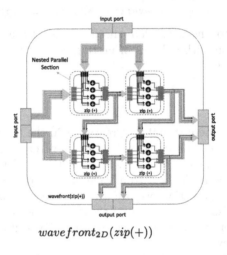

$$wavefront_{2D}(zip(+))$$

Fig. 4. An example of two levels of parallelism in nested composition of skeletons using point-to-point communication between nested sections (shown by dashed line).

While our example only shows two levels of nested-parallelism, nested composition of algorithmic skeletons in SSL allows expressing arbitrary levels of nested parallelism without using any global (or subgroup) synchronization. We discuss initial findings with additional levels of parallelism in Sect. 6.

There are times when it might be preferable to serialize the execution of some levels of the nested parallel algorithm specification. Whether it is insufficient levels of the system hierarchy to map onto or insufficient parallelism in the section to practically exploit, there are times when one may want to suppress some of the available parallelism in the algorithm. For this purpose, we provide execution policy directives that are used to request serial execution *without changing the algorithm specification*. Many of the experimental configurations in Sect. 6 use these directives to mimic the behavior of the reference implementation of *Kripke*. For instance, in $wavefront_{2D}(zip(+))$, user can specify sequential execution policy for execution of $zip(+)$ as shown in Eq. 10.

$$wavefront_{2D}(zip{<}seq\text{-}exec{>}(+)) \tag{10}$$

By using the data-flow model as the internal representation for skeletons, SSL can specify dependences between nodes in data-flow graph at the most fine-grain level, exposing all the available parallelism in the program and enabling an asynchronous nested parallel execution.

5   Kripke, Mini Transport Benchmark

Kripke is a simple mini-app for 3D Sn deterministic particle transport [19]. Mini-apps are importants tools that capture the essential performance behaviors of complex applications and allow rapid implementation of new approaches and exploration of new techniques and architectures. *Kripke*, like its parent application *ADRA*, is implemented with C++, OpenMP, and MPI. We have implemented *Kripke* v1.0 [1] using our skeleton framework and studied the performance of the sweep kernel with varying levels of parallelism and loop nesting orders.

5.1   Problem Description and Reference Implementation

Kripke solves the steady state form of the Boltzmann transport equation and stores the angular flux for every point in the phase space representing every point in the discretized angle, energy, and 3D spatial dimensions. The mini-app has three distinct kernels that perform a discrete-to-moments transformation (LTimes), a moments-to-discrete transformation (LPlusTimes), and a Sweep of the spatial domain for all discretized points in the energy and angle domains. The LTimes and LPlusTimes kernels are completely parallel map operations. We focus on the Sweep kernel and its unique composition challenges in this work.

Algorithm 1. Sweep Algorithm

1: G all groups in the domain problem
2: D all directions in the domain problem
3: Z_p zone-set assigned to the current task
4: **procedure** SWEEP-SOLVER
5:     **for** each G_p in G **do**
6:         **for** each D_p in D **do**
7:             sweep($\{G_p, D_p, Z_p\}$)
8:         **end for**
9:         send/receive local sweep results between MPI tasks
10:     **end for**
11: **end procedure**

The discretized problem phase space $(G \cdot D \cdot Z)$ is partitioned into P subsets, identified by $\{G_p, D_p, Z_p\}_{p \in P}$. Each of these subsets are assigned to an MPI task in the reference implementation. MPI tasks operate on sub-domain of the problem. The choice of the data-layout for storing these subsets and corresponding choice of OpenMP loop-level threading for on-node parallelism greatly affects the performance of the application and is the primary research interest for the mini-app. The reference implementation supports all six layout orders and provides computational kernels written for each layout. The layout/loop nesting order is referred to by the strings (*DGZ, DZG, GZD, GDZ, ZGD* and *ZDG*) that indicate the order of the loops in the Sweep kernel. The Sweep kernel for the DGZ and ZGD nestings are provided as examples in Algorithms 2 and 3, respectively. The *diamond-difference* computation and more details about Sweep algorithm is provided in [19].

Algorithm 2. Sweep Kernel for DGZ nesting order

1: **procedure** $Sweep_{DGZ}(\{G_p, D_p, Z_p\})$
2:     **for** each d in D_p **do**
3:         **for** each g in G_p **do**
4:             **for** z_k in range Z_{pk} **do**
5:                 **for** z_j in range Z_{pj} **do**
6:                     **for** z_i in range Z_{pi} **do**
7:                         diamond-difference computation
8:                     **end for**
9:                 **end for**
10:             **end for**
11:         **end for**
12:     **end for**
13: **end procedure**

Algorithm 3. Sweep Kernel for ZGD nesting order

1: **procedure** $Sweep_{ZGD}(\{G_p, D_p, Z_p\})$
2:     **for** z_k in range Z_{pk} **do**
3:         **for** z_j in range Z_{pj} **do**
4:             **for** z_i in range Z_{pi} **do**
5:                 **for** each g in G_p **do**
6:                     **for** each d in D_p **do**
7:                         diamond-difference computation
8:                     **end for**
9:                 **end for**
10:             **end for**
11:         **end for**
12:     **end for**
13: **end procedure**

The partitioning of the problem phase space across MPI tasks in the reference implementation partitions the spatial dimensions only. The result is that the sweep kernel is a sweep of the spatial domain that is distributed across the nodes of the system. Within each node, OpenMP is used to parallelize the loop iterating over the energy or angle domains, depending on the layout chosen. The outermost of the direction or energy loops is the loop that is parallelized using OpenMP in the reference implementation. In the SSL implementation, we follow the same partitioning of the spatial domain across nodes and explore parallelization at multiple levels in processing a partition of the phase space on a node.

The sweep algorithm across MPI tasks is provided in Algorithm 1. As mentioned above, the sweep is a nested computation since *Zones* are partitioned into P sets by partitioning the spatial domain only. The outer sweep is performed for each direction set (a grouping of directions within the same octant) and energy group set (a grouping of consecutive energy groups). The on-node operation for the Sweep is the call to the sweep function in line 7. The communication of angular flux values from the on-node sweep computation is line 9 in Algorithm 1.

5.2   Kripke Implementation in STAPL

The Sweep implementation of *Kripke* in STAPL follows the same approach for decomposing the domain problem into set of sub-domains and doing two sweeps, one over all subdomains and a nested sweep on each sub-domain. In the STAPL implementation, *STL* containers are replaced by distributed containers called pContainers [2]. pContainers distribute data across the system and provide data access operations that encapsulate the details of accessing distributed data. The STAPL container framework supports composition of pContainers which makes them a natural fit for expressing applications with nested-parallelism. Listing 1.2 describes the data structure to store the angular fluxes in the STAPL implementation of *Kripke* using a *multiarray* container, a generic multidimensional container in the STAPL container framework.

Listing 1.2. Container Composition used for angular flux storage in STAPL Kripke.

```
// storing angular flux storage in
// a 5D space (z_i, z_j, z_k, d, g)
using zoneset_container = multiarray<5, double> ;

// decomposition of zones in a 3D geometry space
using zonesets_container = multiarray<3, zoneset_container>;
```

The Sweep kernel is implemented by nested composition of algorithmic skeletons provided in SSL. A *wavefront* skeleton captures the sweep pattern, and the *zip* skeleton is employed to process the energy and direction domains. In Listing 1.3, sweep skeletons for two nesting orders, *DGZ* and *ZGD*, are shown. In the first level of the composition, *wavefront* is used to sweep across all the *ZoneSets*, regardless of the nesting order. Based on the nesting order chosen, the work-function passed to wavefront skeleton will differ.

The use of SSL algorithmic skeletons to describe the sweep algorithm has several advantages over use of low-level libraries like MPI and OpenMP, besides programming abstraction and concise specification: First, parallelizing the second sweep over each *ZoneSet* using OpenMP is not a trivial task. However, use of the data-flow graph representation as an internal model for skeletons enables parallelizing skeletons regardless of the parallel library chosen for execution. This means the second sweep in the algorithm could be considered as a candidate to be executed in parallel. Furthermore, SSL supports parallel and sequential implementation for all provided skeletons, which allows the programmer to test different execution policies to find the best configuration. Finally, using SSL Algorithmic Skeletons enables nested parallel execution beyond the common two levels, which enables taking advantage of the hierarchical design of new computer architectures.

Listing 1.3. Nested composition of skeletons to describe DZG and ZGD sweep kernels

```
// sweep kernel for DGZ nesting order
auto DGZ_sweep_kernel =
  wavefront(                               // sweep over zone-sets
    zip(                                   // for loop over groups
      zip(                                 // for loop over directions
        wavefront(diamond-difference-wf)  // sweep over each zone-set
  )));

// sweep kernel for ZGD nesting order
auto ZGD_sweep_kernel =
  wavefront(                        // sweep over zone-sets
    wavefront(                      // sweep over each zone-set
      zip(                          // for loop over groups
        zip(diamond-difference-wf)  // for loop over directions
  )));
```

6   Experimental Results

In this section, we compare the performance of the *Kripke* reference code with the STAPL implementation. All experiments are performed on a Cray XK7m-200 with twenty-four compute nodes of 2.1 GHz AMD Opteron Interlagos 16-core processors. Twelve nodes are single socket with 32 GB RAM, and twelve are dual socket with 64 GB RAM. We use *gcc 4.9* with the *O3* optimization flag and *craype-hugepages2M* module. We perform two sets of experiments, one exercising single node scaling and one showing scaling across multiple nodes. In both experiments, the performance of the STAPL implementation of *Kripke*'s sweep computation is compared with that of the reference code.

6.1   Single Node Performance

For the single node performance study all zones are decomposed into just one *ZoneSet*, meaning that there is no sweep over the *ZoneSets* (one element). The reference code uses OpenMP, so we configure the STAPL runtime to use

OpenMP as well. As a result, strong scaling results show the performance of local sweep of different kernels with a varying number of threads used on the node. The problem test used in [19] has $12 \times 12 \times 12$ spatial zones, 8 *DirectionSets*, 12 *Directions* per set (96 total *Directions*) and 1 *GroupSet* with 64 energy groups. The authors refer to it as the KP0 configuration. We use KP0 and also define a KP0′ configuration, increasing the spatial zones to $20 \times 20 \times 20$, number of directions to 348 (48 directions per DirectionSet) and number of groups to 128. Figures 5a and b show strong scaling results for all 6 different kernels with the two configurations of KP0 and KP0′, respectively. For the single node study we use a larger, 32 core node.

For the *DGZ* and *DZG* kernels with the KP0 configuration, STAPL sweep stops scaling after 12 threads since we are parallelizing the second level skeleton (*zip*) corresponding to D, while the reference code parallelizes the third level loop, G, using OpenMP. However, for the KP0′ configuration, due to larger number of directions, scaling continues for the STAPL version and matches the reference code's behavior.

The *GZD* and *GDZ* kernels show the same behavior for the small configuration of *KP0* and the larger configuration of *KP0'*. However, performance of the STAPL implementation of sweep is more sensitive when the program stops scaling, due to a higher overhead of parallelization, which needs to be investigated and optimized.

For kernels starting with Z loops (*ZGD* and *ZDG*), the ability to parallelize the inner *wavefront* skeleton (local sweep) in STAPL version allows scaling to a higher number of threads, while the reference code doesn't scale after 4 and 8 threads, respectively, due to a lack of this functionality.

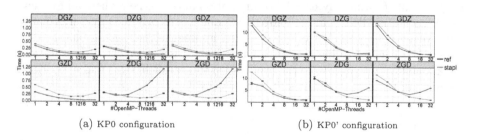

(a) KP0 configuration   (b) KP0′ configuration

Fig. 5. Single node strong scaling for all nesting orders.

6.2   Multi-node Performance

A weak scaling study similar to that in [19] is performed for investigating the scalability of the outer sweeps over the *ZoneSets*. All *ZoneSets* have the *KP0* configuration for Fig. 6a and the *KP0′* configuration for Fig. 6b. Each *ZoneSet* is assigned to one MPI task. We have run this experiment for all kernels up to 64 MPI tasks, each with 8 threads (512 cores in total), to compare the sweep algorithm implemented in STAPL with the reference implementation.

Based on the kernel chosen for MPI scaling, the STAPL sweep is either faster or slower than the reference implementation. The choice of 8 threads per *Zone-Set* is not the best optimal case for on-node computation as shown in on-node scaling study. While this number was a reasonable basis of comparison and supports a large number of possible configurations, we intend to investigate different configurations of the node's cores further.

As can be seen in Fig. 6, the STAPL implementation of sweep shows much less variability in scaling results compared to the reference code. This appears to be due the fact that STAPL is able to parallelize the inner wavefront in the nested section, while the reference's implementation restricts it to parallelizing the next lower loop level, resulting in more parallel sections with smaller granularity and more global synchronizations.

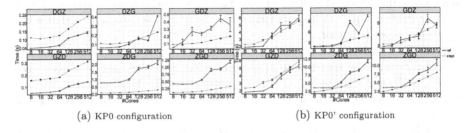

(a) KP0 configuration   (b) KP0' configuration

Fig. 6. Multi-node weak scaling for all nesting orders.

While we only present results with two levels of parallelism, we have obtained initial results for the fully parallel configuration of the kernels where all four levels of nested parallelism are employed. We don't currently see any performance improvements beyond that of the two level approach. While additional investigation is needed, possible reasons for this lack of improvement are insufficient work granularity to overcome the overhead of the parallelization and suboptimal mapping of the data onto the system hierarchy.

7   Related Work

OpenMP [23] supports nested parallelism using the fork-join model. When a thread inside a nested sections finishes, it waits at a global barrier in the nested section for other threads to finish. Inefficiencies can arise due to the global barrier at the end of each nested section. This has lead to the introduction of the *Collapse* keyword in OpenMP-3.0, which flattens the nested parallelism.

Several frameworks employ MPI's ability to partition the MPI communication groups into subgroups for nested execution. NestStep [18] uses this ability to partition communications groups into subgroups and run nested sub-supersteps on these subgroups asynchronously. However, the parent group needs to wait for all subgroups to finish their supersteps before going to next superstep, which can degrade performance. [10] and [20] follow the same approach in assigning nested parallel sections to sub-groups of processing elements.

MPI + OpenMP is a common approach to express two level of parallelism in benchmarks [7,19] and [27]. However, this approach usually results in complex codes which are hard to maintain and are restricted to two levels of parallelism.

Among the frameworks which support task-level parallelism, Cilk [26] and TBB [25] allow spawning nested tasks where the system is responsible for mapping nested sections to the machine, which degrades the performance due to loss of locality. X10 [9], Habanero-Java [8], HPX [15], and Fortress [17] allow users to control task-placement. However, as tasks are independent, there is no communications between nested sections.

Legion [3] partitions memory into regions for spawning independent tasks using its dynamic machine mapping model to improve the locality of tasks. However, there is no support for dependencies between nested tasks, and it is limited to task level parallelism.

Among the previous frameworks with *skeleton* specifications with nested composition support, [16] and [4] only support nesting of task-parallel skeletons and do not explicitly address data communication between nested sections. Skeleton frameworks presented in [21] and [13] support two levels of nesting for data-parallel skeletons. However, due to the use of a *master/slave* scheme, their approach is not scalable, especially on distributed systems.

[11] proposes a construct for modeling the nested data-flow model to analyze the complexity of algorithms with nested parallelism.

8   Conclusion

We present a novel implementation of nested parallelism using STAPL, which allows the expression of arbitrary levels of parallelism using the nested composition of algorithmic skeletons. Choosing a data-flow graph representation for skeletons removes the need for barriers between nested parallel sections, leading to a fully asynchronous implementation of nested parallelism.

While the initial results with the multiple levels of nesting are promising, we want to fully utilize the flexibility of the framework to explore various configuration of execution and extend the current to work to support applications with irregular and dynamic workload. We believe that studying this variety of platforms will provide better insight into how nested parallelism can help programmers cope with the deepening hierarchies and heterogeneity present in modern HPC architectures.

References

1. Co-design: Kripke. https://computation.llnl.gov/projects/co-design/kripke
2. An, P., et al.: STAPL: a standard template adaptive parallel C++ library. In: Proceedings of the International Workshop on Advanced Compiler Technology for High Performance and Embedded Processors (IWACT), Bucharest, Romania, July 2001

3. Bauer, M., Treichler, S., Slaughter, E., Aiken, A.: Legion: expressing locality and independence with logical regions. In: 2012 International Conference for High Performance Computing, Networking, Storage and Analysis (SC), pp. 1–11. IEEE Computer Society Press, November 2012. https://doi.org/10.1109/SC.2012.71

4. Benoit, A., Cole, M.: Two fundamental concepts in skeletal parallel programming. In: Sunderam, V.S., van Albada, G.D., Sloot, P.M.A., Dongarra, J.J. (eds.) ICCS 2005. LNCS, vol. 3515, pp. 764–771. Springer, Heidelberg (2005). https://doi.org/10.1007/11428848_98

5. Buss, A.A., et al.: The STAPL pview. In: Languages and Compilers for Parallel Computing - 23rd International Workshop, LCPC 2010, Houston, TX, USA, 7–9 October 2010. Revised Selected Papers, pp. 261–275 (2010). https://doi.org/10.1007/978-3-642-19595-2_18

6. Buss, A.A., et al.: STAPL: standard template adaptive parallel library. In: Proceedings of of SYSTOR 2010: The 3rd Annual Haifa Experimental Systems Conference, Haifa, Israel, 24–26 May 2010, pp. 1–10. ACM, New York (2010). https://doi.org/10.1145/1815695.1815713, http://doi.acm.org/10.1145/1815695.1815713

7. Cappello, F., Etiemble, D.: MPI versus MPI+OpenMP on IBM SP for the NAS benchmarks. In: Proceedings of the 2000 ACM/IEEE Conference on Supercomputing, SC 2000. IEEE Computer Society, Washington, DC (2000). http://dl.acm.org/citation.cfm?id=370049.370071

8. Cavé, V., Zhao, J., Shirako, J., Sarkar, V.: Habanero-Java: the new adventures of old X10. In: Proceedings of the 9th International Conference on Principles and Practice of Programming in Java, PPPJ 2011, pp. 51–61. ACM, New York (2011). https://doi.org/10.1145/2093157.2093165, http://doi.acm.org/10.1145/2093157.2093165

9. Charles, P., et al.: X10: an object-oriented approach to non-uniform cluster computing. In: Annual ACM SIGPLAN Conference on Object-Oriented Programming, Systems, Languages, and Applications, pp. 519–538. ACM Press, New York (2005). https://doi.org/10.1145/1094811.1094852

10. UPC Consortium: UPC Language Specifications V1.2 (2005). http://www.gwu.edu/~upc/publications/LBNL-59208.pdf

11. Dinh, D., Simhadri, H.V., Tang, Y.: Extending the nested parallel model to the nested dataflow model with provably efficient schedulers. In: Proceedings of the 28th ACM Symposium on Parallelism in Algorithms and Architectures, SPAA 2016, pp. 49–60. ACM (2016). http://doi.acm.org/10.1145/2935764.2935797

12. Fatahalian, K., et al.: Sequoia: programming the memory hierarchy. In: Proceedings of the 2006 ACM/IEEE Conference on Supercomputing, SC 2006. ACM, New York (2006). https://doi.org/10.1145/1188455.1188543, http://doi.acm.org/10.1145/1188455.1188543

13. Hamdan, M., Michaelson, G., King, P.: A scheme for nesting algorithmic skeletons, October 1998

14. Harshvardhan, Fidel, A., Amato, N.M., Rauchwerger, L.: The STAPL parallel graph library. In: Kasahara, H., Kimura, K. (eds.) LCPC 2012. LNCS, vol. 7760, pp. 46–60. Springer, Heidelberg (2013). https://doi.org/10.1007/978-3-642-37658-0_4

15. Heller, T., Kaiser, H., Schäfer, A., Fey, D.: Using HPX and LibGeoDecomp for scaling HPC applications on heterogeneous supercomputers. In: Proceedings of the Workshop on Latest Advances in Scalable Algorithms for Large-Scale Systems, ScalA 2013, pp. 1:1–1:8. ACM, New York (2013). https://doi.org/10.1145/2530268.2530269, http://doi.acm.org/10.1145/2530268.2530269

16. Jocelyn Sérot, D.G.: Skeletons for parallel image processing: an overview of the skipper project, December 2002
17. Jr Steele, G.L., et al.: Fortress (sun HPCS language). In: Padua, D.A. (ed.) Encyclopedia of Parallel Computing, pp. 718–735. Springer, Boston (2011). https://doi.org/10.1007/978-0-387-09766-4. http://dblp.uni-trier.de/db/reference/parallel/parallel2011.html#SteeleACFLMR11
18. Keßler, C.W.: NestStep: nested parallelism and virtual shared memory for the BSP model. J. Supercomput. **17**(3), 245–262 (2000). http://dblp.uni-trier.de/db/journals/tjs/tjs17.html#Kessler00
19. Lawrence Berkeley National Laboratory and United States. Department of Energy and United States. Department of Energy. Office of Scientific and Technical Information: Kripke - a massively parallel transport mini-app. United States. Department of Energy (2015)
20. Mellor-Crummey, J., Adhianto, L., Scherer, I.W.N., Jin, G.: A new vision for coarray Fortran. In: Proceedings of the Third Conference on Partitioned Global Address Space Programing Models, PGAS 2009, pp. 5:1–5:9. ACM, New York (2009). https://doi.org/10.1145/1809961.1809969, http://doi.acm.org/10.1145/1809961.1809969
21. Michaelson, G., Scaife, N., Bristow, P., King, P.: Nested algorithmic skeletons from higher order functions (2000)
22. Musser, D., Derge, G., Saini, A.: STL Tutorial and Reference Guide, 2nd edn. Addison-Wesley, Boston (2001)
23. OpenMP, ARB: OpenMP Application Program Interface. Specification (2011). http://www.openmp.org/mp-documents/OpenMP3.1.pdf
24. Papadopoulos, I., Thomas, N., Fidel, A., Hoxha, D., Amato, N.M., Rauchwerger, L.: Asynchronous nested parallelism for dynamic applications in distributed memory. In: Shen, X., Mueller, F., Tuck, J. (eds.) LCPC 2015. LNCS, vol. 9519, pp. 106–121. Springer, Cham (2016). https://doi.org/10.1007/978-3-319-29778-1_7
25. Reinders, J.: Intel Threading Building Blocks. O'Reilly & Associates Inc., Sebastopol (2007)
26. Robison, A.D.: Composable parallel patterns with Intel Cilk Plus. Comput. Sci. Eng. **15**(2), 0066–71 (2013)
27. Sillero, J., Borrell, G., Jiménez, J., Moser, R.D.: Hybrid OpenMP-MPI turbulent boundary layer code over 32k cores. In: Cotronis, Y., Danalis, A., Nikolopoulos, D.S., Dongarra, J. (eds.) EuroMPI 2011. LNCS, vol. 6960, pp. 218–227. Springer, Heidelberg (2011). https://doi.org/10.1007/978-3-642-24449-0_25
28. Tanase, G., et al.: The STAPL parallel container framework. In: Proceedings of the 16th ACM SIGPLAN Symposium on Principles and Practice of Parallel Programming, PPOPP 2011, San Antonio, TX, USA, 2–16 February 2011, pp. 235–246 (2011). https://doi.org/10.1145/1941553.1941586, http://doi.acm.org/10.1145/1941553.1941586
29. Zandifar, M., Jabbar, M.A., Majidi, A., Keyes, D., Amato, N.M., Rauchwerger, L.: Composing algorithmic skeletons to express high-performance scientific applications. In: Proceedings of the 29th ACM International Conference on Supercomputing (ICS), ICS 2015, pp. 415–424. ACM, New York (2015). https://doi.org/10.1145/2751205.2751241, http://doi.acm.org/10.1145/2751205.2751241. Conference Best Paper Award
30. Zandifar, M., Thomas, N., Amato, N.M., Rauchwerger, L.: The STAPL skeleton framework. In: Brodman, J., Tu, P. (eds.) LCPC 2014. LNCS, vol. 8967, pp. 176–190. Springer, Cham (2015). https://doi.org/10.1007/978-3-319-17473-0_12

HDArray: Parallel Array Interface for Distributed Heterogeneous Devices

Hyun Dok Cho[1]([⊠]), Okwan Kwon[2], and Samuel P. Midkiff[3]

[1] NVIDIA Corporation, Santa Clara, USA
hyundokc@nvidia.com
[2] Apple Inc., Cupertino, USA
o_kwon@apple.com
[3] Purdue University, West Lafayette, USA
smidkiff@purdue.edu

Abstract. Heterogeneous clusters with nodes containing one or more accelerators, such as GPUs, have become common. While MPI provides inter-address space communication, and OpenCL provides a process with access to heterogeneous computational resources, programmers are forced to write hybrid programs that manage the interaction of both of these systems. This paper describes an array programming interface that provides users with automatic and manual distributions of data and work. Using work distribution, and kernel *def* and *use* information, communication among processes and devices in a process is performed automatically. By providing a unified programming model to the user, program development is simplified.

1 Introduction

Both large and small scale multi-node systems with one or more GPUs per node have become common. These systems, however, complicate already messy distributed system programming by adding MPI [13] to proprietary host-GPU mechanisms. Developers must maintain two programming models: one for intra-process communication among devices and one for inter-process communication across address spaces.

Several systems have improved the programmability of multi-node systems with accelerators. SnuCL [16,18], dCuda [15], and IMPACC [17] support transparent access to accelerators on different nodes, and PARRAY [7] and Viñas et al. [32] provide high-level language abstractions and flexible array representations. Programmers can develop high-performance applications but must manage low-level details of accelerator programming or provide explicit communication code. Partitioned Global Address Space (PGAS) platforms for accelerators, XMP-ACC [22], XACC [25], and Potluri et al. [27], relieve programmers from dealing with data distribution, but data is strongly coupled to threads, making

---

H. D. Cho—This work was done while at Purdue University.

O. Kwon—This work was done while at NVIDIA Corporation.

ⓒ Springer Nature Switzerland AG 2019
M. Hall and H. Sundar (Eds.): LCPC 2018, LNCS 11882, pp. 176–184, 2019.
https://doi.org/10.1007/978-3-030-34627-0_13

performance tuning more difficult. Finally, compiler-assisted runtime systems, Hydra [29] and OMPD [20], propose a fully automatic approach that allows OpenMP programs to run on accelerator clusters, presenting an attractive alternative for developing repetitive and regular applications, but the distribution of work and data are limited by OpenMP semantics and expressiveness. Other related work [1–6, 9–11, 14, 19, 21, 23, 26, 28, 31, 33] is discussed in [8].

In this paper, we describe the Heterogeneous Distributed Array (HDArray) interface and runtime system. HDArray targets program execution on cluster-sized distributed systems with nodes containing one or more accelerators, i.e., devices. Work is done by OpenCL work items, and HDArray provides ways to explicitly and implicitly partition work onto devices.

HDArray also provides ways to specify data used by the work on a device. Data read and written is typically relative to work items and can be specified either using offsets from the work item, or with an absolute specification of the data. HDArray then tracks the data defined and used by each work item, which allows communication to be generated automatically, since, in race-free programs, HDArray knows where the last written copy of a datum is, and who needs that value. Importantly, data is not explicitly distributed and is not bound to, or owned by, a work item, but flows from its defining device to the device where it is needed.

Finally, HDArray allows work to be repartitioned at any point in the program. This flexibility allows a programmer to optimize the work distribution and its necessary communication without any changes to the kernel code.

2 Design of the HDArray Interface

The central structure and concept of the HDArray system is the HDArray itself. The HDArray encapsulates a *host buffer* and *device buffer* by keeping necessary state for communication among processes and kernel computation. Each MPI process that maps to a single OpenCL device maintains HDArrays and their structures. The HDArray system provides a collection of APIs and annotations that the programmer uses to access the features of the HDArray system. These APIs and annotations are translated by the HDArray frontend into calls, arguments, and initialization files for use by the HDArray runtime. Detailed information about the interface can be found in [8].

2.1 HDArray Programming Interface

The HDArray programming interface has two types of specifications. First, a single pragma of the form `#pragma hdarray [clauses]` allows user-defined hints to find data to be accessed and partition work item regions to distribute work. Second, HDArray provides library functions, hiding low-level details of distributed device programming. We now show a General Matrix Multiply (GEMM) implemented using HDArray, consisting of C host and OpenCL device code to perform the matrix multiply $C = A \times B$ on three 1024×1024 2D matrices.

Line 6 of the host code (Listing 1.1) initializes the MPI and OpenCL environments. Line 7 evenly partitions the highest dimension of the 2D array domain with regard to the number of devices. The function returns a partition ID, part0, which represents the partitioned region and is used throughout the program.

On lines 8–10, the host allocates host and device buffers of HDArrays with the same size as the user-space arrays. After the allocation, handles (hA, hB, hC) allow users to access device buffers holding data for their respective program arrays (a, b, c). Lines 11–13 write user arrays into the device buffer of HDArrays according to the part0 specification. Therefore, the data is distributed to different devices.

```
1  void main(int argc, char *argv[]) {
2    int ni = 1024, nj = 1024, nk = 1024;
3    float a[ni][nk], b[nk][nj], c[ni][nj], al, be;
4    HDArray_t *hA, *hB, *hC;
5    ... // initialize variables
6    HDArrayInit(argc, argv, "gemm.cl", NULL);
7    int part0 = HDArrayPartition(ROW, 2, ni, nj, 0, 0, ni, nj);
8    hA = HDArrayCreate("a", "float", a, 2, ni, nk);
9    hB = HDArrayCreate("b", "float", b, 2, nk, nj);
10   hC = HDArrayCreate("c", "float", c, 2, ni, nj);
11   HDArrayWrite(hA, a, part0);
12   HDArrayWrite(hB, b, part0);
13   HDArrayWrite(hC, c, part0);
14   HDArrayApplyKernel("gemm", part0, hA, hB, hC,
                        al, be, ni, nj, nk);
15   HDArrayRead(hC, c, part0);
16   HDArrayExit();
17 }
```

Listing 1.1. GEMM host code.

```
1  #pragma hdarray use(A,(0,*)) use(B,(*,0)) def(C,(0,0))
2    __kernel void gemm( __global float *A,
3                        __global float *B,
4                        __global float *C,
5                        float alph,
6                        float beta,
7                        int ni,
8                        int nj,
9                        int nk)
10 {
11   int i = get_global_id(1);
12   int j = get_global_id(0);
13   if ((i < ni) && (j < nj)) {
14     C[i * nj + j] *= beta;
15     for(int k=0; k < nk; k++)
16       C[i*nj+j] += alph * A[i*nk+k] * B[k*nj+j];
17   }
18 }
```

Listing 1.2. GEMM device code.

On line 14, the host launches the "gemm" kernel using part0 for work distribution and kernel arguments. The runtime then binds HDArray handles and host variables to kernel arguments, handles necessary communication, and invokes the kernel. Line 15 reads the result of the computation from the device memory into user array c. Finally, the host frees all the resources, including HDArrays, and finalizes the parallel program in line 16.

The device code in Listing 1.2 shows an ordinary OpenCL kernel to be called, with an annotation added on line 1. The annotation is a #pragma hdarray statement with *use* and *def* offset clauses. These offsets, relative to a work item index, specify slices of the A, B, and C arrays that are used and defined. The code informs the runtime system that a single thread reads all elements of the row of the array A and all elements of the column of the array B. The zero offset indicates that each thread writes the result of the multiplication to its work item index of the array C. With the per-thread array element access (offset) and work partitioning (part0) information, the runtime generates communication and launches the kernel.

The offsets can be used when a kernel's array access pattern is relative to a work item, which is the most common kernel programming pattern. For nonrectangular access patterns, one can use the *absolute section interface* with *use@* and/or *def@* clauses and APIs. The HDArray pragma also enables manual partitions for more programmer control of communication tuning and load balancing.

2.2   Communication Generation Using Array Section Analysis

An HDArray contains sets of array sections: *global*, i.e., across all kernels, definition sections (*GDEF*); *local*, i.e., for a particular kernel, definition sections (*LDEF*); and local use sections (*LUSE*). GDEF is a set of written sections not yet communicated, and two types of GDEFs are maintained: sGDEF to send and rGDEF to receive. LUSE/LDEF is the set of sections each process reads/writes in the kernel. HDArray programs are SPMD programs, and each process maintains coherent local copies of the aforementioned four sets for all processes, and thus each process knows the array access information of all other processes.

When the program invokes a kernel, the runtime analyzes LDEF and LUSE by composing the partitioned work item region with the offset provided by each kernel. The runtime then communicates only necessary array sections by intersecting LUSE with the GDEF. After communication and kernel execution, the system updates GDEF sets for each HDArray for kernel call k to avoid redundant communication and detect new communication in the future kernel call $k + 1$. Handling communication requires the number of array section computations on each process p that is linear in the number of processes. The HDArray system reduces the runtime overhead by maintaining a history of LDEF/LUSE and GDEF, and overlapping communication with GDEF computation [8].

3   Experimental Results

Our evaluation is done using up to 32 OpenCL devices on the XSEDE Comet GPU cluster [24,30], which consist of NVIDIA P100 and K80 nodes. We use six micro-kernel benchmarks from PolyBench/ACC [12]. Baseline numbers are found using the implementations provided by the benchmarks. For HDArray numbers, OpenCL device and C host code includes HDArray pragmas and library calls.

In this section, we focus on scalability of HDArray programs, but details of the experimental setup and the evaluation of runtime overhead can be found in [8].

Figure 1 shows strong scaling with the baseline of an OpenCL device running without HDArray. All the benchmarks perform a row-wise partition using the HDArrayPartition function with a ROW argument for work and data distribution. Most benchmarks running on K80 nodes scale better than those on P100 nodes because the P100 is faster than the K80, and thus the communication overhead on P100 nodes is a larger fraction of the computation time.

GEMM, shown in Sect. 2.1, uses $10{,}240 \times 10{,}240$ matrices with 100 iterations. The HDArray runtime system detects and generates all-gather collective communication because each OpenCL work-item needs row and column elements of arrays for computation. Scaling is good to 32 processes, with similar efficiencies on the K80 (92%) and P100 (90%), due to the low ratio of communication to kernel execution time. 2MM performs two matrix multiplications, $D = A \times B$ followed by $E = C \times D$. It differs from GEMM in that 2MM runs two kernel functions within a loop and exhibits a data dependency because one kernel defines the array D used by the other kernel. With the row-wise partitioning,

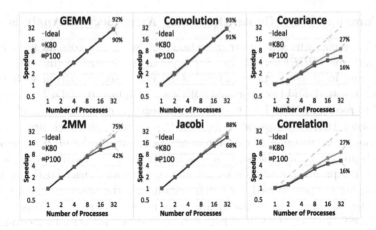

Fig. 1. Scalability for the HDArray runtime system on P100 and K80 nodes. We show the speedup for each benchmark, which is the ratio of the execution time of a single device to the execution time of the number of devices indicated on the x-axis. All the benchmarks use an automatic row-wise partitioning for data and work distribution.

the efficiency drops off to about 75% (42%) on the K80 (P100) at 32 processes because of the communication cost. The cost is proportional to the number of processes, and every iteration requires the communication: once for the array B, and 100 times for the array D.

A different partitioning can be used to reduce the communication cost. 2MM with column-wise partitioning, as shown in Fig. 2, communicates only twice for arrays A and C, and the efficiency is about 98% (96%) on the K80 (P100) at 32 processes. Table 1 shows communication volumes of all 32 processes and a noticeable volume difference for 2MM. This performance tuning was done by simply changing the `PART_T` argument of `HDArrayPartition` function.

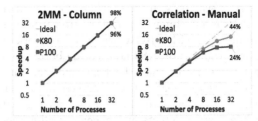

Fig. 2. Scalability for the HDArray runtime system with different partitioning methods. 2MM uses automatic column-wise partitioning, and Correlation uses manual row- and column-wise partitionings.

Both Jacobi and Convolution kernels are iterative 4 and 8 point stencil codes. The *use* clauses for the first kernel of Jacobi specify four offsets $(0, -1)$, $(0, +1)$,

$(-1,0)$, $(+1,0)$ for array B. The second kernel transfers the array A to the array B, and zero offsets are used. Two partition IDs are used: one for entire arrays and the other that excludes the boundary ghost cells. The kernels have a data dependence on the array B. The kernels all use $20,480 \times 24,080$ matrices with 100,000 iterations, and the runtime detects and schedules point-to-point communication. Convolution needs four additional offsets, but has no data dependency. Both benchmarks scale well with an efficiency of 88% (68%) on the K80 (P100) for Jacobi, and 91% (93%) on the K80 (P100) for Convolution at 32 processes.

Table 1. Total communication volume for 32 processes

Partition	Convolution	JACOBI	GEMM	2MM	Covariance	Correlation
Default (Row)	5 MB	473 GB	12 GB	1262 GB	1268 GB	1268 GB
Customized	5 MB	473 GB	12 GB	25 GB	811 GB	811 GB

Covariance and Correlation are data mining benchmarks that compute a measure from statistics that show how linearly related two variables are. These benchmarks have triangular-shape array accesses, requiring the absolute section interface discussed in Sect. 2.1. Both use 10,240 vectors and $10,240 \times 10,240$ matrices with 100 iterations, and the system detects point-to-point and all-gather communication. Scaling is poor with the default row-wise partitioning, with an efficiency of 27% (16%) on the K80 (P100) for Correlation (similar to Covariance). This is because evenly distributing work using `HDArrayPartition` causes poor work and communication load balancing for kernels that have triangular access patterns. The most time-consuming computation is done from the upper-triangular section of an array which later requires communication to make the array symmetric. As a result, each device gets a different amount of work, and a device with the most computation also has the most communication, which leads to an imbalance of computation and communication across the devices.

Manual partitioning with optimized absolute section updates to balance the work and communication among devices, gives better scalability with an efficiency of 44% (24%) on the K80 (P100) thanks to the reduced communication volume as shown in Fig. 2 and Table 1, respectively. This result highlights the value of integrating manual and automatic partitioning. Also, the performance tuning does not require any changes in kernel code, but only a few lines of host code are changed for different absolute section updates and partitioning.

4   Conclusions

We have presented the HDArray interface and runtime system for accelerator clusters. The interface features a novel global programming model that separates work partitioning from the concept of data distribution, enabling straightforward and flexible work distribution. The interface abstracts away many low-level details of multiple address space programming, yet supports a low-level array programming environment through annotations and APIs for performance tuning. The offsets provide an intuitive and simple way to describe kernel access patterns, and the patterns can be easily changed by simply adjusting partitions without the modification of kernel code. Finally, the HDArray runtime system performs efficient and fully automatic communication by managing the array sections.

Acknowledgments. This material is based upon work supported by the National Science Foundation (NSF) under Grant No. CNS-1405954, and uses the Extreme Science and Engineering Discovery Environment (XSEDE), which is supported by NSF grant number ACI-1548562. Any opinions, findings, and conclusions or recommendations expressed in this material are those of the author(s) and do not necessarily reflect the views of the NSF or XSEDE. We thank Prof. Jeffrey M. Siskind and Purdue ITaP for providing GPU resources.

References

1. ArrayFire. https://arrayfire.com/
2. The OpenACC Application Programming Interface Version 2.5 (2015). http://www.openacc.org/sites/default/files/OpenACC_2pt5.pdf
3. Bikshandi, G., et al.: Programming for parallelism and locality with hierarchically tiled arrays. In: Proceedings of the Eleventh ACM SIGPLAN Symposium on Principles and Practice of Parallel Programming, PPoPP 2006 (2006)
4. Bueno, J., et al.: Productive programming of GPU clusters with OmpSs. In: 2012 IEEE 26th International Parallel and Distributed Processing Symposium (IPDPS), pp. 557–568 (2012)
5. Catanzaro, B., Garland, M., Keutzer, K.: Copperhead: compiling an embedded data parallel language. In: Proceedings of the 16th ACM Symposium on Principles and Practice of Parallel Programming, PPoPP 2011, New York, NY, USA (2011). https://doi.org/10.1145/1941553.1941562
6. Charles, P., et al.: X10: an object-oriented approach to non-uniform cluster computing. In: ACM SIGPLAN Notices, vol. 40, pp. 519–538. ACM (2005)
7. Chen, Y., Cui, X., Mei, H.: PARRAY: a unifying array representation for heterogeneous parallelism. In: Proceedings of the 17th ACM SIGPLAN Symposium on Principles and Practice of Parallel Programming, PPoPP 2012 (2012)
8. Cho, H.D., Kwon, O., Midkiff, S.: HDArray: parallel array interface for distributed heterogeneous devices. arXiv:1809.05657 [cs.DC] (2018). https://arxiv.org/abs/1809.05657
9. Consortium, U., et al.: UPC Language Specifications V1.2. Lawrence Berkeley National Laboratory (2005)
10. Cui, X., Li, X., Chen, Y.: Programming heterogeneous systems with array types. In: 2015 15th IEEE/ACM International Symposium on Cluster, Cloud and Grid Computing (2015)
11. Ernsting, S., Kuchen, H.: Data parallel algorithmic skeletons with accelerator support. Int. J. Parallel Program. **45**(2), 283–299 (2017)
12. Grauer-Gray, S., et al.: Auto-tuning a high-level language targeted to GPU codes. In: 2012 Innovative Parallel Computing (InPar), pp. 1–10, May 2012. https://doi.org/10.1109/InPar.2012.6339595

13. Gropp, W., Lusk, E., Skjellum, A.: Using MPI: Portable Parallel Programming with the Message-Passing Interface, vol. 1. MIT Press, Cambridge (1999)
14. Gupta, M., et al.: An HPF compiler for the IBM SP2. In: Proceedings of the 1995 ACM/IEEE Conference on Supercomputing, Supercomputing 1995. ACM (1995). https://doi.org/10.1145/224170.224422
15. Gysi, T., Bär, J., Hoefler, T.: dCUDA: hardware supported overlap of computation and communication. In: Proceedings of the International Conference for High Performance Computing, Networking, Storage and Analysis, SC 2016 (2016)
16. Kim, J., Jo, G., et al.: A distributed OpenCL framework using redundant computation and data replication. In: Proceedings of the 37th ACM SIGPLAN Conference on Programming Language Design and Implementation, PLDI 2016 (2016)
17. Kim, J., et al.: IMPACC: a tightly integrated MPI+ OpenACC framework exploiting shared memory parallelism. In: International Symposium on High-Performance Parallel and Distributed Computing, HPDC 2016 (2016)
18. Kim, J., et al.: SnuCL: an OpenCL framework for heterogeneous CPU/GPU Clusters. In: Proceedings of the 26th ACM International Conference on Supercomputing, ICS 2012 (2012)
19. Klöckner, A., et al.: PyCUDA and PyOpenCL: a scripting-based approach to GPU run-time code generation. Parallel Comput. 38(3), 157–174 (2012)
20. Kwon, O., et al.: A hybrid approach of OpenMP for clusters. In: Proceedings of the 17th ACM SIGPLAN Symposium on Principles and Practice of Parallel Programming, PPoPP 2012, pp. 75–84 (2012). https://doi.org/10.1145/2145816.2145827
21. Lam, S.K.: NumbaPro: High-Level GPU Programming in Python for Rapid Development. http://on-demand-gtc.gputechconf.com/
22. Lee, J., Tran, M.T., Odajima, T., Boku, T., Sato, M.: An extension of XcalableMP PGAS lanaguage for multi-node GPU clusters. In: Bosilca, G., et al. (eds.) Euro-Par 2011. LNCS, vol. 7155, pp. 429–439. Springer, Heidelberg (2012). https://doi.org/10.1007/978-3-642-29737-3_48
23. Majeed, M., et al.: Cluster-SkePU: a multi-backend skeleton programming library for GPU clusters. In: Proceedings of the International Conference on Parallel and Distributed Processing Techniques and Applications (PDPTA) (2013)
24. Moore, R.L., et al.: Gateways to discovery: cyberinfrastructure for the long tail of science. In: Proceedings of the 2014 Annual Conference on Extreme Science and Engineering Discovery Environment, XSEDE 2014. ACM (2014). https://doi.org/10.1145/2616498.2616540
25. Nakao, M., et al.: XcalableACC: extension of XcalableMP PGAS language using OpenACC for accelerator clusters. In: Workshop on Accelerator Programming Using Directives (WACCPD) (2014). https://doi.org/10.1109/WACCPD.2014.6
26. Numrich, R.W., Reid, J.: Co-array Fortran for parallel programming. In: ACM SIGPLAN Fortran Forum, vol. 17, pp. 1–31. ACM (1998)
27. Potluri, S., et al.: Extending openSHMEM for GPU Computing. In: 2013 IEEE 27th International Symposium on Parallel and Distributed Processing (IPDPS), pp. 1001–1012 (2013)
28. Rice University, CORPORATE: High Performance Fortran Language Specification. SIGPLAN Fortran Forum, December 1993. https://doi.org/10.1145/174223.158909
29. Sakdhnagool, P., Sabne, A., Eigenmann, R.: HYDRA: extending shared address programming for accelerator clusters. In: Shen, X., Mueller, F., Tuck, J. (eds.) LCPC 2015. LNCS, vol. 9519, pp. 140–155. Springer, Cham (2016). https://doi.org/10.1007/978-3-319-29778-1_9

30. Towns, J., et al.: XSEDE: accelerating scientific discovery. Comput. Sci. Eng. **16**(5), 62–74 (2014)
31. Viñas, M., Bozkus, Z., Fraguela, B.B.: Exploiting heterogeneous parallelism with the heterogeneous programming library. J. Parallel Distrib. Comput. **73**(12), 1627–1638 (2013)
32. Viñas, M., et al.: Towards a high level approach for the programming of heterogeneous clusters. In: 2016 45th International Conference on Parallel Processing Workshops (ICPPW), pp. 106–114. IEEE (2016)
33. Yan, Y., et al.: HOMP: automated distribution of parallel loops and data in highly parallel accelerator-based systems. In: 2017 IEEE International Parallel and Distributed Processing Symposium (IPDPS), pp. 788–798. IEEE (2017)

Automating the Exchangeability of Shared Data Abstractions

Jiange Zhang[1(✉)], Qian Wang[2], Qing Yi[1], and Huimin Cui[3]

[1] University of Colorado, Colorado Springs, USA
{jzhang3,qyi}@uccs.edu
[2] NVidia, Shanghai, China
traz0824@gmail.com
[3] Institute of Computing, Chinese Academy of Science, Beijing, China
huimin.cui@gmail.com

Abstract. This paper presents a framework to support the automated exchange of data abstractions in multi-threaded applications, together with an empirical study of their uses in PARSEC. Our framework was able to speedup six of the benchmarks by up to 2x on two platforms.

1 Introduction

Software applications need to use synchronous data abstractions, e.g., queues and hash maps, to store shared data. The relative efficiency of these abstractions are not easily predictable when used in different scenarios. To demonstrate, Fig. 2 shows the measured speedups when using C11 queue, TBB concurrent queue, and Boost deque, to replace a default ring-buffer task-queue on two hardware platforms. On both platforms, the TBB concurrent queue performs the best when the batch size is 1 but poorly when batch size is 20, where the C11 queue is the best on the AMD and the Boost deque the best on the Intel. There is not a single implementation that always performs the best.

This paper aims to support the automated exchange of abstractions in multi-threaded applications. Figure 1 shows our overall workflow, which includes (1) an *abstraction adapter interface* that documents the relations between different abstraction implementations and (2) an *abstraction replacement compiler* that automatically substitutes abstractions in applications with alternative ones based on the adapter specifications. Offline profiling is used to drive the optimizations.

Fig. 1. Overall Workflow

The abstraction adapter interface, manually written by developers, is used to ensure correct optimization. Our technical contributions include the following.

This research is funded by NSF through award CCF-1261584.

M. Hall and H. Sundar (Eds.): LCPC 2018, LNCS 11882, pp. 185–192, 2019.
https://doi.org/10.1007/978-3-030-34627-0_14

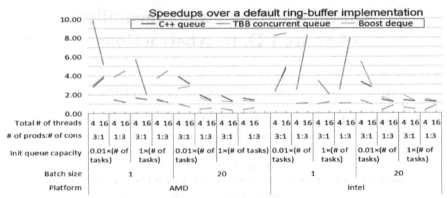

Total # of threads	4	16	4	16	4	16	4	16	4	16	4	16	4	16	4	16
# of prods:# of cons	3:1	1:3	3:1	1:3	3:1	1:3	3:1	1:3	3:1	1:3	3:1	1:3	3:1	1:3	3:1	1:3
Init queue capacity	0.01×(# of tasks)		1×(# of tasks)		0.01×(# of tasks)		1×(# of tasks)		0.01×(# of tasks)		1×(# of tasks)		0.01×(# of tasks)		1×(# of tasks)	
Batch size	1				20				1				20			
Platform	AMD								Intel							

*batch size: the number of tasks a thread can push into or pop from the queue each time;
# of prods: # of cons: the number of threads pushing into vs popping from the queue

Fig. 2. Efficiencies of three task queues on a 12-core Intel and 24-core AMD

- A programming interface for documenting the relations between different abstraction, thus allowing them to be used interchangeably in applications.
- A source-to-source compiler that automatically replaces existing uses of abstractions in multi-threaded applications with alternative implementations;
- An empirical study of optimizing the use of data abstractions in PARSEC [4].

The rest of the paper presents each of the above components in more detail.

2   The Abstraction Adapter Interface

Figure 3 shows some example adapters defined using our interface, each in the form of *adapt x as y* {body}, where *x* is an existing abstraction being adapted; *y* is an abstract type name; and *body* is a sequence of interface functions, each defined by borrowing a subset of C++, enhanced with the following notations,

- *this*, which refers to the abstraction object being adapted;
- *val_type*, which refers to the type of values stored in abstraction *x*;
- *ref(t)*, which defines a pointer type to objects of type *t*;
- *array(t, n)*, which defines an array type with *n* elements of type *t*;
- the () notation, which refers to an empty type (the void type);
- $t_1 \rightarrow t_2$, which defines a function type that maps type t_1 to t_2;
- the | operator, which connects multiple implementations of a function;
- *syn._mutex_lock(v)*{s}, which uses mutex lock *v* to synchronize block *s*;
- *syn._wait(c, v)*, which blocks a thread until the condition variable *c* is set;
- *syn._broadcast(c)*, which wakes up threads blocked on condition variable *c*;
- *foreach v in lower .. upper .. step do s enddo*, which repetitively evaluates statement *s* while setting variable *v* from *lower* to *upper* by *step*.

For two existing abstractions x_i and x_j to be exchangeable, two adapters a_i and a_j must be defined to respectively adapt them to a common abstract type. Further, the common interface functions in both a_i and a_j must be sufficient to cover all uses of x_i in the application. Our compiler checks these requirements and performs the substitution only when all the requirements are satisfied.

```
(1) adapt struct ::_ringbuffer_t {int head=0; int tail=0; int size=CONFIG;
                    val_type data[size]; } from dedup/{queue.h,queue.c} as task_queue {
_empty = () -> (this.tail == this.head);
_full = () -> (this.head == (this.tail - 1 + this.size) % this.size)
             | (this.tail == (this.head+1) % this.size);
_erase_1 = (val : ref(val_type)) -> syn._mutex_lock(&this.mutex) {
                val = this.data[this.tail];
                this.tail = this.tail +1; if (this.tail == this.size) this.tail=0;
           }
_insert_1 = (x : val_type) -> syn._mutex_lock(&this.mutex) {
                this.data[this.head] = x;
                this.head = this.head + 1; if (this.head == this.size) this.head = 0;
           }
_syn_erase_n = (val : array(val_type,1), n:int, lock : mutex, f1 : ()->(), f2 : ()->())
        -> syn._mutex_lock(lock) { f1;
                            foreach i in 0 .. n ..1 do
                              this._erase_1(val[i]); if (this._empty()) { i=i+1; break; }
                            enddo
                            f2; return i; }
_syn_insert_n = ...... };
(2) adapt tbb::concurrent_queue as task_queue {
_empty = () -> this.empty();
_full = ()->false;
_try_insert_1 = (x : val_type) -> this.try_push(x);
_try_erase_1=(val : ref(val_type))-> this.try_pop(val);
_syn_erase_n = (val : array(val_type,1),n:int, lock : mutex, f1 : ()->(), f2 : ()->())
        -> {syn._mutex_lock(lock) { f1; }
           foreach i in 0 .. n ..1 do if (!this._try_erase_1(val[i])) break; enddo
           syn._mutex_lock(lock) { f2; }
           return i;  }
_syn_insert_n = ...... };
```

Fig. 3. Example: abstraction adapter interface

3   The Abstraction Replacement Compiler

Our abstraction compiler takes three inputs: the user application to modify, the adapter interface that relates different abstractions, and a set of optimization configurations. The developer is expected to invoke our compiler with the same configurations on all files to ensure consistency of the substitution results. Each configuration instructs the compiler to convert an abstraction x_i to x_j, based on their adapters a_i and a_j. To do this, the compiler first finds the abstraction type and the adapter definitions to make sure they are consistent with each other. It then tries to convert each variable v_i of type x_i in each function f of the input application, by first outlining all uses of v_i into invocations of abstract interface functions in a_i. Then, it modifies the type definition of x_i: if only a subset of its member variables are used in a_i, a new member variable of type x_j is added to x_i to replace these member variables; otherwise, the type of v_i is simply changed from x_i to x_j. Finally, it inlines each abstract interface operation over v_i with implementations defined in adapter a_j over the new v_j variable.

The key of the compiler is its outlining algorithm, which includes three steps: (1) normalize the input code to use higher-level notations defined in the adapter interface; (2) sort all interface functions in increasing granularity and convert each interface function f_a into a set of patterns, where variables, e.g., *val*, *n*, *lock*, *f1*, *f2*, and *this* in _syn_erase_n of the *task_queue* in Fig. 3, are converted to pattern parameters that can be matched to different expressions and statements; and (3) use each implementation pattern generated in step (2) to match against existing input code, while outlining each matched code fragment into an invocation of the corresponding interface function. Figure 5(a–b) illustrate the results of these steps when outlining the dequeue function in Fig. 4, with the result of instantiating the outlined code by using the TBB concurrent queue adapter shown in (c). Here the original mutex protected critical section has been split into three subsections, with the middle section no longer protected by the lock and instead invoking the already synchronous *try_erase* function of the TBB queue. Such algorithmic changes are enabled by the adapter definitions, which can be made quite powerful by integrating knowledge from developers.

```
struct queue {
      int head, tail, size; void** data;    int count, threads;
      pthread_mutex_t mutex; pthread_cond_t empty, full;
};
int dequeue(struct queue *que, int *fetch_count, void **to_buf) {
1.   pthread_mutex_lock(&que→mutex);
2.   while((que→tail==que→head)&&(que→count<que→threads))
3.        {pthread_wait(&que→empty,&que→mutex);}
4.   if((que→tail==que→head)&&(que→count==que→threads)) {
5.        pthread_cond_broadcast(&que→empty); pthread_mutex_unlock(&que→mutex); return -1;}
6.   for((*fetch_count)=0; (*fetch_count)<16; (*fetch_count)++) {
7.        to_buf[(*fetch_count)]=que→data[que→tail]; que→tail++;
8.        if (que→tail==que→size) que→tail = 0;
9.        if (que→tail==que→head){(*fetch_count)++; break;}}
10. pthread_cond_signal(&que→full); pthread_mutex_unlock(&que→mutex); return 0;}
```

Fig. 4. An example queue abstraction

Our compiler follows two steps to outline each implementation pattern from an input code. First, it traverses all statements in the input code while matching each of them against all parts of the given pattern, with each successful match remembering the required values for each pattern parameter. Then, it examines the saved matches to see whether they can be outlined without violating dependences of the original function, while performing the outlining transformation only when safe. Specifically, each outlining transformation requires a sequence of statements in the input code that are matched precisely to the sequence of statements in the given pattern, without any conflicting assignments of values to the pattern parameters, and with no dependence cycle involving any other intervening statements in the input code. Note that single pattern parameters such as variables $f1$ and $f2$ in _syn_erase_n of adapter (1) in Fig. 3 can be matched to a sequence of statements in the input code, to enhance effectiveness.

4   Experimental Evaluation

We have implemented our infrastructure using the POET language [16] on top of the ROSE C/C++ open-source compiler [12]. We used our adapter interface to manually document a set of queue and map implementations from the PARSEC benchmarks [4] and from C++11 std [2], TBB [13] and Boost [1] libraries. We also identified a number of simple mutex-based synchronization patterns and automatically correlated them with equivalent non-blocking synchronizations, illustrated in Fig. 6. We then tried to optimize PARSEC [4] 3.0, by replacing their existing uses of queue, map, and synchronization abstractions. We used offline profiling to determine the performance of different abstractions in different use cases.

We evaluated all benchmarks on two platforms, shown in Table 1. All benchmarks were compiled using *icc* with -*O3* on the Intel machine and using *g++* with -*O3* on the AMD. Each benchmark is evaluated by using its *native* input (the largest input set) and with a thread configuration that provides the best performance. Each measurement is repeated 10 times, and the average used to calculate performance speedups. The variations across different runs of the same code are $\leq 5\%$.

Our framework is able to support the exchange of all uses of pre-defined queue, map, and synchronization abstractions in PARSEC (they are used in 10 of the 13 available benchmarks). Figure 7 shows the overall performance speedups attained by our compiler, together with a breakdown of the speedups from tuning only the queue, map, and synchronization abstraction implementations respectively.

Four PARSEC benchmarks (Dedup, Bodytrack, Ferret and Facesim) use the queue abstraction. However, they are all designed to minimize contention among the threads

```
int dequeue(struct queue *que, int *fetch_count, void **to_buf) {
1.   syn._mutex_lock(&que→mutex): {
2.     while((que._empty()&&(que→count<que→threads)) {syn._wait(&que→empty,&que→mutex);}
3.     if((que._empty()&&(que→count==que→threads)) { syn._broadcast(&que→empty); return -1;}
4.     foreach i in 0 .. 16 .. 1 do
5.       to_buf[i]=que→data[que→tail]; que→tail=que→tail+1; if (que→tail==que→size) que→tail = 0;
6.       if (que._empty()){i=i+1; break;} enddo
7.     (*fetch_count)=i; syn._signal(&que→full);}; return 0;}
```
(a) after normalization and outlining _empty

```
int dequeue(struct queue *que, int *fetch_count, void **to_buf) {
1.   (*fetch_count) = _syn_erase_n(to_buf, 16, &que→mutex,
2.   /*f1*/{ while((que._empty()&&(que→count<que→threads)) {syn._wait(&que→empty,&que→mutex);}
3.     if((que._empty()&&(que→count==que→threads)) { syn._broadcast(&que→empty); return -1;}},
4.   /*f2*/ { syn._signal(&que→full);}); return 0;}
```
(b) after outlining _erase_1 and _syn_erase_n

```
struct queue {
       tbb::concurrent_queue<void*> *tbb_que;   int count, threads;
       pthread_mutex_t mutex; pthread_cond_t empty, full; };
int dequeue(struct queue *que, int size, void **to_buf) {
(1)    pthread_mutex_lock(&que→mutex);
(2)    while ((que→tbb_que→empty())&&(que→count<que→threads))
(3)      {pthread_cond_wait(&que→empty,&que→mutex);}
(4)    if ((que→tbb_que→empty())&&(que→count==que→threads)) {
(5)      pthread_cond_broadcast(&que→empty); pthread_mutex_unlock(&que→mutex); return -1;}},
(6)    pthread_mutex_unlock((&que→mutex);
(7)    for(int i=0; i<size; i+=1) { if (!que→tbb_que→try_pop(to_buf[i])) break;  }
(8)    pthread_mutex_lock(&que→mutex); pthread_cond_signal(&que→full);
(9)    pthread_mutex_unlock(&que→mutex); (*fetch_count) = i; return 0;}
```
(c) after replacement

Fig. 5. Example: substitute the queue in Fig. 4 with TBB concurrent_queue

```
adapt { x : val_type; pt : syn.mutex; } as atomic_var {
(1) _syn_fetch_add = (incr: val_type) →
        { syn._mutex_lock(this.pt) { tmp : val_type =this.x; this.x=this.x + incr; } return tmp;}
(2) _syn_add_fetch = (inc:val_type) → { syn._mutex_lock(this.pt) { thix.x=this.x + inc; } return this.x;}
(3) _syn_set_value = (v : val_type) → { syn._multex_lock(this.pt) { this.x=v; } }
(4) _syn_set_and_broadcast = (pc : syn.cond_var) →
        { syn._multex_lock(this.pt) { this.x=v; syn._broadcast(pc) } }
(5) _syn_wait_cond = (cond : bool, pc : syn.cond_var) →
        { syn._multex_lock(this.pt) { while (cond) syn._wait(pc, this,pt); } } }
(6) adapt ::pthread_barrier_t as thread_barrier {
    _barrier_init = (n_threads : int) → {pthread_barrier_init(this, NULL, n_threads);}
    _barrier_wait = () → {pthread_barrier_wait(this);}
    _barrier_destroy = () → {pthread_barrier_destroy(this);} }
```

Fig. 6. Example adapters for synchronization operations

over the queue operations. Due to low contention, a better synchronized queue implementation does not produce any speedup, unless the overall application is modified to increase concurrency among the threads. The map abstraction is also used in four PARSEC benchmarks: Canneal, Dedup, Raytrace and Vips. Speedups of 1.255–1.806x are achieved for Canneal and Raytrace, by replacing their uses of the C++ std::map, which is internally a red-black tree. with the faster C++ std::unordered_map, which is internally a hash table. No speedups were attained for Dedup and Vips because their maps are already quite efficient. Most speedups (1.08–2.35x) are attained by replacing the underlying implementations of synchronizations in Canneal, Bodytrack, Fluidanimate, and Streamcluster. All four benchmarks benefited from replacing their uses of Pthread barriers with a lighter weight implementation using atomic operations followed by spin waiting. Bodytrack and X264 also benefited from using atomic operations to replace their mutex-based synchronizations over single global shared variables.

Table 1. Platform configurations

CPU	Freq.	L1 Cache sz	L2 Cache sz	# of cores
Intel E5-2420	1.9 GHz	32 KB	256 KB	12
AMD Opteron-6128	2 GHz	64 KB	512 KB	24

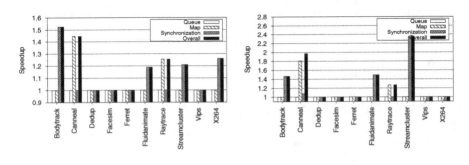

(a) on the Intel Platform   (b) on the AMD Platform

Fig. 7. Performance speedups attained by our compiler

The results across platforms are mostly consistent. We have observed from tuning these applications that their uses of abstractions are tightly connected with other aspects of application design, and replacing a single abstraction in isolation is often not rewarding, unless the abstraction itself is complex enough to offer significant opportunities.

5 Related Work

The idea of automated data structure selection originated in the context abstract data types [9]. More recent work has studied the automatic selection of abstraction implementations for performance optimizations [5,10,14] and the use of nonblocking synchronizations in multi-threaded applications to enable better load balancing and scalability [3,7,8,11,15]. In this paper, we develop compiler support to automate the deployment of alternative abstraction implementations. Existing frameworks on abstraction-aware optimizations mostly focus on optimizing a specific type of data abstraction, e.g., matrices [6] and arrays [17]. Our framework aims to support the automated selection of general-purpose abstractions in multi-threaded applications.

6 Conclusion

This paper presents a framework for automatically exchanging abstraction implementations in multi-threaded applications to enhance performance portability. The framework is used to optimize the use of queues, maps, and synchronization abstractions in the PARSEC benchmarks.

References

1. Boost 1.56.0 Library Documentation (2014). http://www.boost.org/doc
2. Standard C++ Library reference (2014). http://www.cplusplus.com
3. Barrington, A., Feldman, S.D., Dechev, D.: A scalable multi-producer multi-consumer wait-free ring buffer. In: Proceedings of the 30th Annual ACM Symposium on Applied Computing, Salamanca, Spain, 13–17 April 2015, pp. 1321–1328 (2015)
4. Bienia, C., Li, K.: Parsec 2.0: a new benchmark suite for chip-multiprocessors. In: Proceedings of the 5th Annual Workshop on Modeling, Benchmarking and Simulation, June 2009
5. Cho, D., Pasricha, S., Issenin, I., Dutt, N., Paek, Y., Ko, S.: Compiler driven data layout optimization for regular/irregular array access patterns. In: Proceedings of the 2008 ACM SIGPLAN/SIGBED Conference on Languages, Compilers, and Tools for Embedded Systems (LCTES 2008), Tucson, AZ, USA, 12–13 June 2008, pp. 41–50 (2008)
6. Cui, H., Yi, Q., Xue, J., Feng, X.: Layout-oblivious compiler optimization for matrix computations. ACM Trans. Archit. Code Optim. 9(4), 35:1–35:20 (2013). https://doi.org/10.1145/2400682.2400694
7. Dechev, D., LaBorde, P., Feldman, S.D.: LC/DC: lockless containers and data concurrency a novel nonblocking container library for multicore applications. IEEE Access 1, 625–645 (2013)

8. Feldman, S.D., Bhat, A., LaBorde, P., Yi, Q., Dechev, D.: Effective use of non-blocking data structures in a deduplication application. In: Proceedings of the 2013 Companion Publication for Conference on Systems, Programming, & #38; Applications: Software for Humanity, SPLASH 2013, pp. 133–142. ACM, New York (2013)

9. Low, J.R.: Automatic data structure selection: an example and overview. Commun. ACM **21**(5), 376–385 (1978). https://doi.org/10.1145/359488.359498

10. Majeti, D., Barik, R., Zhao, J., Grossman, M., Sarkar, V.: Compiler-driven data layout transformation for heterogeneous platforms. In: an Mey, D., et al. (eds.) Euro-Par 2013. LNCS, vol. 8374, pp. 188–197. Springer, Heidelberg (2014). https://doi.org/10.1007/978-3-642-54420-0_19

11. Michael, M.M., Scott, M.L.: Simple, fast, and practical non-blocking and blocking concurrent queue algorithms. In: Proceedings of the Fifteenth Annual ACM Symposium on Principles of Distributed Computing, Philadelphia, Pennsylvania, USA, 23–26 May 1996, pp. 267–275 (1996)

12. Quinlan, D., Schordan, M., Yi, Q., Saebjornsen, A.: Classification and utilization of abstractions for optimization. In: ISOLA 2004: The First International Symposium on Leveraging Applications of Formal Methods, Paphos, Cyprus, October 2004

13. Reinders, J.: Intel Threading Building Blocks, 1st edn. O'Reilly & Associates, Inc., Sebastopol (2007)

14. Rubin, S., Bodík, R., Chilimbi, T.M.: An efficient profile-analysis framework for data-layout optimizations. In: Conference Record of POPL 2002: The 29th SIGPLAN-SIGACT Symposium on Principles of Programming Languages, Portland, OR, USA, 16–18 January 2002, pp. 140–153 (2002)

15. Tsigas, P., Zhang, Y.: Integrating non-blocking synchronisation in parallel applications: performance advantages and methodologies. In: Workshop on Software and Performance, pp. 55–66 (2002)

16. Yi, Q.: POET: a scripting language for applying parameterized source-to-source program transformations. Softw. Pract. Exp. **42**, 675–706 (2012)

17. Yi, Q., Quinlan, D.: Applying loop optimizations to object-oriented abstractions through general classification of array semantics. In: LCPC 2004: The 17th International Workshop on Languages and Compilers for Parallel Computing, West Lafayette, Indiana, USA, September 2004

Author Index

Printed in the United States
By Bookmasters